SHARKEY'S KID

SHARKEY'S KID

A MEMOIR

Leroy Ostransky

WILLIAM MORROW AND COMPANY, INC.
NEW YORK

Recognizing the importance of preserving what has been written, it is the policy of William Morrow and Company, Inc., and its imprints and affiliates to have the books it publishes printed on acid-free paper, and we exert our best efforts to that end.

Library of Congress Cataloging-in-Publication Data

Ostransky, Leroy.
    Sharkey's kid : a memoir / Leroy Ostransky.
       p.   cm.
    ISBN 0-688-10325-1
    I. Title.
    PS3565.S835S47   1991
    813'.54—dc20   90-13558
                                                  CIP

Printed in the United States of America

First Edition

1 2 3 4 5 6 7 8 9 10

BOOK DESIGN BY M. C. DEMAIO

To Natalie and Sonya

FOREWORD

THIS ACCOUNT OF the relationship between my beloved friend Leroy Ostransky, and his father, Sharkey, is intensely personal. I therefore feel quite comfortable in offering an intensely personal foreword.

When I was a college freshman at the University of Puget Sound in Tacoma, Washington, I had only one class that I ran to on Tuesdays and Thursdays so that I could get a front row seat. Big Leroy would hold forth in a course entitled "Introduction to Music Literature" and I was not about to miss a word that this man offered. He knew things about music history that would just crack you up, and he snuck these items into a lecture in the most creative and profound way. He was one of the finest teachers that I had ever met, or have met since.

Though Leroy has always been somewhat of an eccentric character he has always shown a bit of patience with his students, though a strange sort of patience that could only come from a fine teacher. I will never forget the concert reviews that were assigned the class. One student, and I knew this kid well, handed in a concert review. It was a fine review of the Mozart we had heard a week before, and I was impressed. The paper was returned to my acquaintance with the following remark hastily written in the margins:

"This is one of the finest reviews of a Mozart concert that I have ever read. It is terrific and insightful. The only problem is that the first time I read it was in the *Harvard Review of Music*. Excellent. You flunk. L. Ostransky."

Dr. Ostransky spent several hours in the library locating that original review. He remembered reading it years before, but he could not remember where. He was not about to let a loose student put one over on him . . . and the student did not.

Sitting on the front lawn during a class one day . . . we could do that sort of thing in Tacoma . . . the professor claimed that repeated listenings of a particular piece could help you learn to love it. A student, a rather dull one, as I recall, said, "But, Dr. Ostransky, how can you love something that you cannot understand." Leroy replied in his best Brooklyn tongue, "Ya know, that's what my wife, Natalie, says about me." That is how this man taught.

During the 1970s *People* magazine called him "one of the 12 best college professors in the nation." I didn't have to read *People* to know that!

I returned to Tacoma in 1966 and was appointed to a small United Methodist parish on the edge of the city. I wanted my flock to know more of my affections for the newly renamed University of Puget Sound and so we had a series of guest lecturers come to our parish. Ostransky was one of the guests. The lecture series centered around current theological concerns and I was a bit nervous about the content of Leroy's lecture. After all, he was an internationally known teacher, composer, and one of the great authorities on jazz. But theology? Jazz, he explained in his lectures, was that freewheeling attitude of creativity, a creativity that is not bound by such set and narrow rules. I was ready to print the announcement of his coming to our theological lecture series. "What will your talk be called, Leroy?" "God Needs Jazz!" he responded. It was terrific, just terrific.

During those days in Tacoma, Leroy wrote a column for our local newspaper, a column entitled "Musical Notes and Comments, by Leroy Ostransky." It started as a concert review column . . . but Leroy has such a wide grasp of the humanities, such an incredible insight into so many fields, that he seldom stuck to music. Pretty soon the column was just called "Notes and Comments." That was fine with me and I loved reading it each week. I remember how he would discuss his relationship with his wonderful daughter, Sonya. He would quote her in the column as calling him "Big Daddy!" That became the word for him in our household and then he started writing about his father. He talked of his childhood in Brooklyn, of his father's insistence that

8

he study the "fiddle," and of the lengths to which his father would go to see that Leroy received lessons from the best teachers in Manhattan. His ability to discuss daily things in a fascinating way gave rise to my next request. I wanted him to speak in chapel at the University of Puget Sound.

My bishop appointed me chaplain to the University, and one of my favorite tasks was that of preparing chapel services for the community each week. We, meaning the students and I, decided to do a series on the creative process. We asked each speaker to talk about the sources for creative thought, the meaning of the whole process, the function of creative thinking in our lives . . . and, of course, we asked Big Daddy to speak.

I was a bit upset that week over the fact that I could not find Ostransky and confirm the title of his talk. He was "out of town," whatever that means. I heard nothing from him the week prior to the chapel session but I went to chapel fully confident that somehow he would show up. We, meaning the students and I, entered the building to get ready for the event. We found the professor seated at the grand piano at the front of the chapel. He was playing "All the Things You Are." I knew better than to interrupt him when he was at the keyboard, so we all sat down. Leroy continued to play until everyone was present and then he stood at a music stand. He had some notes or a manuscript or something. He explained that the creative process involves a collection of all the things that have influenced you, and thus the music that he had just played. One of the things that had influenced him was his father. And now, he said, "I am going to tell you about him!" He began to read from portions of this manuscript that you are about to read. He read for two minutes, perhaps three at the most, and then stopped. He totally stopped! I could not imagine what was going on since this man was one of the great lecturers that I have known. "I can't do it, Jeff, I just can't." He closed his notebook and walked from the platform. As he passed my pew he mumbled, "My father died this week!"

That was where he was! He had been in Brooklyn . . . and burying this man that had such an influence on his life.

The manuscript that he was working on at the time has not been published until now. I am sorry that you have had to wait so long to gain an insight into one of my dearest friends. But now you have the book in hand and you may proceed with affection, as I have.

—Jeff Smith
The Frugal Gourmet

SHARKEY'S KID

PROLOGUE

FROM THE TIME he arrived in America in 1904, when he was fifteen, my father worked hard to become "somebody, a big shot," as he put it. I suppose he would have loved to be rich and famous and have his picture in the newspapers. That didn't happen. However, later on he did become acquainted with Lower East Side gangsters. The most powerful of these was a man called Big Jack Zelig, who befriended my father in small ways—taught him a little East Side English; paid him to run errands—to pick up Zelig's shirts at the laundry, buy liquor for him, place bets at his bookie's, bring him the latest newspapers. Zelig was murdered in 1912. My father had come to the party, but nobody asked him to dance.

Although my father was born in 1889, as far as my mother was concerned he was born in 1917, on the day they were married. It was nobody's business—including her four children's—how he had occupied himself before she met him. The customers in my father's saloon, including famous East Side gangsters, racketeers, con men, and gamblers, were, when my mother spoke of them, very interesting people. Those who called me by name were indeed interesting people, and to my childish eyes their flashy clothes, easy way with money, and soft conversation were mysterious and attractive.

My mother and father spoke of his customers often, and if there was anything I missed in my daily visits to the saloon I could hear the stories recounted each night as I lay awake in the bedroom adjoining the kitchen while my father, after he had closed the saloon, sat at the kitchen table with his glass of tea and regaled Mama with the highlights of the day's activity. I listened carefully and discreetly. I tossed and turned, and squeaked the bed, pretending to make sleep

13

noises. My father's stories were exciting enough so I couldn't afford to miss even a word of these lessons. He spoke to my mother mostly in Yiddish, and thus, in a small way, helped to increase my own vocabulary. What I remember best were his stories of crimes of the past and present in streets I roamed regularly, his facile use of underworld nicknames, and the relationship among various gangs and the police.

Until I started working on this memoir in the eighties, I thought I had almost enough collected information to cover the dominant theme of my youth: the relationship linking my quasi-irreligious Jewish father and his desire to make me into a virtuoso violinist, my reluctance to have him do so, and our relation to my religious maternal grandfather, who abhorred my father's ways and who wished to turn me into a proper Jew—and, of course, my reaction to these inescapable conflicts.

What I still lacked, I believed, were a few essential facts. I sent out a batch of questions to the family and old friends, and as letters, old photographs, and personal memoirs reached me, I made up several tentative chronologies in order to produce some dependable biographical data on my father's European family, where he stood in the order of the brothers and sisters he left behind, and so on. For example, I knew when he arrived in America, and I knew about his first job as a cigar maker and something about a job he held in 1917 in a Ford factory on Long Island just before I was born.

Years ago I learned he had arrived in New York accompanied by an older brother, and that they were met by still another brother named Hymie, who (my mother hinted before she died) was executed in the electric chair before I was born. That, of course, was an interesting piece of news, and I guessed that old newspaper reports, if I could find them, would provide me with Hymie's age, and, no doubt, why he was electrocuted.

I set to work. In the *New York Times Index* I found references to two stories on Hymie. (We'll return to them later.)

CHAPTER ONE

On New York's Lower East Side in the 1920s, my father was the only Jew with a knife scar on his jaw, a tattoo on his left forearm, and tears in his eyes every time he heard a cantor chant the Kol Nidre on his Victrola. Tears among East Side Jews were commonplace; they cried easily and almost always with justification. Women wept because it was so difficult to be a Jewish woman, while their men congregated several times daily in the local synagogues to cry their special kind of blues. Immigrant Jews wore beards and occasional earlocks, and among those on the road to assimilation were clean-shaven faces; but there were no knife-scarred faces. Hardly ever. A knife-slashed face in their midst would be singular indeed; and the odds that the owner of such a face was tattooed as well would be impossible. And, as if the scar and tattoo weren't enough, this strange Jew was known as Sharkey. A truly un-Jewish ghetto Jew.

The scar on Sharkey's face wasn't much of a scar. It was about two inches long and was the result of a late-night street brawl in 1922, when he was in his early thirties, during which he knocked out two assailants while a third (according to my mother, who stood by, terrified) slashed Sharkey's face and ran off into the darkness beneath the Manhattan Bridge.

The resulting scar suited his strong features. His nose might have been borrowed from Jack Dempsey; his eyes, never fully open, studied the world with quiet impatience; and his heavy jaw was plainly grim and tough. Still, his broad smile, when he laughed at the sort of physical violence ordinary East Siders avoided, made him impudently attractive, and, not surprisingly, brought him many hardnosed admirers.

...key's tattoo must have been inscribed early in his life, because, as I remember it, there wasn't much tattoo left to see. On the inside of his left forearm, just above the wrist, was a small, pale blue anchor. As he moved about quickly behind his bar, his biceps filling the sleeves of the expensive sport shirt he wore tucked daintily under his sparkling-white floor-length apron, Sharkey presented his customers not so much with any one notable physical feature, but rather with his total physique; thus his pale, tattooed anchor stood out no more than it would on a battleship at sea.

Zaida, my maternal grandfather, was not one of Sharkey's saloon customers. He was a devout orthodox Jew. To him, my father's pale blue anchor was more like a pale blue cancer; or, if the tattoo was glimpsed from a certain angle, he saw a Latin cross. Cancer or cross made little difference to Zaida, because in those years good Jews did not sport tattoos. (Some twenty years later, all of my father's European family would be transported from Bialystok to Treblinka, where tattooing had become the fashion; not one of them survived.)

Perhaps scars and tattoos were *de rigueur* for the owner of a saloon, for if among East Side Jews in the twenties my father wasn't especially distinguished as a family man, as a saloonkeeper he was unique. Although Jewish and Gentile customers alike referred to his saloon as Sharkey's (and to my father as Sharkey), I myself never called him Sharkey where he could hear me. He would have nearly killed me if I had. In the years I was forced to practice my violin in the back room of the saloon, I was required to call him Daddy. It was my mother's idea, and I was never very comfortable with it. But then, East Side children weren't expected to be comfortable.

"I'll see you in Daddy's saloon right after school," Mama would say (as if I had a choice of several saloons I could visit). Now Mama, as I called my mother, called *her* father Papa. Perhaps Mama thought Papa for our Daddy was too old-fashioned, too green, and therefore didn't fit the husband of a woman who had finished high school and business college, and had worked in an office. Mama was a great one for the elegant variation, and Sharkey—aspiring American robber baron—respected Mama's ability with a language he could barely speak. I was a grown man before I realized that "Daddy" was not just a family term. Daddy and Sharkey were different men.

Asked for a simple favor of any kind, Daddy would respond tolerantly and, on occasion, warmheartedly. When Daddy was "up," it would be fair to say he had a pleasant nature. In his private relations with Mama he was gentle. He was tender. And given the right circumstance, I can imagine him as romantic and (not to get soppy about it) even dreamy. I have seen him that way, and I know Mama did.

But Sharkey would have been embarrassed to be called dreamy—that was a young girl's word, a word used by sissies. Considering the amount of money Sharkey spent on "good" clothes, there was still something coarse about him, but anyone who called him coarse could expect a fast knockout. He enjoyed being known as rough, tough, violent, harsh, demanding, and—if he had known the word—aggressive. And Sharkey was aggressive if he was anything. Aggressiveness, I would say, could have been my father's middle name, an essential part of his *unpleasant* nature.

While Daddy was gentle and sentimental and Sharkey was brutal and reckless, they both loved music. Not all music, of course (neither had ever heard of Bach, say, or Mozart), but the music that had touched their lives: the music of the Pale in Daddy's boyhood, and the music of the Lower East Side as he grew up flexing his muscles. And while it isn't likely that Daddy had heard "Mother Machree" sung in Bialystok, much of what he had heard there as a boy was still with him, in muddled memories, years later.

Daddy soon learned he was one of a great variety of Jews on the East Side. There were fellow Bialystokers, of course, but Bialystok was only one small city in what used to be the Kingdom of Poland. Russia eventually annexed all of Poland and took three million Polish Jews, added three million Russian Jews, and (to help solve their ongoing "Jewish Problem") confined them to an area called the Jewish Pale of Settlement. These Jews, and others, soon discovered America, and by the time Daddy was twenty, in 1909, about a million Jews from Russia, Austria, Hungary, Romania, Syria, and Lebanon were panning the Lower East Side streets for gold (and finding dung), and singing the songs of their homeland.

German Jews, who had arrived in New York long before the Russian Jews, now lived uptown and were hardly considered real Jews. Why, they didn't speak Yiddish, for one thing, and even their so-called music sounded odd, somehow non-Jewish. It was said that *Deitchin* families like the Schiffs, the Lehmanns, the Warburgs, and the Guggenheimers went to symphony orchestra concerts, the ballet, and the opera, and there were strong rumors that their synagogues used choirs and, if you can believe it, the organ!

The poor Russian Jews and the rich German Jews regarded each other with undisguised contempt. Often I would hear Daddy and his customers sing, to a German folk tune, "*Alle Deitchin shtinken, alle Deitchin shtinken, nur dee vyblakh shtinken nit*" (All the German Jews stink, all the German Jews stink, only the young wives do *not* stink). It was more Sharkey's song than it was Daddy's.

On the Lower East Side there was, of course, other, "uptown" music which I discovered as I grew older—choral and orchestral concerts and solo recitals in the settlement houses on Madison and Henry streets, and at the Educational Alliance on East Broadway, all just a few blocks from Daddy's saloon, but Daddy would have been bored by such staid music and its lack of true Jewish emotion. He would have pointed out that certain music *sounds* Jewish, and for Daddy that was pedigree enough.

The Sabbath sounds from the synagogue, just up the street from the saloon, filled Daddy with exultation, particularly the coloratura cantillations evoking the pleasure of the great holidays. His face lit up with enthusiasm as he heard the genuine folk songs and dances from any Jew's homeland, and for the composed "folk" songs of the Yiddish musical theater he clapped his hands zestfully. When Daddy heard anything played on the fiddle, the most typically Jewish instrument, he became a child, and when he listened to Elman or Heifetz or Menuhin, he would shake his head in wonder and say, "*Yiddle mitten fiddle*" (a Jew with a fiddle).

I thought his words made a jovial, bouncing rhythm, a rappity-tap expression Daddy had invented; later, I learned that Irving Berlin (Israel Baline, an East Side songwriter) composed a piece in 1908 called "Yiddle on Your Fiddle," and Daddy's phrase, I realized, must have been more common than I supposed. The song's full title was "Yiddle on Your Fiddle—Play Some Rag Time." Daddy would have understood the yiddle-fiddle part, but Sharkey would also have known something about ragtime.

If Daddy's musical taste leaned toward the sacred, or at least the quasi-religious, Sharkey's musical taste was essentially profane. There was, of course, bound to be some common ground: a preference for vocal over instrumental music, say, or a penchant for yesterday's traditional dance tunes. Sharkey was fond of shevelehs, frailachs, Romanian horas, Russian kasotskis—all snappy, boisterous foot-tappers played at weddings, Bar Mitzvahs, dances, and other celebratory occasions in any of the East Side's dozens of halls or "mansions," where the East Side elite danced the night away.

These dance halls played a significant role in Sharkey's youth. He had the powerful young legs of a prizefighter—constant practice had made him light on his feet—and he was always a ready but not necessarily graceful dancer. As he danced his way along East Broadway, between Houston and Grand, his then favorite neighborhood, he had his choice of thirty-one halls, several of which he and his bosom friends came to know intimately.

He had also become a spiffy dresser. His husky young body was made to order for whatever he wore. The men in his circle favored expensive items of apparel, stylish in themselves but often made cheap by curious juxtapositions—a three-piece blue serge suit worn over an open-collared maroon sport shirt; or a chinchilla overcoat worn over a champagne-colored Hong Kong summer suit. The result was often the impression of a large, chic primate sporting the Crown Jewels. The jewels, somehow, seemed out of place anywhere but in the East Side halls and grandly termed mansions.

(And while we're on the subject of halls and mansions, it may be useful to know that he and Mama were married in a place called the Pearl Mansion, owned by the Pearlmans, parents of a promising boy cantor later to be known as Jan Peerce.)

Sharkey picked up much of his taste for the profane in music in the cabarets and saloons he frequented from the time he was old enough to box until he was in middle age. In the East Side cabarets and saloons patronized by the enclave's freewheeling big-spending mobsters, toughchiks, racket guys, and con men, he found the spirit, impetus, and financial support that would eventually lead to his simultaneous ownership of two saloons, a restaurant that served booze in teacups, a hotel resort in the Catskill Mountains called the Maple

Grove House, and a cabaret on Rivington Street known as the American Casino.

From the time the Volstead Act—prohibition of liquor—became law in 1920, the word "cabaret" meant, on the East Side, any place you could eat, drink illegal booze, and be entertained. The entertainment would include a singer, an accompanist, and perhaps a Gypsy violinist who moved from table to table. The right sort of female singer, singing the right sort of songs for the right sort of customers, invariably brought the house down; it was the work of these singers and their songs that helped shape my father's taste in vocal music.

I was taken to the American Casino on rare occasions and I could hear these songs for myself, but my memory of them comes mostly from hearing my father sing parts of them to me or to Mama, or to his saloon customers. There were songs in English that were currently popular and had special meaning for the Casino clientele ("My Yiddishe Mama—I need you more than ever now"); the lament in what we may call the Tin Pan Alley–Yiddish minor ("Take me in your arms, before you take your love away"); songs from the Yiddish musical theater which pine for the primitive ways of home ("*Belz, mein shteteleh Belz*"—a townlet in Galicia, a thousand miles from Bialystok); songs at once philosophic and ironic, with biblical allusions ("*Vu zynen meine ziben gute yor?*"—Where are my seven good years?); and, finally, the blue-comedy songs in doggerel Yiddish, sung late in the evening when the customers were happy and the spirit naughty ("Cockeyed Jenny, *mit dee ferfoylteh tsayn*/Cockeyed Jenny, *zee lekt a bayn*"—Poor cross-eyed Jenny, with her bad teeth—all she can do is lick a bone).

As Sharkey, my father had a firm grip on Cockeyed Jenny and her bad teeth, and as Daddy, his hand held firmly the little town of Belz. In the oral tradition, these picturesque, sometimes elegiac songs were handed down from father to son. I knew other music—the saloon songs especially, and the pieces in his record collection (which still surprise me when I think of them)—but these deserve some special attention.

My father, obviously, loved to sing. With his head back and his eyes peering upward as if he were searching for stars, Daddy sang out in his thin, high tenor with just a smidgin of static around the edges, while his heaving burly chest showed him as a legitimate whiskey tenor. Like a *tenore robusto* forever poised to reach his highest note, Daddy's voice remained pretty much in its falsetto range, which was no great handicap, because in his musical circles the ability to join in often counted for more than the quality of one's voice.

I have heard my father sing with his saloon crowd; I have heard him when he thought he was alone; and I have heard him when he sang especially for my benefit, carrying on the oral tradition, as it were. I can still recall Daddy's gentle rendition of "Offen Pripetchuk," a song about a little fire burning in the fireplace as the rabbi teaches small children their ABCs. Two other songs come back to me that I may have heard Daddy sing in my first two or three years—the touching lullaby "Raisins and Almonds" (although Mama, too, may have sung this song to me, I still associate it with Daddy); and the rousing children's song "*Pot-cheh, pot-cheh, kichelach*"—clap hands, clap hands, little cakes—and the pleasure Daddy took in the rhyme *schichelech* and *kichelach* (little shoes and cakes) because it meant that come what may, Daddies provide their good little sons with shoes.

When Daddy thought he was alone I would hear him hum something rather Middle Eastern, a melody he may have heard as a child in a Bialystok synagogue; or I would hear him sing *sotto voce* the words "Romania, Romania, Romania" as if he had been born there. In a quite different mood he would intone such Chassidic nonsense syllables as "dye-dye-dye" or "bim-bim-bim" as he paced the floor, bearing up under the Czar's cruel persecution like a poor Jew from *Fiddler on the Roof*.

But one of his all-time favorites, encompassing five thousand years of what it was like to be a Jew—pale old men in long black coats, patriarchal beards, prayer shawls, and skullcaps; and the compassion, the fervent soul, the Yiddishkeit of ancient cantors—all of this Daddy found in the melody and words of "Eili, Eili," a lamentation especially composed for the New York Yiddish theater.

Daddy never got through the entire piece; the first few lines were enough to bring tears to his eyes. On those high occasions when the family gathered for a meal in Zaida's house to celebrate Passover or a special Sabbath, and Daddy had had a few shots of Zaida's homemade cherry brandy (Zaida called it firewater), Daddy's neck would bulge and he would have a go at the opening line, "*Eili, Eili, lomo azavtoni*"

(My God, my God, why has thou forsaken me?), and Zaida would sit quietly at the head of the table, listening to the bum his daughter had married against his wishes, and the sadness in his face told me God should have complained to this bum "why hast thou forsaken me"—instead of the other way around. But it was not a bum who sang "Eili, Eili," it was Daddy.

He picked up tunes rather quickly, but the words seemed to matter little to him after the first line or two, lines he would often use as catchphrases to bolster or enliven sagging saloon conversations. (Genet once said, in effect, that the lyrics of popular songs provide illiterate lovers with ways of expressing themselves that would otherwise never occur to them; for Daddy, the words provided him with ready-made comments on life in general, a not insignificant asset for a bartender).

When a customer in Daddy's saloon tried to burden him with a long tale of hard luck, Daddy would wait for the proper opening. Whatever hard lines were in his face would disappear; the patience in his usually fierce blue eyes, and his unthreatening posture, presented a simple rendition of unbounded tolerance. He was merely biding his time—waiting for his client to have his say. If the customer spoke Yiddish, Daddy would repeat the first line of a popular song: "*Vus iz geven iz geven, iz nishtaw.*" And if the hard-luck story came from an Irishman, Daddy would give him the English equivalent: "What's past is past," he'd say, "It's over with. No use worrying about it. It's gone!" He would mop the bar a bit and move along to the next victim.

As I have said, Daddy had one criterion for all music. Either it sounded Jewish or it did not. Like Frederick of Prussia, who believed he was musical because he could distinguish "God Save the King" from anything that wasn't, Daddy thought he could distinguish Jewish music from anything that wasn't. If a tune was in the Yiddish minor mode it had a good chance of moving into Daddy's heart and, eventually, into his vocal repertory.

During all those hateful years he forced me to practice the violin and endure his brutal beatings in the back room of his saloon, it seemed to me he always listened more intently when I practiced pieces in a minor key. He would sit on his bar stool, chin in hand, elbow on knee, deep in his own system of concentrated thinking, while his aesthetic sense seemed bound up in the smaller (minor?) of two musical modes. The minor keys were the only keys which counted; pieces in major keys were . . . well, tolerated.

Although my father could not have had firm knowledge of any authentic Jewish musical tradition, he simply knew that somewhere in the past, someone on high—who knows? God perhaps?—had passed down unique music composed of intervals faintly Persian, Arabic, Turkish, Romanian, and Russian; and Oriental-Spanish melodies called Sephardic; and the Palestinian-German melodies called Ashkenazic. All these heavenly sounds came to him in a muted falsetto, and, as evident from the distant, serene expression on his face, from a long way off—Babylonia, say, or the Yiddish Art Theater on Second Avenue.

When Daddy got the notion a piece of music was Jewish, it was impossible to convince him otherwise. He knew, for example, the popular song "Take Me in Your Arms" was a Jewish song (he thought it was translated from the Yiddish) because it *sounded* Jewish. He felt the same way about a song called "When a Gypsy Makes His Violin Cry." Both songs are in a minor key, of course. Once, when he was in a music store selecting a record to add to his bizarre collection, he heard Caruso for the first time. Daddy bought the record because it sounded Jewish. The record turned out to be the principal tenor aria from Halévy's operatic masterpiece *La Juive*, and when he learned what *juive* meant in English, he beamed. "You see," he exclaimed, "you can tell a Jewish piece even when it's sung by a wop!"

Few people argued with Sharkey about music, or, for that matter, anything else. He was too stubborn, too tough. A 1920 photograph, taken when he was thirty-one and a sophomore saloonkeeper, shows him as a nattily dressed, square-jawed, rugged but handsome man, about five-ten, a light heavyweight (175 pounds) with powerful shoulders, and hands like a pair of oversized work gloves. The dominant impression is one of seriousness, confidence, ambition, and strength. What the hand-tinted photo does not show is his lack of formal education, his ambivalence about being a Jew, and his apparently uncontrollable temper.

If you were foolish enough to oppose him because his view was wrongheaded and yours was right, because your argument was based on fact and was sound, logical, and up to the minute while his was medieval and full of holes, you'd be lucky to get off with just a punch in the mouth—Sharkey's standard method for ending all arguments. Nobody on the Lower East Side ever really won an argument with Sharkey. With Daddy, yes! But not with Sharkey. And when it came to questions of what was "Jewish" and what wasn't, he tolerated no opposition. Like it or take your lumps.

Any music that was not Jewish was likely to be, as he put it, "Crap"—an indispensable term he used any way he wanted to. When Daddy broke a drinking glass he'd say, "All the glasses today are made of crap." When he caught me pasting down my hair with Vaseline he'd say, "Jesus! Take that crap off your head!" When he said a certain piece of music was crap, it didn't mean he didn't like it, it meant it just wasn't Jewish. In fact, he enjoyed certain pieces of what he called crap. Among his favorites were snatches of songs he had picked up from his Irish customers: "When Irish Eyes are Smiling," "Mother Machree," and "Where the River Shannon Flows"—this last became "Where da River Shannon Flows."

Daddy understood the sentimental spirit of these songs of the Ould Sod, and he often joined the Irishmen when the spirit moved them; but, alas, he seldom was able to remember more than the first two lines or the last two. The Irishmen were nonetheless delighted to have Daddy's high tenor join their chorus even if it was only for the final cadence, and after the teary singalong, one of the men would pay him the ultimate compliment: "Sharkey," he would say, "you're a real *Irish* tenor." Daddy would beam. "Not bad for a Jew-boy, eh, ya mick?" he'd reply, smiling. Then he would buy a round for the boys and the singing would continue. Ah, Sharkey was an all-right Jew, and that was no crap.

That the Jews were the chosen people was a constant in my father's philosophy of life. Anything a Gentile could do, a Jew could do better. People, places, things, were all rapidly classified—Jewish or not Jewish; and since Daddy could neither read nor write (he had great difficulty even learning to write his name), all his information was hearsay. But hearsay is better than no information at all, and Daddy had his favored sources: Mama, who read the *Daily News* and passed on bits she thought would interest him; his saloon customers, some of whom worked uptown and were, in a sense, Daddy's stringers; and, of course, the inevitable neighborhood gossip, some of which no doubt started in the saloon itself.

The East Side network of information—a sort of Mogen David grapevine—rose to its peak when any personage, historical or contemporary, unexpectedly turned out to be Jewish. These included movie actors, politicians, industrialists, musicians, athletes, and even the cop on the beat. For Daddy to be in possession of such news bolstered his confidence in himself, and reinforced his view that Jewish was better. He made it a paternal duty (as I discovered early) to impose this view on his firstborn son, to show me the importance of being Jewish in a world of Gentiles, to show me that a Jew can *do* it, and for these reasons I was often the first recipient of Daddy's underground intelligence.

One day Daddy received word that Oskar Straus, composer of *The Chocolate Soldier*, was Jewish. "Did you know Straus is a Jew?" he asked, tossing away the line. I said I didn't, and moreover that I thought he was German. "That shows how much you know," he said. "He's a Jew. Take my word." I took it; I didn't dare not to. When Sharkey made up his mind you were Jewish, it was as if he were the *mohel* and you had just been circumcised. Later, Johann Strauss, the waltz king, became one of Daddy's favorites. Because Daddy couldn't spell, he saw no difference between Oskar Straus and Johann Strauss; he treated them like brothers. Anyone named Straus(s) was Jewish, whether *he* knew it or not. Even years later, I never mentioned *Richard* Strauss. Too complicated.

Such great Gentile composers as Bach, Mozart, Beethoven, Brahms, meant little to Daddy. He never mentioned their names and he never played their music on his Victrola. There was one master, however, whose name he knew well: Mendelssohn. Mendel is a common Yiddish name, and only a simpleton would suggest that Mendel's son could be anything but Jewish. Even I could make that connection. Still, one day, when I was old enough to read a biography of Mendelssohn, I discovered what I thought was sufficient evidence to prove that Mendelssohn was not a *real* Jew.

He had been born a Jew, all right, but when he grew up and had a choice he renounced his Jewishness. I was excited by my golden discovery. At last I would have a chance to show my father I knew something he did not. Knowing how easily he was baited on questions of Jewishness, I told him what I had uncovered—the possibility that Mendelssohn was not a Jew.

"Don't tell me any old wives' tales," Daddy said in Yiddish, and I knew he meant business. "Once a Jew, always a Jew. Don't tell me about that crap you get in books." His tone indicated the conversation was over. But I persisted. I had taken on Daddy's world and I had not done so lightly, because I had been *thinking*. "What about his first name?" I asked. "Felix isn't a Jewish name. I never heard of a Jew called Felix."

Daddy looked at me quizzically. "His name was *Felix?* Where did you hear that crap—that his name was Felix?"

I now understood that the name Felix was new to Daddy. Obviously, I had slowed him down some. I sensed he was stalling for time. "It says right on my violin music his first name is Felix."

But Daddy moved in quickly for the kill. "Felix," he said, "is his name in *English*. His Jewish name is Faivel—just as your friend's name is Faivel. Understand, you stinker?" My friend was indeed Faivel; his parents called him that. But at school his teacher called him Philip, a name we agreed on. Furthermore, I had pressed Daddy as far as I dared. Common sense, experience, and fear told me to keep my mouth shut, so I withdrew.

I thought I had my father on the ropes. But, as it turned out, I was wrong. Years later, while I was doing some research on Mendelssohn, I learned that his father, Abraham, on learning of his son's apostasy, urged Felix to gloss over his Jewishness by adding part of his mother's maiden name—Bartholdy—to Mendelssohn, so his name would be Mendelssohn-Bartholdy. In a letter to Felix, his father said, "A Gentile by the name of Mendelssohn is an absurdity." Exactly Daddy's point.

Daddy's saloon appealed to Jews and Gentiles alike. He quickly picked up the Gentile words and expressions, and in his turn tried to teach them his favorite Yiddish expressions. I don't know the influence of Daddy's language on his Gentile customers, but despite the rapid increase in his English vocabulary, he managed to keep his own heavy

Yiddish accent. The language of the Jews in Bialystok had been Yiddish, sprinkled with Polish and a smattering of Russian. Yiddish was my father's mother tongue, which of course he spoke during his Bialystok years, and even his Yiddish, therefore, was limited to the vocabulary and thought patterns of a Bialystoker boy's world.

Unlike Zaida and other immigrants who arrived in America grown men and who regularly read one of the Yiddish newspapers available at all East Side newsstands, Daddy never learned to read a paper. Perhaps Mama's good intentions were at fault. Despite his longing to speak English at least as well as Mama could, no day passed in which Daddy and Mama did not speak some Yiddish. Mama had become Daddy's executive administrator. What she bought, what she sold, for how much, their cash flow—all these matters had to be discussed in Yiddish if Daddy was to have any clear idea of what was going on. And so while he used his special brand of English in the saloon, at home we were bilingual. He spoke to Mama and me in Yiddish; Mama answered him in Yiddish, and I answered him in English.

The use of language alone, of course, was not my father's main strength. When Isaac Bashevis Singer remarked that Yiddish may be the only language on earth that has never been spoken by men in power, it's plain he didn't know about Sharkey. While Daddy had charm and grace and an open, comforting sentimentality, Sharkey, with his good-fellow approach to one and all, his overwhelming obsession with what he considered fair play, his obvious physical superiority and brute strength, made his Gentile customers regard him as a "good" and powerful Jew.

For the goyim, as he called the Gentiles, Sharkey's saloon was a good place to trade language, booze, stories, gossip, bar tricks, ballads, songs, and snatches. For me, my father's saloon was home for at least an hour a day seven days a week. The back room, which my father envisioned as his Conservatory of Music, I saw as my disciplinary cell, my school of hard knocks. Daddy meant well, but I always had Sharkey to contend with.

Daddy opened his saloon in 1920 at 55 Rutgers Street, between Monroe and Cherry, close to the wharves, warehouses, and marine bustle of South Street, the East River waterfront. The waterfront was good for the saloon business, but it was bad for Jews. For age-old reasons—looks, speech, religious habits, social habits—Jews were not eligible to work the East River piers and warehouses, or the ships being loaded and unloaded; and since the saloon drew much of its trade from the waterfront docks, its morning and late-afternoon customers were mainly working stiffs.

Among the saloon regulars, I remember some Italians, some Dutchmen, some Englishmen, a craggy fellow called Joe Welsh (a Welshman?) who taught me a good way to tie my shoelaces; a small group of Americans (those who spoke without a recognizable foreign accent); and a large clique of young Irishmen who lived in the neighborhood and used Daddy's saloon as a way station to and from work on the waterfront. There were Jewish customers, too, but they came mostly in the evening, and from outside the immediate neighborhood.

But my clearest memory of Daddy's saloon dates from the summer when I was eight, after Daddy had moved us from our flat above the saloon into 60 Rutgers Street, a tenement directly across the street. I remember crossing the cobbled street, avoiding a broken line of fresh horse manure, skipping over the cracks in the sidewalk just for luck, and pausing in front of Daddy's saloon. The lower half of the storefront plate-glass window was painted dark green and the only way to see what was going on inside was to push against the swinging doors. The push had a good feeling, like going downhill on a pushmobile.

The saloon was long and narrow and cool, running straight from the street to the back yard. On summer afternoons when I entered with my fiddle case under my arm, I would see a clutch of ordinary bums—the everyday hangers-on—sitting around the small tables near the swinging doors, smoking, sipping beer, looking at an old newspaper, or sometimes sleeping it off in fragile ice-cream-parlor chairs tilted against the scaly gray-buff wall.

Set on the sawdust floor was the bar, a dozen or so feet long, with its brass railing and brass spittoons, and, beyond that, a door opened into a small hall, a vile-smelling toilet, and two back rooms —my practice room, bare except for a music stand; and the other (boasting a barred window), which looked out on the back yard. This last room contained empty cartons, mops and brooms, a workbench, some tools, and a large wire cage which served its special function late on Saturday nights when sporting customers with strong stomachs watched intently as an alley cat fought a water rat to death. The crowd bet on the outcome, and Sharkey was, of course, the trusted stake-holder.

Sharkey was full of surprises. All my life he continued to surprise me. One hot day when I came into the saloon for a bottle of lemon soda, several customers were standing at the bar singing a song, while Daddy accompanied them on a harmonica. Where he had learned to play the harmonica only God knows. On another occasion, I found him with a pair of spoons in his outsized hand, and he rapped out a rhythm—clickety-clack, clickety-clack—while a half-loaded Irishman staggered through a reel. And when the singing and handclapping and shouting faded away, everyone laughed and there was a call for fresh drinks.

But woe to the occasional innocent fresh up from the docks, who, unaware of his surroundings—cocky, provocative, goyisher, unfamiliar with Sharkey's house rules—dared give the impression that Sharkey's harmonica-playing or his singing or his Yiddish accent were in any respect laughable. If he did, he would wake up later in the back room not remembering who had hit him, or why. And when he eventually found his way back to the bar, Sharkey would look at him and grin. "Waddya say, tough guy, can I buy you a drink?" And it was plain that Sharkey had forgiven his innocent indiscretion.

The saloon give-and-take, the animated conversation of the goyim, seldom failed to inspire Sharkey. From them he picked up new words: useful expressions, songs, poems, and considerable trivia—considerable even for a bartender. He could make you believe he had been to Dublin, seen the Liffey, and watched da River Shannon flow, and knew the exact location of County Cork. He could toast you in Gaelic—*Pug ma hone!* (Kiss my ass!)—and laughingly remind you that while there were no Irishmen in Palestine, there were plenty of Jews in Dublin.

While the Irish taught him their most popular Irish songs, it was from his Italian regulars that he first heard "O Sole Mio," "Marie," and a swinging tarantella full of engaging rhythms and Neapolitan obscenities. His speech came to be flavored with such expressions as *paesan'*, *pasta fazool*, and *capisc' italiano?* and a string of authentic Sicilian curses.

On the wall behind his bar hung a framed certificate showing King Neptune rising out of the sea—testimony that its owner had crossed the equator. Sharkey had acquired it one evening in exchange for a couple of drinks, and as a bonus had received pertinent information on the shipboard ritual, the location of the equator, and a lot of stuff about degrees of longitude and latitude, tonnage, stability, Plimsoll marks, and other instruction useless to anyone except a bartender. Or another sailor. Add to these his salty expressions in his kitchen Yiddish, his stockpile of Polish and Russian street phrases, his ability to sound like an ex-con when he wanted to, and you had the East Side's all-time great bartender.

My father, I realized years late, simply had *flavor*. The way he gestured affirmation corroborated his customer's view, supported his position, made him feel at home, and provided the appropriate "bullshit." That's what his customers wanted to hear, and—as he put it—not some crap you could get out of a book. When Joe Welsh, who worked on a coal truck, came in for his eye-opener, Sharkey would say, "Waddya loadin' today, Joe, ant'racite?" Sharkey couldn't tell anthracite from anthrax, but it gave the coal man a warm feeling to know that somebody *cared*. Once, when an off-duty Irish cop named Finney mentioned that he sang second tenor in the Police Department Glee Club, Sharkey said, "It's a fuckin' shame! When they gonna make you foist?" He wanted *all* his customers to be first.

To be a right guy—according to his own standards, his own code—was my father's greatest strength, his greatest weakness, and his true religion. While his Gentile customers found this quality admirable, Jews in the immediate neighborhood found his right-guyness incomprehensible. In the new Pale they had fashioned for themselves they were again pious, meek, and self-effacing.

They feared Sharkey; he dressed up like the enemy, often talked like the enemy, did not keep the Sabbath, and—mystery of mysteries—he appeared *unafraid of the enemy*. After a thousand years of persecution, he acted as if nothing had ever happened—the Diaspora, the oppression, the pogroms—nothing. A strange Jew. And for this reason the neighborhood garment workers, peddlers, pieceworkers, never entered Sharkey's saloon.

Sharkey's Jewish customers were a different breed. They came to the saloon from other parts of the East Side and from as far away as Brooklyn and the Bronx. I once asked Mama why one of Daddy's good customers, who lived in the Bronx, came all the way down to Daddy's saloon on the East Side. Didn't they have saloons in the Bronx? "They come down to give Daddy a play," she said, meaning they came to pay their respects, to put some money on the bar, to build up a debt of goodwill they might call in at a future date, and (as I had little reason to suspect then) to pay off old debts to the man who had been Big Jack Zelig's admirer and errand boy.

Sharkey's high-roller Jewish customers, unlike their sober, circumspect, and fearful brethren, were ambitious and successful, and wanted their share of what America had to offer, not sometime in the messianic future but right now! Unlike the Jews in the slum tenements on Rutgers, Monroe, and Madison streets, Sharkey's prized Jewish customers lived in a world of silk shirts, pearl-gray fedoras, illegal booze and firearms, heavy tips, willing women, and the certain knowledge that power achieved through terror and brutality and fear and the cooperation of crooked cops, corrupt officials, and an unprincipled judiciary was more likely to produce the good life than all the promises of ancient rabbis. These were the mobsters, the strongarm guys (the *shtarker*), the gamblers, pimps, con men, stickup artists, fellow saloonkeepers and cabaret owners—the riffraff who made up New York's netherworld.

These were Sharkey's friends, friends of friends, old sidekicks, or young ambitious hoods, all hustling, dealing, mingling, waiting for the main chance. And the saloon was a good place to wait, to talk, to negotiate, to leave compromising packages in Sharkey's hands for safekeeping and then retrieve them when the coast was clear, to pick up instructions, to give and receive what were often false promises, to have a drink, sing a song, and to enjoy the companionship of other fearless Jews on the make.

For Jews they were: immigrant Jews like Sharkey, or sons of Orthodox immigrant Jews—non-practicing second-generation Jews but Jews nonetheless. They were those whose first language was Yiddish and who still spoke more easily in Yiddish than in their East Side English, who sang the Yiddish songs arrogantly, defiantly, who viewed themselves and each other as big shots, smart-money boys, the *cha-*

varim, colleagues, supporters and henchmen of such Jewish saloon idols as Kid Dropper, Big Jack Zelig, Joe the Greaser, and Arnold Rothstein. Each night I listened, full of anticipation and excitement, as Sharkey related the exploits of these and others to Mama—not the stories from the *Daily News*, the *Mirror*, or the *Evening Graphic*, but the *true* events leading to the imprisonment of this one, the murder of that one, the electrocution of still another.

Their swashbuckling names, as Sharkey whispered them to Mama late at night, have stayed with me, for over half a century inscribed on my mind, a child's catalogue of heroes: Kid Dropper, Monk Eastman, Kid Twist, Gyp the Blood, Lefty Louie, Herman Rosenthal, Johnny Spanish, Little Kishkey, Dopey Benny, Nigger Benny, Yoshe Nigger, Little Augie, Monkey Levine. And, as I learned years later, the names of their immigrant parents: Kaplan, Horowitz, Rosenberg, Rosenthal, Rosenzweig, Fein, Toplinsky, Schneider, Orgen, Fisher, and so on. As Zaida often said, "For shame!"

I eased past men like these on Saturday and Sunday late afternoons on the way to the back room to practice my violin. Standing at the bar, at leisure, they drank quietly and carried on hushed conversations; they were boisterous only when they sang. Arriving as they did after a midday meal, they were usually well insulated by East Side Jewish fare, and carried enough carbohydrates and chicken fat to power a seven-passenger Packard, and the quantities of gaseous seltzer accompanying their chopped liver, roast chicken, and potato pancakes would have kept the *Graf Zeppelin* aloft for a week. It was therefore no surprise that the whiskey they drank, Sharkey's most expensive bourbon—his own Old Grand-Dad—appeared to have little effect. Jewish drinkers, it was believed, held their liquor better than Gentiles did. They probably did not; their stomachs were simply better insulated.

Sharkey used the words *nikhter* (sober) and *shikker* (drunk) extensively; shikker was not only an adjective ("He is shikker"), but also a most important noun ("He is a shikker"—a drunkard). While Gentiles see drunkenness as having degrees—tight, inebriated, blind, paralyzed, loaded, tipsy—my father saw no gradations, no fine lines; a Jew was either sober or he was shikker.

On those rare occasions when a misled Jew lost his perspective

and set out to drink whiskey like a goy, he forfeited the respect of his
friends, his drinking partners, and perhaps the Jewish community at
large. When such a tragedy befell, Sharkey summed up the group
feeling. "A Yid a shikker," he said to his customers, "*zul geharget
verren!*"—A Jew who is a drunkard ought to be killed! Sharkey did
not realize that, considering his audience, he had just invented a new
form of tragic irony.

Although the saloon Jews did not have a true "drinking" song,
there was seldom a singing session that did not include the song I
remember as "Oy, Oy, Shikker Iz a Goy"—the Jewish drunkard's
theme song, full of comfort and joy. The goy is drunk, the song goes,
and he *must* drink because he is a goy; the Jew, however, is sober,
and he must pray because he is a Jew. Sharkey's chosen saloon few
had of course long ago given up prayer for bribery, theft, and assault
with a deadly weapon, but that didn't stop them from believing in
the message and spirit of the song. It seemed so inexpressibly Jewish!
Immanuel Kant said, "Women, ministers, and Jews do not get drunk";
it's clear he had never visited Daddy's saloon.

In my saloon experience as a child and as an adult, I have seen
Jews barely able to walk straight, lunging against walls, careening
against doors, bars, windows, falling-down drunk, their firewater faces
aflame, their eyes glazed, as they continued to bellow "Oy, Oy, Shikker
Iz a Goy" until they collapsed unconscious. (After a male infant is
circumcised, the *mohel* touches the child's lips with wine; my father
used to say some Jews never got over it. Still, during the many years
I knew him, I never heard Daddy speak a harsh word to Mama and
I never saw Sharkey drunk.)

Aside from raising himself to the top of a saloon world which
was sentimental and at the same time incorrigibly violent, my father's
principal activity was his attempt to create a child prodigy, a boy
wonder of the musical world, a virtuoso in the image of the great
Jewish violinists, by inspiring in his feckless and unwilling son anxiety,
cold sweat, fear, and ultimately hatred.

For eight years—commencing when I was five years old—Sharkey's harsh and heavy whip hand frequently brought me to tears as
part of the price of my own clumsiness and failure to please him. In

all that time, no one questioned Sharkey's authority or ability to transform me into something *he* wanted. That unnecessary, unasked question, put in the way I intend to put it now, seems preposterous: should a father (whose favorite instruments are the harmonica and the spoons, but who can nevertheless hum the first few phrases of Kol Nidre) expect to take his young and untalented son, who thrills to the exploits of Kid Dropper, Little Augie, and Gyp the Blood, and make him—for a dollar a lesson with a neighborhood teacher and an hour of daily practice in the back room of the family saloon—into another Heifetz or Elman or Menuhin?

The question seems foolish, but it isn't. It omits two important elements: my father's ambition, and whatever inspired his apparently odd and whimsical record collection—a collection that I believe more accurately reflected his eclectic taste and artistic sensitivity than did his favorite saloon music. It was indeed this collection of records that helped counterbalance the crap—Sharkey's word—that for a time had been the musical substance in my life and, for that matter, in his.

It all began about 1922 when Daddy bought what he called the Machine, a handsome mahogany Victor Talking Machine, better known as a Victrola. It stood chest-high, and came furnished with a dozen empty record albums stamped in gold with letters of the alphabet—A-B through W-Z—concealed on a shelf under the turntable behind a pair of doors. A gracefully curved lid protected against dust and maltreatment both the turntable and a gilded tone arm that, as I remember it, was about the size and weight of a bowling pin.

Daddy was overelaborately concerned with the operation of his Machine. The brass crank for winding it was kept hidden from the rest of the family. He was dead certain that neither Mama nor I— especially I—had the intelligence and mechanical aptitude required to insert the crank into the hole in the side of the Machine and wind it up. The task was too delicate, too complicated, and so the Machine was to be played only in Daddy's presence and under his personal supervision. (Later, when he brought home an Atwater Kent radio about the size of a small coffin, he wouldn't let anyone in the family touch that either, or tune it, or change stations without his approval. I have been notably unhandy with mechanical and electrical devices ever since.)

Daddy loved his Machine as if it were an animate object. Mama told me he had paid two hundred dollars for it, and two hundred dollars was a tidy sum on Rutgers Street in the early twenties. Rent in the tenement at 55 Rutgers, from which we had just moved and where my grandfather's family still lived, ranged from twelve to fifteen dollars a month; thus, the cost of Daddy's Machine was well over a year's rent. But it was worth it. The Machine was the best on the block and could be heard all up and down Rutgers Street, particularly in the summer months when the front-room windows were kept wide open.

Daddy played his Machine day and night, whenever he had any free time. "Come here," he would order, "and listen to some *real* singing." Considering his lack of formal education—who in the world would dare become his musical mentor?—his record collection was quite remarkable in both range of price and taste. Daddy's collection included a large number of Victor Red Seals heavily in favor of Enrico Caruso (twelve-inch Caruso solos sold for three dollars each; duets, four dollars; the "Quartet" from *Rigoletto*, six dollars; the "Sextet" from *Lucia*, seven dollars—all of which were in Daddy's collection, along with records with the Columbia, Vocalion, Brunswick, and Pathé labels, among those I recall. As Roland Gelatt, the phonograph's historian, put it, "A collection of Red Seal Records established one as a person of both taste and property." On Rutgers Street, anyway, Daddy fitted that description perfectly.

Opera and Italian tenors were among his principal interests, and he never tired of pronouncing the names of Enrico Caruso, Giovanni Martinelli, Antonio Scotti, Tito Schipa, and Beniamino Gigli, as if these lovely Italian sounds were a conjuration. Where he learned to pronounce them I do not know—an Italian customer perhaps. Over and over he would play Caruso's best-known arias from *Aida*, *La Bohème*, *La Juive*, *Tosca*, and others, and as Caruso would reach a climax, Daddy would look at me and say, "Well? Well? What did I tell you?" Sometimes he would hum and sing along with the soloist. His range, of course, was no match for Caruso's—still, Daddy was a tenor, wasn't he?—and he enjoyed taking a stab at the high-flying florid cadenzas, which he somehow made sound cantorial.

While Daddy favored tenors, he did not neglect the other voices: Chaliapin sang something from *Boris*, Titta Ruffo sang the "Largo al factotum" from *The Barber of Seville* (I listened to it so many times I can still remember most of the words), Galli-Curci sang the "Sempre libera" from *La Traviata*, Schumann-Heink sang "Silent Night," and so on. Old war horses even then, but they were new to Daddy and me, and we both loved them.

When Daddy brought home a new record, he played it over and over and over, and I would hear the words and tune repeated until, willingly or not, I had memorized them. By the time I was eight I could sing, approximately, the melodies of the *Rigoletto* "Quartet," the *Lucia* "Sextet," and John McCormack's version of "Danny Boy" (the "Largo al factotum" was more difficult; I couldn't fake that until I was twelve).

My memory of the order in which I learned these pieces, or the order in which Daddy bought them, is uncertain; while I can recall the words and tunes on many of Daddy's favorite records, I can no longer say which tenor sang what aria. But Daddy always would. (A year before his death at eighty-three, he recalled for me a melody from *Aida*. He hummed a phrase. "Remember that?" he asked, as he came out of his falsetto. "Ah-h-h, that Martinelli used to sing that song so that you wanted to give him a kiss.")

Daddy loved the sound of his Machine, but he had little or no notion of the literal meaning of any of the words of the arias. Nor did I. However, I'm convinced that he caught the sense of what was being sung, and that his emotional response was appropriate. To Daddy, literal meanings were crap; literal meanings were not his forte. It was spirit that counted, and soul. And except for Jewish music (which was, of course, in a class by itself), only the Italians had it. By choice or accident, Daddy's Machine almost never said anything in French or German. Except for the Russian *Boris* (parts of which he claimed he understood) and his favorite aria from *La Juive* (which I am not at all certain he recognized as French), his heart lay with those operas that were, for him, unmistakably Italian—the arias of Puccini, Verdi, Bellini, Donizetti, or Leoncavallo. I doubt whether in those years the names Mozart or Debussy or Wagner had any meaning for Daddy.

I'm sorry he missed Wagner. Since he was unaware of Wagner and therefore of his anti-Semitism, I think he would have enjoyed particularly the overblown, brassy preludes, because even then my father had a special fondness for marching-band music—a fondness he passed on to me. He owned a number of records made by Sousa and by the U.S. Marine Band, and Mama's dish cupboards frequently rattled to the zoom-bang of the "Washington Post March" and "Stars and Stripes Forever." The march he enjoyed most (or, at any rate, played most) was the "Jack Tar March," and when his Machine boomed out the one-*two*, one-*two*, one-*two* rhythm of this jiggling, foot-tapping piece, he *whistled* this fine tune to its rousing finale. (Years later, after several drinks in good company, I found that I too could whistle the "Jack Tar March," albeit fuzzily.)

Daddy's musical tastes ranged even further afield. When he wasn't listening to his "classical" records, he took a childish pleasure in requiring Mama and me to listen to what I remember as "the laughing record." This musical oddity began with a straightforward unaccompanied performance of "The Last Rose of Summer" by a competent if undistinguished cellist. Before long, the cellist was joined by a man's voice laughing at first in rather short, perfunctory bursts, progressing to steadier, sustained laughter, and finally (now joined by a female voice) turning into a laughing-crying uproar.

The performance was so blatantly idiotic and the laughter so infectious that by the time the record had run its three-minute course we were all guffawing uproariously. Mama never laughed hard without crying, and the nonsensical whole was further protracted by Daddy's Dick-and-Jane cries: "Look at your Mama! She cries! Why does she cry? Look, she's going crazy!" and we would shake our shoulders, stamp our feet, look through our fingers, and laugh and laugh and laugh with simple pleasure—while Mama laughed and cried.

One day Daddy brought home a ten-inch record called "Red Hot Henry Brown" (in Daddy's house, ten-inch records were not to be taken seriously). The vocalist, whose name I can't remember, sang something like this:

I'm Red Hot Henry Brown,
I'm the hottest man in town.
That redheaded mama that you heard about,
Took one look at me and the fire went out.

The record was clearly intended to shock Mama. While Mama's language was occasionally salty, she was essentially a modest woman, and Daddy enjoyed teasing her. Perhaps he thought there was something rather dirty about Red Hot Henry Brown, that stuff about "the hottest man in town," and "that redheaded mama." And Mama enjoyed playing into his hands. "Feh!" she would say, imitating Zaida. "That's music?" And Daddy would raise his arm and move his hand rapidly in a gesture of dismissal. "Go on," he would say, mockingly, "what do *you* know about music?" But he was teasing and she knew it, and she played the game because she knew he enjoyed it.

Somewhere in the process of putting together his record collection (I must have been four or five), Daddy decided it would be nice to have his son become a great violinist. Jews had always ranked high among the world's greatest fiddle players, and such names as Mischa Elman and Jascha Heifetz were, in Jewish households, household names. And on the Lower East Side, even among the poorest of the poor, the idea of successfully raising a child prodigy was not considered outrageous or even strange; even God might be persuaded to intervene, and which poverty-stricken Jew did not consider himself an old pro at that Holy Game?

Daddy, however, obviously felt strong enough to fulfill my destiny on his own, without His help. At the time, his ambition for me was sparked by two recorded examples he owned of the virtuoso fiddler's art: Elman's tender version of the "Meditation" from *Thaïs*, and Heifetz's highwire performance of Sarasate's *Zigeunerweisen*, more easily pronounced *Gypsy Airs*. Some time after Daddy brought these records home, listened to them, and made up his mind what my role in his life was to be, his pronunciamento was handed down to my mother and me.

When he first brought the Elman and Heifetz records home, they were not intended to suit *me*—they simply conformed to his criterion for building his collection. If Daddy was moved to sing along with a record, or whistle even some part of it (he wasn't greedy), he would buy it. Everything else was crap; and in this spirit of utter simplicity, Daddy and Mama and I were never forced to listen to such crap as symphonies, concertos, oratorios, ballet music, orchestral preludes, overtures, tone poems, jazz, chamber music, or even folk music (unless it happened to be sung in Yiddish).

The final group of Daddy's records—selections he considered to be representative of the cantorial art—is another matter altogether, to be taken up presently. It includes the records of the performing cantors over whom Daddy and Zaida were to have their greatest disagreement in their long history of bitter conflict. Meanwhile, Daddy continued to play his Machine, and to dream his dreams. But his dreams, he would have been astounded to learn, were not mine.

CHAPTER TWO

Next to Daddy's Caruso records, his favorites were those by *hazzanim*, the world's most famous cantors. True cantors sang authentic selections from prescribed or authorized synagogue services—the sort of music Christian churches call "liturgical." Other cantors sang pieces in Yiddish embroidered with religious or sacred phrases; mixed Yiddish and Hebrew texts with rich instrumental and choral backgrounds; genuine folk songs and "folk songs" written for popular theater productions; ballads, flagwavers, and tearjerkers.

While Daddy loved all cantors and would-be cantors equally (as I did), Zaida despised the second-rank cantors and didn't always agree with Daddy's view of the true cantors. The difference between how Daddy listened and how Zaida listened was evident: Daddy listened purely for musical virtues, and Zaida evaluated the effectiveness and authenticity of the religious communication. While they heard the same musical language, each was his or her own translator, and much was lost in both private interpretations. I think Daddy would have accepted the conclusions of Zaida's expeditions in search of error if Zaida had been willing to discuss the principles of his evaluation. But Zaida never would. It's possible his refusal was prompted by spite.

Once, after he and Daddy had argued at length the vocal and musical ability of one of their cantors and the appropriateness of his interpretation, Daddy left in a huff (only Zaida or Mama could get away with provoking my father), and Zaida turned to me and quietly observed that the so-called cantorial selection Daddy had been carrying on about should be sung not at the synagogue lectern but on a stage, in a theater—a point he had never raised with Daddy. If Zaida had played fair, the match between the two would clearly have been no contest.

Daddy was a pushover for anything that plucked, as they say, at his heartstrings, but a *hazzanishe* piece—authentic or not—moved him not so much for its religious message as for its musical wallop. Daddy had little respect for organized religion, a view painful to Zaida but one he would never openly challenge. They both loved good singing, and Zaida, outside Daddy's presence, once acknowledged that Caruso would have made a true cantor had he been trained properly, and, of course, had he been Jewish. Daddy, for his part, had an unrestrained admiration for virtuosity whether he found it in a boxer, a thief, or even a cantor.

The cantorial style, make no mistake, requires vocal virtuosity equal to anything found in Verdi or Puccini. The accomplished cantor is the highwire artist among singers; high above the crowd, his co-loratura atremble, he jumps and sways dramatically from one brilliant ornament to another, each more difficult, more dazzling than the last. His unique voice—part male, part female, with the beauty and power of old-time castrati—soars to heaven pleading for justice and mercy and love, and even the unfaithful might suspect that the Lord of the universe pays attention and listens. Daddy, too, listened. And when the Machine's needle reached the last groove, he often murmured a solemn amen.

Daddy admired high voices more than all others. To be sure, Daddy was a saloonkeeper, but only because he was a realist; if he had an occupational fantasy at all, I know he would have liked to be a cantor. Height is what moved him. He preferred coloratura sopranos to lyric sopranos, tenors to baritones, and in later years tried never to miss a yodeler named Elton Britt, who sang regularly on the *Grand Ole Opry* radio program and whose specialty was hitting a high falsetto tone and sustaining it forever.

Thus Daddy was obsessed with the cantorial art, or what he *thought* was the cantorial art. For Zaida, here was a made-to-order opportunity for further instruction—shaping and affirming Sharkey's faltering Jewishness. No one was better qualified to do so than Zaida, the acknowledged leader of the Rutgers Street congregation, synagogue scholar, authentic and respected *baal t'fillah* (master reader of the

Sabbath services), and cantor—albeit a minor one—in his own right. Why, then, had he let slip this chance to instruct, to fashion, to persuade, to win Sharkey over, and to raise (even a jot) his own level of Jewish consciousness?

Why, instead, had he chosen to discuss and argue points on which Sharkey's views were, in truth, as valid as his own: questions of pitch, timbre, tempo, dynamics, interpretation, and the *musical* significance of a recorded cantorial performance? These were questions in which Zaida was clearly out of his element; besides, this was a subject Sharkey knew enough about to have a strong, informed opinion, and he kept in trim defending it against other lovers of the cantor's art, however less distinguished than Zaida they might be.

What seems strange to me now is Zaida's lack of encouragement and sympathy even when Sharkey showed a flicker of contrition or repentance, some indication that he remembered he had been raised as a Jew, that there was such a thing as Yiddishkeit, and that, despite appearances, he had not forgotten his birthright and his and Zaida's common heritage. Such occasions brought out the worst in Zaida, his *own* hostility. There were those times, for example, when Daddy offered to buy tickets for High Holiday services in one of the East Side's most prestigious synagogues, featuring an internationally known cantor, so that he and Zaida and I could attend the services together. Zaida would most often refuse. He would not be seen walking through the East Side streets accompanied by Sharkey; nor would he be seen entering the synagogue with this near-Gentile whose saloon remained open on the Holy Days. It would make more sense, Zaida observed, if Sharkey stayed in his saloon and Zaida took me to the synagogue alone.

Sometimes late at night I would overhear Daddy pleading his case to Mama, appealing to her sense of fairness. He *had* reformed, hadn't he? It *was* a good idea for him to go to the synagogue at least once in a while, wasn't it? He wished to be seen and remembered as a Jew, and what was wrong with that? It was not *right* for Zaida to make it so difficult for him, to resist his pleas, to be so obstinate, so mean, so *unfeeling*. Perhaps she could talk to Zaida; she could persuade him that it would be good for me to see the inside of the great synagogue on Rivington Street in the company of my father *and* my grandfather.

Perhaps Mama did. Some years, Zaida relented and the three of us went together; in other years, Daddy and I went without Zaida.

Through the years, Zaida persisted in challenging Sharkey on his own ground, to debate who sang best, an issue Sharkey had already settled for himself. Why Zaida chose to give his opponent an unnecessary advantage—he avoided raising the religious questions of the cantorial art—was beyond my understanding. After the usual Friday Sabbath dinner in Zaida's kitchen, they debated and argued, and I listened. I wanted Zaida's soft-spoken opposition to win out, but it never did. Sharkey, frustrated to the end, always had the last word.

"Go on, Shvair," he said, "you're truly a learned man, but when it comes to talking about a voice like Rosenblatt's, you're not really an authority." Zaida would tighten his lips indicating the debate was over. His expression would be calm, but his small white goatee would move ever so slightly. He would reach up to adjust his yarmulke, and he would shrug his shoulders as if to say there was nothing left to talk about, and the best thing Sharkey could do now was go back to his saloon and its Friday-night bustle, where, if his odd views did not prevail, he could always punch somebody in the nose.

Between Zaida and Sharkey there were, of course, certain visible differences: their taste in clothes, their speech, the company they kept, and the physical environment in which they chose to work. At first glance, their disagreements were unremarkable—Sharkey the immigrant Jew with his visions of becoming rich and powerful and less Jewish, and Zaida the immigrant Jew, poor, helpless, powerless, who clung to the vision of greater salvation through becoming even *more* Jewish.

Sharkey believed America's streets were paved with gold, that is, just beneath the manure, while Zaida saw only the manure. Sharkey was willing to fight like a Gentile—while Zaida, like a Christian, found his defense in turning the other cheek. Sharkey was the Jew who saw the East Side's huddled masses as a manipulated group of passive *luftmenschen*—a people from whom to distance himself—while Zaida saw these same people as a transplanted religious community of which he was not only a charter member but a member forevermore.

Sharkey and Zaida were as different from each other as night

44

from day, good from evil, or—and this is perhaps closer to the truth—war from peace. It is not enough for me to seek the differences, as I have been doing, only in what I was able to observe between them in the muddle of the Lower East Side. The origins of these deep differences go much further back, and I think may be found in the circumstances of their birth.

Sharkey grew up in Bialystok, an important industrial and textile manufacturing city, in a household entirely dependent on the garment industry. Samuel, my paternal grandfather and head of the household, had saved enough money to acquire a buttonhole-making machine. Each day, as a Bialystok visitor told me, the male members of the family picked up bundles of vests, jackets, and coats from factories in various parts of the city and brought them back to the house, where the girls and women, under Grandfather Samuel's supervision, fashioned the required buttonholes, after which the clothes were returned to the factories.

Because payment was reckoned on piecework, all members of the family old enough to help were expected to pitch in. Thus the household was, in effect, a tiny factory on its own. Although Daddy grew up in a Jewish household and in an atmosphere that emphasized the value of industriousness, his environment could not have been conducive to scholarship and the contemplative life. Thus, there were no luftmenschen in Grandfather Samuel's household—all members were usefully employed. In Bialystok, the Astrinsky family were known as the Holemakers.

Zaida was brought up in Kovno. He was born into a family with a tradition of scholarship, and had Zaida remained in Kovno he would no doubt have pursued his studies until a discerning congregation chose him to be their rabbi. This was to be his life's work; in Kovno, as on the East Side, he was most comfortable in the company of students, aspiring scholars, sages, and other exemplars of the spiritual life. It was this pervasive spirituality of his early life in Kovno that gave gentle, bookish Zaida his air of quiet piety and elegance.

The hearts of Zaida and his East Side companions in blessed misery clung to the old ways: the melancholy rituals they believed would finally bring them joy and happiness and triumphant justification. Sharkey and his peers had little time for contemplative remorse praying for mercy and forgiveness. Their ideal was not to be realized by asking a stern and often seemingly indifferent God for joy and happiness and the wherewithal to make these delights possible, but by *demanding* that their fellow men satisfy their needs with money.

In this world, the reasoning went, the odds were against those who lived merely with hope and prayer—life was a game of winner take all. In America, to win meant to take on as rapidly as possible those qualities that had made Americans winners and Jews losers and victims. To ignore this fact of life, to delay or resist assimilation, was thus, inevitably, the mark of a loser. Sharkey recognized this ignoble truth almost as soon as he and his brother Muttel made their way from Castle Garden to the Lower East Side. To Zaida, this defection, this near-apostasy, was incomprehensible. Sharkey had concluded that being a Jew was in itself not enough; for Zaida, it was total deliverance.

For the young Sharkey, America was somewhere to *go*. He came to America not with a sense of relief but with enthusiasm and the anticipation of fun and adventure—an extension of the spree that had started when at age twelve he had tossed a homemade bomb into a Bialystok police station. Mama later told me how he escaped through the narrow streets, how his terrified family sent him off to a relation in the country, how he was hidden there inside a kitchen stove, how he was joined by his older brother Muttel escaping the wrath of a cuckolded husband, how they made their way to another brother in London, and then to still another brother, Hymie, who lived on the Lower East Side. What headiness, what excitement, what flaming exhilaration—off to America, the Goldeneh Medineh, land of the free! Sharkey would grow to love it, Zaida to hate it and yearn for Kovno, the *old* Kovno, as if for Jews there ever was such a welcoming place.

That Sharkey and Zaida differed in so many respects may be attributed not only to the difference in their early intellectual training, but also to the social and economic values of their respective families in Bialystok and in Kovno. Even as a child I was not surprised to find that Sharkey's penchant for physical combat—violent competition as a valid way of life—led me directly to his fanatical love of sports, particularly boxing, and his vanity. He was a professional boxer for a while.

For years I heard him explain to Mama what it was like to be a boxer. "The main thing was to keep in shape," he said. "First I'd punch the light bag, then I jumped with a rope, then I'd bang the heavy bag, and then my trainer would try to find somebody I could spar with." Above all, he protected his face, which, except for the bump on his nose, remained unmarked. A cauliflower ear, as he put it, was the mark of the punch-drunk rumdums who hung around the gym, with their slack jaws and bobbing heads. Getting hit was apparently not his style, but it was plain that he enjoyed the impact *his* bandaged fists made when they thumped home; he learned to slip punches, to feint, to jab, to hook, and other refinements of the fighter's trade.

Although he had shown considerable promise at the outset, he soon discovered he had neither the inclination nor the dedication necessary to fight a long series of three- and six-round bouts for five or ten dollars each. (It was during this period that he received his new name—his trainer said he moved like Sharkey, the famous fighter who ran a saloon on 14th Street. My father had never heard of Tom Sharkey, but the name seemed to be a lucky one, and after his first few bouts as "Young Sharkey" everyone called him Sharkey.)

Zaida viewed boxing with distaste and no little revulsion. A prizefight had as much meaning as a cat-and-dog fight or last week's garbage. Zaida had been trained for the traditional Jewish intellectual life; by flickering candlelight he had spent thousands of hours on wooden benches at old wooden tables studying textbooks compiled by wise old rabbis after centuries of scholarship, so that perhaps someday he too could live out his life as a scholar, could comment on the commentaries, to add to the ancient interpretations of what it meant to be a Jew.

How in God's name had he acquired Sharkey as a son-in-law? Having Sharkey in the family was a crushing blow to the heart and as bitter as gall. Why had his daughter chosen this man? It was as shameful as if she had taken up with a boisterous, culturally insensitive, illiterate Polish peasant. Worse, his son-in-law had never been seen to open a book. (Years later, when I asked Mama why we never had any books or magazines around the house, she said, "You know Daddy couldn't read; to have books in the house would remind him he couldn't, and I didn't want him to feel bad." "But what about me?" I wanted to say, but didn't; I was just beginning to understand how deeply she must have loved him.) In any case, Zaida's antagonist, the self-satisfied, cocky, aspiring American roughneck, remained (outside of saloon life) stolidly ignorant.

In the saloon, however, his primary quality was audacity. Sharkey and his company of *shtarker* saw themselves as soldiers, as part of the forward guard, boldly and confidently moving ahead to previously unexplored and perhaps dangerous territory—certain that somewhere out there they'd find a prosperous and assured future. Sharkey laughed about the future. "One day everybody thinks you're dead and the next day you're laughing at the world," he told Mama, as he related what happened once, after the celebrated Zelig had been shot, and, seemingly close to death, was hurried to a hospital.

A group of Zelig's boys, as I recall Sharkey's narrative, directed a spray of bullets at a saloon on the Bowery owned by a competitive gang leader who had ordered Zelig's death. In turn, the two gangs, with knives and guns, went at each other for six days and nights. At the end there were no winners—only the lucky, the wounded, and the dead. Meanwhile, Zelig was recovering nicely. "The big joke," Sharkey said, "was that Zelig, who was supposed to be dying by inches, came out smelling like a rose. So don't tell *me* about the future."

Zaida, in wholehearted opposition to Sharkey's values, saw himself as part of the rear guard, the true conservatives; despite his experience as a Jew in Kovno, he still embraced the fantasy that wherever he and his companions had been was safer than wherever Sharkey and his shock troops appeared to be going. The distant past, calculated in centuries, seemed more attractive than the future. In any case, one could at least *read* about the past.

Zaida's daily life was uncomplicated by East Side temptations. For him, how to live a good life was clearly set out in the *Shulchan Aruch's* 613 rules of daily living—a code which told Zaida when to eat, when to pray, how to pray, when to work, when to rest, what to wear on Mondays as distinguished from Saturdays—in short, how to be a good Jew in the eyes of other good Jews, and, of course, how to please the Lord.

Everything about Zaida suggested pride and dignity. A turn-of-the-century photograph taken after he arrived in America shows him with a dark, bushy beard, which by the time I knew him had become a Vandyke, white and neatly trimmed. His face was rosy and always looked freshly scrubbed, his clothing neat, his bearing distinguished. I remember Zaida best in a blue serge suit, a white shirt with a celluloid collar, and a ready-made black bow tie; in the winter he wore a bulky, handsome black chinchilla overcoat with a black velvet collar, and a black homburg. I don't know the color of his hair, because I never saw his head uncovered, indoors or out. No smoking (but a pinch of snuff harmed no one). No drinking (except as a ritual). His wife, Chana, kept a kosher table, and with God's help they had raised seven children as orthodox Jews.

I knew without being told that Zaida believed there was grace in being honest, in telling the truth, in keeping promises. Sharkey believed honesty had its place provided it was self-serving; that keeping a promise was·a surrender by the weak and helpless; that promises were devices to gain time or advantage, and when used properly were invaluable instruments of expediency. Zaida feared only the Lord, his God; Sharkey feared law and order as practiced by Irish cops.

Sharkey already enjoyed the respect of his particular congregation, but respect was only a low rung on the ladder of power. Respect was nice, but it was fear that brought home the bacon. As for pride (called *nachis*), Sharkey wanted Mama to be proud of him; that came first. And if his son happened to turn out the way he hoped he would . . . well, that too would be a source of pride.

There were rules to be followed, all right, but not someone else's rules. In the saloon, rules were made to fit circumstances. Sharkey had his own *Shulchan Aruch*; there may even have been *more* than 613 rules, but they were easier to remember because they were *his* rules, *his* laws. His daily life was controlled not by laws laid down by ancient rabbis but by strict nonobservance of the liquor laws of the State of New York. His saloon's opening and closing hours, its busy periods and slow periods, the likes and dislikes of his customers—these dictated when he worked and when he rested, the significance of the Sabbath, his eating habits, the clothes he wore, the company he kept, and his relation to Mama and to me. Only Mama could frustrate him, irritate him, anger him, and still avoid his wrath. He feared little else.

Maintaining law and order in his saloon was only a matter of muscle and money. There was convincing evidence of Sharkey's muscle; as for money, with the help of Mama's unaudited accounting procedures, the saloon profits deposited in the bank daily (I frequently delivered the sealed envelope myself) grew beyond Sharkey's dreams, despite the requisite payoffs to local and state cops and federal revenue agents.

As an example of the saloon's increasing success, when my sister Dorothy was born in the summer of 1920 we moved from the 55 Rutgers Street three-room cold-water flat we rented for thirteen dollars a month, to a four-room apartment with steam heat and hot water at thirty dollars a month, at 60 Rutgers Street; and soon after, into the next apartment as well (the landlord tore down the wall between), making seven rooms at sixty-five dollars a month. Sharkey was the sybarite at 60 Rutgers Street; Zaida was the ascetic at number 55. For Zaida his tenement flat was not home, but just a place to eat and sleep; the true life, spiritual and intellectual, was found in the synagogue.

In Zaida's traditional view, a Jew went to the synagogue to worship, not to be entertained; the synagogue was not created to be a theater with the hazzan as the featured attraction. Daddy believed synagogue services were boring and lifeless, redeemed only by the hazzan's exciting vocal flights. Zaida wasn't against employing a hazzan (after all, he was one himself) but he would have preferred the hazzan to function as in olden times, as the chanter and prayer leader.

Since the hazzan's tasks required no specialization, his job was easy enough, and because he received no salary there was often no audition. But as times changed and the hazzan's duties were revised, it became a full-time job for those blessed with *bel canto* voices. The brilliant voice took precedence over the colorless liturgy, and congregations rejoiced.

As the number of new-style cantors grew, attendance at synagogues burgeoned. Good news travels fast, and the best cantors became as famous and well paid as opera stars. Cantor Yussele Rosenblatt was hired by a New York congregation at what was then the astonishing salary of twenty-four hundred dollars. Fees of a thousand dollars for the religious holidays were common, with journeyman cantors commanding two hundred dollars. Despite the prices, customers stood in line for tickets as if they were about to receive a message from the Messiah himself.

Among East Side hazzan buffs, the ranking cantors were discussed with the same busy interest and missionary enthusiasm as Daddy's saloon customers discussed Jewish prizefighters, or the kids on the block discussed baseball players. By the time I was ten or twelve, the names Gershon Sirota, Zavel Kwartin, Mordecai Herschman, Yussele Rosenblatt, Berele Chagy, and Moishe Oysher were as familiar to me as Rabbit Maranville, Miller Huggins, Waite Hoyt, Rogers Hornsby, Burleigh Grimes, and Ty Cobb.

Opportunities to hear the great cantors in person were of course rare, and for this reason Zaida could be persuaded to cross the street from his tenement to ours to hear Daddy's recordings. These occasions offended Zaida's taste. He suspected Mama did not keep a fully kosher house, and he sat and listened as stiffly as if he were in a church pew. Mama kept what might be called a semi-kosher house, but for Zaida there were no halfway measures or halfway houses—a Jewish house was either a kosher house or it was not.

Once the recording had ended, Zaida would sit silently for a moment, perhaps wondering whether to commit himself, and then say, "We'll have to talk about it." What he meant was: This is no house for a serious discussion.

Daddy found the apex of musical arts in Moishe Oysher's version of "A Hazzandl oif Shabbes" ("A Cantor for the Sabbath"). Zaida couldn't believe his ears. Daddy simply liked the way Moishe and Oysher rhymed. I remember the special delight he took in rhyming the words as if they made a perfect rhyme. And the way Moishe Oysher sang "A Cantor for the Sabbath"—that was perfect! But not for Zaida.

The song tells of an itinerant cantor who comes to a tiny village to lead the Sabbath services. To hear the new arrival are three solid citizens: a tailor, a blacksmith, and a coachman, who are so overwhelmed by the cantor's magnificent singing and praying that each in turn sings and shouts his praises to the world. In short, "A Cantor for the Sabbath" brought together those thoughts and sentiments dearest to Daddy's heart. Only Zaida—when he heard Moishe Oysher's recording of this work—remained unmoved. Zaida had listened to the record once, and once was enough. The case was closed! That Zaida could announce this information to the world (that is, up and down Rutgers Street) caused Daddy conspicuous frustration.

As Sharkey he reinforced his arguments with his fists, but he would never strike his father-in-law. Obviously, the safest course was to avoid arguing with him. Yet that was dangerous, because Zaida might come to believe his own opinion was correct, which would, in turn, make Daddy's opinion wrong. And that would be an intolerable strain on Daddy's or Sharkey's ego—take your pick.

Zaida's arguments merely frustrated Daddy, but they made Sharkey apoplectic. (I didn't understand Daddy/Sharkey at that time. I lived in fear of him, remembering the welts on my legs and bottom, and I often wished he were dead.) The wrangling between Sharkey and Zaida was in Yiddish, of course, and Zaida's language was more graceful and precise than Sharkey's, which Sharkey considered to be still another unfair advantage. Especially when Zaida deliberately used words or expressions not in Sharkey's vocabulary. He looked also upon Sharkey's rough English and his English-speaking customers with disgust and disdain. Whether intentional or not, Zaida's way of putting things kept Sharkey in his place. A saloonkeeper arguing with the synagogue's master reader and keeper of the faith? The very idea was an abomination to Zaida.

Does a good Jew blame God? Perhaps. But not for long. All his life Zaida had tried to act like a *mensch*, to exemplify what was decent, honest, worthwhile, noble. And as a reward his oldest daughter, Sophie, took up with a *Sharkey*. She had brought home a roughneck, a prizefighter. A knife in the heart. But then, who can understand God's strange ways?

Sophie Friedman met young Sharkey in 1916. She was twenty, tall, with attractive, regular features. By East Side standards, her English was excellent (occasional lapses of grammar and a faint New York Yiddish accent). She lived with her parents, four brothers, and two sisters in a tenement on Monroe Street, which stood in the center of a bustling open-air pushcart market, and she worked uptown as an office girl. Sunday evenings she often went to the movie house known locally as the Dump, around the corner on Rutgers Street. For ten cents she saw a full-length movie, a comedy, a serial episode, and several short subjects, and her ticket gave her an opportunity to participate in a drawing for a set of dishes given away by Jacobson, the owner, to stimulate trade. On Sundays the Dump was crowded, and the crowd was noisy and (in the excitement of the drawing) frequently unruly.

Young Sharkey, a handsome, tough twenty-seven, protected the Dump for Jacobson as part usher and part bouncer. For some time he'd had eyes for the good-looking, somewhat haughty brunette; he made sure that she always had a good seat and that no one annoyed her. He waited for her after the show was over, and she permitted him to walk her home. On occasion they stopped at the corner restaurant for cheesecake and coffee. He called her Suffih; and while everyone else called him Sharkey, she called him Millie—short for Milton. Apparently she didn't like Max, his first name; Max, she pointed out, could be the English equivalent of his older brother's name, Muttel, and how can brothers have the same name? For her, he would now be Millie.

She enjoyed his company, his protectiveness, his intense desire to get ahead, and his obvious wish to include her in his future. At twenty it was important for a Jewish girl to seriously consider all proposals. Her greatest concern, of course, was the near certainty that a man like Sharkey would not meet with her father's approval. Over a period of months, Sharkey had told her of his youth in Bialystok, how he had arrived in America, how his brother Muttel went to work in a saloon and left him living with Hymie and his wife; he told her how Zelig had befriended him and of his excursion into the ring. He knew he could make good—with her help. She believed him, but she knew her father would not, and that was her immediate problem.

One Sunday when she entered the Dump, ticket in hand, Sharkey took her to one side and handed her a fresh ticket. "Here's your ticket," he whispered. "I fixed it up."

She now had two tickets, and when Jacobson appeared on the

stage at intermission and drew a ticket out of a glass bowl and called out the winning number, she was thrilled to discover that it matched one of the tickets in her hand. She duly appeared on the stage and waited nervously while Jacobson validated her ticket. After the show, she went to the box office, where she found Sharkey waiting to help carry home her prize. Here, then, was a good opportunity to introduce Sharkey to her father. He would enter the Friedman house carrying a carton of free dishes, and that would be as favorable an introduction as any.

As Mama told me in later years, Zaida was not impressed. He knew his daughter had been walking around with this toughchik; he had heard disagreeable gossip among members of his congregation. He had asked his two older sons, Mike and Harry, for a report on his daughter's suitor, and he did not like what he had been told. Not a bit. "In the beginning," Mama told me, "Zaida was so ashamed of Daddy that he refused to allow me to bring him into the house again."

Zaida never liked Daddy. He didn't like his ways, his dress, his overbearing confidence, his physical power, his reputation. Zaida saw Daddy as a bully, and what Mama admired as Daddy's hearty, outgoing nature Zaida saw as unadorned, un-Jewish arrogance. Mama, however, had her own mind.

She decided to resist her father. She was, after all, twenty, and her two younger sisters, Bella and Gussie, were waiting for their turn to get married, too. She was, by East Side standards, an educated person; she contributed most of her wages to the family purse, and while it may have been true that Millie had been, well, uneducated and belligerent, he was at heart a good man; he wished to marry her, and with her guidance and moral support he would become a person the family would be proud of. And besides, he loved her.

Zaida was appalled at his oldest daughter's resistance, her inability to see Sharkey as *prost*—vulgar, ill-mannered—just another East Side cabdriver or gambler or saloonkeeper or prizefighter. What sort of pride could he take in this unprincipled, unlettered Philistine? And where was the possibility of *koved*, what chance was there that such an unlearned man would be able to produce a learned child, a potential scholar?

"If Zaida would have just given Daddy a chance," Mama told me, "I knew he would like him."

Sophie Friedman was dreaming. What she had hoped for was unlikely. Zaida would eventually come to know Daddy better than he cared to, but he would never like him. He would always be Sharkey, the street tough, from whom there would never be *nachis, yichis, koved*—all forms of pride. Still there was one last hope, one last appeal. He would force her to choose between her father and a man she had known for less than a year. "I worried," Mama said, "and I trembled. Your grandfather promised that if I didn't stop seeing Daddy, he would kill himself. He said he would jump off the roof."

At the time, Zaida's threat was credible; suicide among East Side Jews was common. The Yiddish press reported suicides daily, and several years earlier Mama's aunt, a woman Zaida had been fond of, had done just that—jumped from a roof and killed herself. Zaida's threat was therefore nothing to joke about. The tenement roofs were four, five, and six stories high, and were easily reached on the spur of any hotheaded moment, and jumping off the roof was foolproof. "I'll tell you," Mama said, "I was really worried."

But she remained unshaken in her conviction that while Zaida's talk of suicide might be appropriate as the expression of an angry father, he would not kill himself. Once she and Daddy were married, Zaida would see that Daddy was not as bad as he had been made out to be. She was fortunately right on the first count—Mama and Daddy were married on St. Patrick's Day in 1917, just three weeks before the United States declared war on Germany—and, unfortunately, wrong on the second; Zaida's revulsion grew steadily.

Mama and Daddy began their marriage with no money to speak of. Mama, of course, had to quit working—on the Lower East Side a working wife meant the husband was a bum and thus unemployable—and Daddy carried with him the walking-around money he was able to con out of Jacobson the theater owner. He had been living in a tiny flat with his brother Muttel, who had promised him a chance to work into the saloon business—an opportunity Daddy believed was just in the offing. For this reason, there seemed little sense in trying to find even a temporary job while he was waiting for the Main Chance. Now that he and Mama were married they were supposed to live together; the question was where, and how to do it.

Zaida solved the young couple's financial problems by bending the traditional Jewish marriage agreement called the *kest*, which enables a couple to live with the bride's parents and be supported by them so the young man can continue his scholarly career. The "scholarly career" rule distressed Zaida, but his concern for Mama was strong, and when he offered Daddy and Mama sleeping space in his four-room flat on Monroe Street, they accepted gratefully, and moved in.

"Even though your grandfather never had any money," Daddy said to me years later, "he wanted me and Mama to save up some, and that's why he asked us to move in. Your Zaida was a good man, but he didn't know that in America if you have no money you're nothing." Daddy was of course right. Zaida never had any money, and Sharkey eventually made loads of money, but Zaida never let him forget that in all other ways, excepting brute force, he was Sharkey's superior.

Four months after the wedding, Zaida wished he had never heard the name Ostransky. The entire East Side rang with the name of Hymie Ostransky, Sharkey's brother. All the newspapers in the city, including the Yiddish press, headlined the accursed name, and his daughter Sophie was three months' pregnant with a child who would bear that name. Zaida attended his daily services with a broken heart, and must have wondered where his God was hiding.

The press reports told of the relationship between Hymie Ostransky and a Mrs. Dora Cohen, a former neighbor. Mrs. Cohen and Hymie developed a more than neighborly relation, and, to kill their flowering romance, Hymie's wife, Minnie, moved her family to a tenement some distance away. Mrs. Cohen, the mother of five and not to be outdone, also moved so that she could be closer to Hymie.

Apparently their affair was resumed, because one summer Wednesday, on July 25, 1917, Hymie packed a suitcase, told Minnie he was leaving on a solo vacation, and made his way directly to Mrs. Cohen's flat. Minnie followed him. Entering Mrs. Cohen's kitchen, she confronted them, and, holding up an infant child she had brought with her, she pleaded with Mrs. Cohen to stop seeing Hymie.

Mrs. Cohen, perhaps moved by the child, walked to the hallway door to gather up her own five children and asked Hymie to leave, this time for good. Hymie pulled a gun and shot Mrs. Cohen. Minnie screamed, put down her child, and lunged at Hymie's gun arm. Hymie shot two bullets into Minnie's arm. Minnie continued to scream, Mrs. Cohen was now on the floor, and in the next instant Hymie turned the gun on himself and pulled the trigger.

Soon after, the police arrived to take Hymie, Minnie, and Mrs. Cohen to Gouverneur Hospital, only five minutes away. The attending surgeon announced that Minnie was superficially wounded, Hymie was critically wounded, and Mrs. Cohen was dead. Hymie was then operated upon successfully, after which he was tried for murder, convicted, and sentenced to die in the electric chair at Sing Sing during the week of June 10, 1918. Minnie appealed to the governor for clemency, on the grounds that Hymie had been so insane with rage that he hadn't known what he was doing, but her appeal was denied.

The news brought Zaida deep embarrassment. Instead of offering Sharkey comfort and sympathy for his brother's tragic end, he offered only quiet disdain. He could, and did, frustrate his son-in-law at will, and when he wished to, he could push him to fury. Still, as I think back on it, these gambits could not really have brought my grandfather any satisfaction. Sharkey was not a truly worthy opponent, and for Zaida it must have been all too easy. Perhaps he felt that his treatment of Sharkey compensated in some small way for the loss of his own integrity. After all, he had promised his daughter he would jump off the roof and kill himself if she married Sharkey. And she did. He had made a *promise* he hadn't kept.

CHAPTER THREE

The Talmud is a monumental armamentarium of commentaries and interpretations and decisions on traditional Jewish laws, customs, and issues, some of which are at least two thousand years old. The first division of the Talmud is called the Mishna, and the Mishna warns good Jews that male children, at age five, must start to "read" the Old Testament. Most Lower East Side parents took the Mishna's admonishment seriously, and training young boys to mouth, in Hebrew, "Moses commanded us the Law, a heritage to the congregation of Jacob" was a tenement industry.

Almost every East Side block of tenements housed its share of *melamdim*—teachers of elementary Hebrew—who, by relentless rote drill, could teach even a five-year-old to speak phrases as if he understood what he was saying. When a young boy's English (let alone his Hebrew) was still unformed at this freshman stage of his life, he found himself in the hands of one of these teachers—"going to *heder*"—which often meant seven or eight years of learning to repeat ritual petitions and benedictions without understanding their theological or social meanings.

There were, however, good Hebrew schools scattered through the district, where competent teachers offered boys several hours of late-afternoon instruction after public school and on Sundays. Such a school—a Talmud Torah—is what Zaida had in mind for me. Zaida's view was that the average *melamid* was to be avoided like a bad cold; he was usually an otherwise unemployed immigrant who scraped a living teaching ungrateful children their ABCs in a language they would never understand. The teacher's object was to gather together half a dozen students (at a dollar a week each), whose financial support would make his life not quite so meaningless. Because of his questionable ability to teach unknowing and uncaring boys, the neighborhood scholars gave him short shrift. According to Zaida's standards, his first grandson was not to be the victim of a grown-up know-nothing. A good Talmud Torah, with solid, selected teachers who would help me become a good Jew, was the place for me. Or so he hoped.

The nearest Talmud Torah was on Henry Street—three and a half blocks from the saloon and, according to Mama, an enormous distance for an unaccompanied Jewish infant to travel. (Had Zaida forgotten that on the corner of Henry and Rutgers streets stood a *church*?) She managed to avoid the subject of my attending heder as long as she could, until shortly before I was eligible to enroll in the public school on Madison Street, a block *before* Henry Street and the church, which was—thank God!—only *two* blocks from the saloon.

Daddy's view about heder made more sense, at least to me. Once I started the first grade I was required to practice my violin daily, immediately upon my return from school, and since classes at the Talmud Torah ran from three-thirty to five-thirty, that was obviously out of the question. If I was to attend a heder, Daddy said, it would have to be close to the saloon and take up no more than half an hour a day, and—above all—I could not attend Sunday sessions. (Sunday meetings were common; Saturday was our Sabbath, and Daddy was not going to have his Sunday morning sleep-in disturbed by outside influences.) Daddy's view prevailed.

"I don't want any trouble with your father," Daddy said to Mama. "If you want the boy in a heder, find one that's close to the house. You're so smart, *you* find a rabbi. He's your son too."

Mama accepted the challenge. She spoke to a few knowledgeable women in the neighborhood, and a few days later she walked me around the corner and introduced me to my new Hebrew teacher—a *rebitzen*. Her name was Mrs. Zuckerman. She was a kind woman in her sixties, short and squat, who, it occurs to me, looked like Charles Laughton with a shawl on his head. Mama explained to Daddy that Mrs. Zuckerman's husband had been a rabbi, and after his death she eked out a living teaching young boys Hebrew, taking up where her husband, may he rest in peace, left off.

She lived alone on the second floor of a Cherry Street tenement in unbelievably poor circumstances, even for the Lower East Side. The rent for her three-room flat, pitifully furnished with several home-painted chairs and a round dining-room table covered with cracked white oilcloth, was eleven dollars a month. The rebitzin may have had additional income, but certainly the fees from her six or eight heder students kept her alive. I was, of course, a bonanza, because I brought my dollar bill regularly once a week and she didn't have to see me on Sundays, and when I was older and began to cut classes once or twice a week to roam the waterfront streets, our secret was revealed to no one.

For Mama, Mrs. Zuckerman's value was that I could go to heder each day after school without having to cross even one street. Cherry and Rutgers intersected, and all I had to do was walk around the corner. When Zaida discovered who was to be my new "rabbi," he was beside himself. He fussed and he fumed as he must have when Mama first introduced him to Sharkey. How, he asked, can a boy learn from an old woman how to become a man? And why was I not being sent to a Talmud Torah where I could be trained by a genuine rabbi?

Mama's stance was firm. The rebitzen's house on Cherry Street was just around the corner; the Talmud Torah and Zaida's proper rabbis were miles away and, en route, millions of young goyim lay in waiting. There was risk. Uncertainty. Danger. My safety, she insisted, was obviously more important than the quality of my training; the object was to keep me alive until I was at least thirteen—a Bar Mitzvah boy. What was the value of Talmud Torah training to a dead boy?

Zaida was stumped. His daughter's argument was one he could understand. Mama reminded him of the Henry Street church looming over the entire neighborhood. A fact well noted, and, against his weakening judgment, he gave way, not at all gracefully. I don't believe he ever discovered my daily lessons were for only a half hour, and there would be no Sunday sessions. Mama saved him those secondary concerns, and now my Hebrew lessons began.

In the beginning it was fun. What English I had was, of course, an ultimate waste—Mrs. Zuckerman spoke to me in Yiddish. It was her job to teach me to read aloud from the Pentateuch, published in Hebrew, and to read and write Hebrew in a script of funny little curves and lines used to simulate the printed Hebrew alphabet (a simulation I didn't notice until I was past fifty). I remember the innocent pleasure with which I learned to read the Hebrew characters in the normal backward direction (since I could barely read English, reading Hebrew from right to left seemed no great trial); it was as if I were studying a secret code.

As Mrs. Zuckerman and I sat side by side studying the handwritten alphabet from an old, yellowed card, I can still recall the joy I felt when, after pronouncing a letter or two that satisfied the rebitzen, a penny would drop down on the card—a penny for *me*, perhaps from God Himself, and certainly (when I finally figured out what was happening) a reasonable investment for my teacher.

Mrs. Zuckerman taught in the traditional manner, that is, by rote. I learned the alphabet, how to translate diacritical marks into vowel sounds, how to combine these with consonants into simple words, and after some years, how to race through the traditional three daily services and the Sabbath prayers, known as the Siddur. My written work was another matter. I grew quite facile at handling the letters of the alphabet, but since I knew no Hebrew, I used the letters to create words in Yiddish—plainly but badly spelled. (I am sorry now that Mrs. Zuckerman was unable to teach me Hebrew properly, so I could use it to firm up my kitchen French, German, and Italian.)

In the Talmud Torah, as I discovered later, the rabbis provided their students with a translation (in Yiddish, of course) of the Hebrew they learned to read and write. Such good fortune was not to be mine, except in the lessons I learned from the Haggaddah—the story of Israel's bondage and flight from Egypt. It is the custom that during the Passover celebration, the youngest child at the festive table asks his father four questions from the Haggaddah narrative. Mrs. Zuckerman taught me both the Hebrew and its Yiddish translation so I could read the printed text (presumably for the women who did not understand Hebrew) and translate immediately word by word. (In later years, I did my French that way: *Où* where *est* is *la plume?* the pen?)

Altogether it helped my Hebrew very little. I suppose Mrs. Zuckerman taught me to read and write as well as anyone could have done, and I know she grasped the overall sense of what she tried to teach me, but I am equally certain she had no more idea of even literal translation than I did. Still, I enjoyed the pennies. In 1924 you could buy a good-sized kosher dill pickle for two cents, fished right out of the barrel.

One Saturday morning Zaida took me with him to his regular synagogue service. After listening to my fluent pronunciation and the speed of my lambent tongue, he reported to Mama that considering everything (including my not having to pass the church on Henry Street), my progress was satisfactory. For a dollar a week the rebitzen was worth every penny she was being paid, but as soon as I was ready to prepare for my Bar Mitzvah, he would have to find me a proper teacher. Until then, he was satisfied with both my fluency and my understanding. Zaida must have expressed the opinion with tongue in cheek. To this day, nearly sixty years after my Bar Mitzvah, I can read Hebrew like a whiz; I can read it, all right, except for one small point: I can't understand what I'm reading. I am unable to understand one word now, and I was unable to understand one word of what I read for Mrs. Zuckerman. No, to tell the truth—there was one word: *Ahdonoy* means God.

For six years in Mrs. Zuckerman's scantily furnished front room I bravely recited words and phrases from various holy texts. Resting my book on the white, fly-specked oilcloth where figures of bluebirds alternated with gray spots where the oilcloth had cracked and rubbed off after thousands of scrubbings, I droned on. The days of pennies from heaven had long since gone. Perhaps I ought not to be blamed for eventually growing tired of Mrs. Zuckerman's good will, her piety, her unquestioning obligation to have me repeat again and again those curlicued configurations of Hebrew characters which represented Pharaoh, Eleazar, Ben Ezra, and other less significant sounds.

It is just possible that my still developing mind was too full of running and jumping and playing up-and-down scales and chords to understand the immutable necessity for making these foreign sounds. I had yet to understand that for an Orthodox Jew, a *real* Jew, the mere utterance of these sounds—comprehensible or not—is proof of faith. The Mishna, after all, does not say it is necessary for mere boys to understand. It is enough that Zaida (and God, of course) understands. "So," as Mrs. Zuckerman put it for six years, "read!" And I did.

The day finally came when my studies with Mrs. Zuckerman ended. I had just passed my twelfth birthday and Zaida's interest in my formal Hebrew education had reached its peak. I now had one year to prepare correctly for my Bar Mitzvah, and Zaida convinced Mama, who no longer feared for my safety, that I ought to complete my studies with a genuine rabbi. By this time, too, I had learned to move through the house stealthily on Sunday (or any other day) while Daddy's sleep remained unbroken. Daddy was beginning to enjoy the idea of his son's imminent manhood, my feelings aside, and he began to look forward to my Bar Mitzvah with genuine anticipation.

And so with everyone's good wishes (except, of course, Mrs. Zuckerman's; I lacked the knowledge and sensitivity to sense the sorrow she must have felt), Zaida arranged for me to take lessons with a true, one-hundred-percent-male rabbi. I can't remember his name, since I addressed him only as "Rebbe"—which is the Yiddish word for "rabbi." Daddy was especially happy with Zaida's choice. "He *must* be a good rabbi," he said. "He charges fifty cents a lesson."

My father's enthusiasm guaranteed that my Bar Mitzvah would be no small celebration. Sharkey saw this event as an appropriate occasion for bringing together all his saloon colleagues in what he called "a catered affair." For me, however, the Bar Mitzvah preparation brought about the most difficult year of study in my short life. The new rabbi, a dour-faced man with a black beard, taught me privately for an hour a day, six days a week, working and reworking several long sections from the Book of Moses which I would be called upon to read out loud to Zaida and his congregation from the synagogue scrolls, on the Sabbath following my thirteenth birthday.

Hebrew characters in the scrolls (which were not printed but hand-done) lacked the diacritical marks found in published works, and you either knew how to pronounce the vowels or you were up the creek. Furthermore, these passages were not simply to be recited, but sung by the Bar Mitzvah boy and responded to by his father. Further, I was required to present in Yiddish a speech of deliverance releasing me from my flaming youth, and, later, its English equivalent during the evening banquet before the guests got drunk, after which I would become the fortunate recipient of Bar Mitzvah gifts—fountain pens and wristwatches from aunts and uncles; from Zaida, a beautiful white prayer shawl for my very own, and a deeply mysterious set of phylacteries—two small cubes filled with ancient Jewish laws, tied with leather straps to arm and head to remind me I was a Jew; and from Sharkey's best customers, at least two handfuls of five-, ten-, and twenty-dollar gold pieces handed to me undisguised or in little sealed envelopes.

(During the evening banquet I would slip into the men's room so I could hide a handful of gold pieces in my shoes, for my own benefit, thus proving I was Sharkey's kid indeed; and at the same time I also demonstrated the timeliness of my father's synagogue prayer where he thanked God "for having freed him from further responsibility for laws transgressed by his son.")

The Bar Mitzvah was a grand success. I performed in the synagogue like the true grandson of the Master Reader, I made speeches with depth and feeling. Hundreds of friends and relatives came to the banquet afterward to celebrate the steady rise of Sharkey's kid, and to eat, drink, and admire my picture on the rear of the four-page menu, where I appeared complete with black skullcap and Zaida's handsome white prayer shawl. Daddy laughed, Mama cried, and I was happy the affair was over. And, don't forget, there were those heavenly gold pieces.

Except for this night in question, I had long since lost interest in Zaida's version of the making of a Jew. Much as I admired Zaida, his goodness, his righteous concern, I resented the time I had to spend learning how to become a proper Jew. Add to this my dislike for studying the violin and Sharkey's resentment of my reluctance to follow his will. He had approached the challenge correctly: he had paid one hundred dollars for a fiddle; he had paid out fifty to two hundred and fifty dollars a year for lessons; he was fearful of a street-gambling career for one age thirteen; and he had relieved the pressure of the challenge by brutally beating his son in the back room of the saloon. Sharkey and his kid were to have a difficult relationship.

I don't remember the first time Sharkey whipped me. I remember the pain, all right, because for several years I was beaten at least once a week in the back room of Sharkey's saloon. The back room was not very large, probably nine feet by twelve feet. Except for two pieces of furniture Sharkey had built with his own hands—a table that would hold my music and my violin case, and a music stand made from a two-by-four upright and sawed-off chunks of legs that may have weighed more than I did—the room was empty, and even with its high metal ceiling and its stained linoleum floor, the space was small. And for an eleven-year-old trying to avoid being hit by his father's whip hand, the room seemed like a cell.

To avoid the brunt of Sharkey's blows I found myself darting to one corner, then another, holding my hands over my face, crying out my pleas for mercy, and suffering blows on whatever part of my body lay exposed. I discovered, as time went on, that my tactics were in vain. Sharkey's hand was faster than my quivery legs, and the game we played was no contest at all. On various occasions I was hand-whipped, struck with a leather belt Sharkey removed from his trousers, and, during one terrible period, flayed with a cat-o'-nine-tails.

While there were many *good* reasons for these beatings (I was late when I should have been early; I didn't do what Sharkey had ordered me to do; I had broken a promise of one sort or another), the true reason, now that I think back on it, was evident: every time, I had committed a mutinous act which forced me to miss my violin practicing. To Sharkey, there was no greater sin. I was frustrating his plans for my life, whether I intended to or not.

If he couldn't help me draw my bow smoothly across the strings, he could always draw forth my screams and tears: "Please, please, I won't do it again!" or "Please, give me another chance!" while he alternated his crashing blows with "*I'll* give you another chance!"—slam! "*I'll* give you another chance!"—slam! And when he had had his fill, he would stomp out of the room with his final word: "Now, *practice!*" After which, I always practiced hard.

Although the beatings never curbed my rebelliousness, they apparently made Sharkey feel better. Through those early years I blamed not only Sharkey for the marks along my back and sides and thighs, but I also blamed Yehudi Menuhin, the great violinist and prodigy Sharkey wanted me to be. What may be amusing now was, for me at the time, dead serious. Although I have never met Menuhin, any published notice of his career—even the mere mention of his name —still recalls the terror of my youth.

When I was about ten years old, Yehudi Menuhin became the ruling boy-hero of the Lower East Side's poor but discerning Jews. This situation was due of course to no special, arrogant ambition of Yehudi's. All great Jewish fiddle players were heroes, but Yehudi's position was something extraordinary, exalted, venerated. He was more than just a great fiddle player, he was an unusual kind of Jew. In a world of Abes, Samuels, Josephs, and Meyers, just imagine the courage it took to go through life in America bearing a name like Yehudi! Insiders spread the word that Yehudi's family were all made of the same stuff—even his sister was named Hephzibah! There was no doubt that certain astute critics could detect this wonderful ballsy quality in Yehudi's performances. Certainly Sharkey did.

There were times in Sharkey's saloon when the image-worship of Yehudi was given as much time as local prizefighter heroes, such as Sid Terris, Benny Leonard, or Kid Kaplan. The connection between prizefighting and fiddle playing was for Sharkey an important one. In his youth, we may recall, Sharkey had been a prizefighter, appearing under the name Young Sharkey. When I was old enough to understand the meaning of "fight"—on the East Side that would have been at about age five or six—he taught me to jab, feint, hook, and keep-your-chin-down. Perhaps what he had in mind was raising a champion boxer, but whatever his intent, it was all spoiled when, at the age of six, I brought home a note from school indicating my need for eye-glasses, which I have worn ever since.

I cannot imagine my father's frustration at this unwelcome news, and it is just possible that soon after, he decided to turn me over to a local fiddle teacher. To the best of my knowledge, for several years nothing of any exceptional musical significance took place, and for a while it appeared that my father's interest in my musical progress seemed to be waning. My own feelings were straightforward and less mixed. I hated whatever the violin represented.

When Menuhin first appeared on the scene, Sharkey and his Jewish customers agreed that anyone named Yehudi had to be an Orthodox Jew; furthermore, he was a "Russian" Jew (as opposed to a "German" Jew), and a Russian Jew, in Sharkey's eyes, was somehow more Jewish than other Jews. Despite my three years of violin lessons, I had not yet heard of Yehudi Menuhin. My teacher, however, had mentioned the names of other great violinists—Heifetz and Elman and Zimbalist, of course, and others. I was not entirely without sustenance. These men, after all, were not only world-famous fiddle players but they were Jews—an important point in building pride in a young Jewish violinist.

The names of these men, however, could have been the names of characters in Zaida's folk tales. They performed on records, they could be heard in London, Paris, Odessa, you could hear them on the radio; but they were not real persons, they were figures on a stage. My first trouble with Menuhin came when I realized he was not a man, but a boy. He was *real*. Frighteningly real. According to Sharkey's cool reasoning—drawn from saloon customers who kept abreast of Jewish culture, or from a reporter who worked for the *Jewish Daily Forward*, or from the owner of the music store where he bought his records—Menuhin was a boy not unlike his own boy. They were both boys. Children. Perhaps one could not expect his boy to play like a Heifetz or an Elman, but like another *boy*? Why not? A boy is a boy. And so the winter of 1928, the year of Menuhin's debut, became the winter of my discontent, and a previously unknown boy became my *bête noire*.

Then, for years and years (or so it seemed to me), my father would ask anyone who would listen, "Why can't my son play like Yehudi?" as if there were a true comparison to be made. When I learned, as I did, that Menuhin was in fact about a year and a half older than I was, I often wished to scream out to my father, "He's *older* than me!" but I never did.

Sharkey tolerated no back talk, and the best I could do in the circumstances was to look aggrieved. On Sharkey's lips, Menuhin's name became a conjuration. Yehudi became "Yehu*deh*," and Menuhin became "Men*uch*in" the way Germans say *ach*! And this pronunciation surely evoked a picture of Yehu*deh*, the contemplative, all-purpose Hebrew scholar, complete with skullcap, prayer shawl, phylacteries, and earlocks, intensely playing Kol Nidre on the G string. And if I only had the sense to model myself after Men*uch*in, perhaps the East Side would someday beat a path to *my* Kol Nidre. ("But Daddy, he's *older* than me!")

In this same period, along with the name of Menuhin, Sharkey now picked up another name with which to plague me: Ruggiero Ricci. Ricci made his New York debut in 1929, when I was eleven, but perforce couldn't match Menuhin's impact on East Side Jews. Sharkey was not likely to have come across Ricci's name in his usual circles, and he may have first heard of Ricci from Sarno, a spry old Italian with a genuine waxed mustache, who owned the barbershop next door to the saloon, and from whom Sharkey probably learned the correct, Italian way to say Ricci's name. "Ree-chee," he would say, "have you heard about Ree-chee?"

That Ricci was Italian was more than offset by his age. When I was eleven he was nine. "Nine!" Sharkey said. "You hear what I'm telling you? Nine!"

Ricci's debut concerto (chosen perhaps by a manager sensitive to New York's musical preferences) was the Mendelssohn. That choice alone would have had Sharkey's stalwart support. Mendelssohn may have preferred the Gentile life to the Jewish one, and Ricci—poor thing—had never had the choice. Still, the facts of Mendelssohn's (or Ricci's) history notwithstanding, for a violinist to play the Mendelssohn concerto was, in Sharkey's books, the highest manifestation of the Jewish spirit. Both Mendelssohn and Ricci were Jews, of one sort or another. Whether they liked it or not.

My own daily round was set, forever for all I knew. Sharkey had no idea how much I resented taking violin lessons plus my daily practicing, plus my daily Hebrew lessons, plus my trying to read in a house where any except school books were forbidden. No wonder, then, that for quite a while my fiddle playing was slipshod, lackadaisical, and, as Sharkey frequently put it, crappy. Nobody really cared what I wanted to do, I thought. All Sharkey cared about was the fucking fiddle, and he was a man whose mind was not easily turned around.

And now, in the light of Menuhin's brilliant debut, Ricci's emergence, and their growing fame, Sharkey's aspirations took on a new intensity, a new turn. He decided that whatever faults I might have (and I had many indeed) were not altogether of my own doing and might easily be attributed to some insufficiency in my violin teacher's methods. This notion may have been suggested to him by a flashy, fast-fingered fiddler then working at the American Casino—Sharkey's new night club—where he was known as Mischa Hoffmann, King of the Gypsies.

Sharkey's response was to fire my neighborhood teacher at one dollar a week and hire the Gypsy King for three. Moreover, he increased my practice time to two hours a day in the old back room where he could keep an ear on me, as it were, and, at the same time, this would cut down the time I had been spending running around the streets with the gang. His experience as an East Side youth made it clear that without his close supervision I was on my way to becoming a truly bad East Side boy. Daddy could only smell this situation, but Sharkey knew all about it, and the beatings became even more frequent.

I chafed at the time wasted indoors, the appalling injustice of not being allowed in the street with the gang to play games, gamble, tease girls, steal fruit off pushcarts, sneak into the movies; Sharkey had denied me the exciting life of a poor East Side delinquent. Now, however, that I was held captive by Menuhin, Ricci, Sharkey, my new Gypsy teacher Hoffmann, and what seemed to be endless hours of back-room practicing, it was not long before my violin playing took on a new dimension.

In a queer but marvelous way I began to sound transiently like a virtuoso. Under the Gypsy king's tutelage I kept playing faster and faster—perhaps trying to make the practice time go faster. The longer I was forced to practice, the better I sounded, and the better I sounded the longer Sharkey forced me to practice. I was in a snare, with no escape, and I hated it. Sharkey could have his Riccis, his Menuhins, his Gypsy kings—his lions—I thought, but I'll take my fakes every time. I yearned for the company of my peers: the street punks, the famous neighborhood no-goodniks whom I envied.

Sixty-year-old memories are like old-fashioned hand-tinted photographs. The pinks and yellows and sky blues are conceived in perfection that never really existed, not at any time. My street friends seemed ideal (except to Sharkey, of course), and the Lower East Side streets became not so much a welter of dirty brick-red tenements and their jumbled backyards as my place to run, play cards, shoot craps —my bright and sunny playing fields.

Summertime weekends were best of all. I recall especially a sunny Saturday afternoon—no school, no heder, no practicing until late in the afternoon. I was in my grandparents' flat, having just finished the Sabbath lunch (my sister Dorothy, seven, and my just-born brother were in our new flat across the street with Mama), and my object was to make my way out of the building and into the streets without being observed by Daddy from the saloon doorway. If Daddy saw me he would find something for me to do, something to keep me off the streets. It was an old game, and I was determined to win.

On sunny days Daddy kept the saloon door open to let the sunshine in, and from his post behind the bar he commanded a clear view of everyone going into or coming out of the building. I prayed he would have a few customers to engage his all-seeing eye. There was, however, an even worse possibility: if the saloon was empty of customers, as it frequently was early Saturday afternoon, Daddy would sit out in front, his chair tilted back against an iron railing separating the saloon entrance from the building entrance, watching his world go by. For me, that would be death.

Alert and cautious now, I tiptoed down the four flights of creaky stairs, each landing dimly lighted by a single small bulb. As I reached the ground floor I paused to peek around the edge of the stairwell, hoping I would not catch a glimpse of Daddy's lavender silk shirt. Happily, the God of Isaac and Abraham was with me—Daddy was in the saloon. Skittering away from the main entrance, a quick dash and a single hop-skip-and-jump took me into the back yard. I shinnied up the board fence, dropped to the other side, scooted across two more back yards, over two more fences, and entered the rear hallway of a building around the corner from Daddy's saloon. Now shifting to my second wind, I darted down the dark hall and emerged into the sunshine of Monroe Street, home safe.

I was looking for my two best friends—Peter Federinchik and Joseph Turano. To me they were Petey and Joey—Petey lived with his parents across the hall from Zaida, and Joey's father was a part-time bartender in Daddy's saloon. To Sharkey, they were Petey the Polack and Joey the Wop, mildly contemptuous names to remind us —especially me—that he did not approve of our hanging out together. Usually I took Sharkey's discomfiture to heart (even if I didn't act on it), but his disapproval of Petey and Joey had small effect on our friendship, because he knew, and I knew he knew, that Petey and Joey—compared to the rest of the gang of mostly tough Jewish kids —were relatively good boys.

"He's growing up to be a bum!" Daddy once said to Mama. "He don't wanna practice, he don't wanna go to heder, all he wants to do is play in the street with those two little punks—the goyim."

"Don't worry your head," Mama said, sticking up for me. "They're better than those Yiddishe bums on the corner. Better he should play with honest goyim than with those Yiddishe thieves."

Daddy pouted. Only Mama could make him pout. "According to you," he said in Yiddish, ending the conversation, "*everybody's* a thief!"

It was impossible for Daddy to understand that I was attracted to Petey and Joey just because they were *not* Jews. They were my exotics, my contact with the Outside World. I was in Petey's house one afternoon when his mother, a strong, flat-nosed woman Mama called Kotzeh, gave me my first ham sandwich. I loved it. And who else but Petey had a father who worked in the Cherry Street stable and was unafraid of horses? Who else on the East Side—outside of my movie-cowboy heroes—had anything to do with horses? And with whom else could I walk down nearby Gentile streets knowing that Joey was my safe conduct, my assurance that I wouldn't be beaten up by kids who were unaware that my father's name was Sharkey?

Because Petey and Joey weren't chained to the fiddle, weren't force-fed Hebrew, weren't running from one corner of the back room to another screaming *Please!* but were out roaming the back alleys, the back yards, running up the tenement stairs so they could jump from one roof to another—they were free!—exactly during the times I saw myself imprisoned just like George Raft, James Cagney, and other famous Hollywood convicts. And while Sharkey forced me to serve long years at hard labor, Petey and Joey were out on bail, stealing empty milk bottles and turning them in for the two-cent deposit, having fun, living it up, enjoying themselves, like kids on a *Saturday Evening Post* cover.

Of my two staunch friends, Petey, a chunky ten or eleven, with a round face, his mother's flat nose, and shaggy blond hair, was the more sensitive. He knew everyone called him Petey the Polack, and it filled him with a gnawing bitterness. "I'm *not* a Polack," he complained to me. "I'm a Russian!" And to prove it, he recited a Russian poem I thought worth learning. Here it is (phonetically—the way I remember it after fifty years):

> Ponyamayish parussky?
> Nazhna chuy na zakussky!

It loses its force in translation:

> Do you understand my Russian?
> Then here is my cock for an appetizer!

Petey's poetic blandishment (in what may have been Russian or Chinese for all I knew or cared) moved no one but me. Petey was my friend, and if he wished to be Russian, that was good enough for me.

Joey, on the other hand, never complained when he was called Joey the Wop. Once when someone knocked at the door, Mama called, "Who's there?" and Joey answered, "It's me—Joey the Wop!" Perhaps like me, he too enjoyed our differences. I taught Joey to swear like a Jew and he taught me to swear like a Wop. (Years later I discovered that Joey profited most by the exchange; the obscenities I taught him still had currency wherever Yiddish is spoken, while the expressions he taught me had meaning in Palermo but not in Rome.)

Joey also taught me to count to ten in Italian and Petey introduced me to Russian numbers, while I taught them to count in Yiddish. Joey—small, dark, neat, sharp, and always aware, always impatient to grow up—got the best of this exchange, too. At sundown each Friday, the start of the Sabbath, Joey went from one tenement flat to another, climbing up and down stairs, making the rounds of his "gas" route, when he would turn on the gaslight and fire it up for those housewives forbidden by Talmudic law to strike a match once the Sabbath had begun. Joey's price for this act of selflessness had always been one cent. After I taught Joey to count, he informed his customers that his new price was *tsvay cent* (two cents). While Sharkey had little use for Petey the Polack, he admired Joey the Wop's shrewdness. All of Joey's actions proved he was *alert*, and Sharkey knew the value of alertness.

My own sympathies lay with Petey. How I envied Petey his freedom! Nobody to tell him what to do, where to go—his mother worked as a seamstress in someone's sweatshop and his father worked in the Cherry Street stable—no fiddle lessons, no heder. Always available to play cards, dice, jump roofs, stone cars; to walk down to the river and watch used Trojans drift past, to wonder by what magic they stayed afloat, who had used them, to dream, to wet dream. And while Petey could go anywhere, could explore the seven seas, I had to listen to Sharkey's fretful voice reminding me that if I went near the river he would break every bone in my body.

As I came out of the dark hallway into the sunshine of Monroe Street, the outdoor market now closed up tight for the Sabbath, the pushcart tops tied down with assorted rags or old blankets or faded black oilcloth covers, there was Petey kicking a can down the street in one of our favorite games. It was all right with Monroe Street immigrants for Petey to play kick-the-can on the Sabbath because Petey was a goy—look at that flat nose, that yellow hair, his shabby clothes, that lack of Jewishness. I ran up to Petey at top speed, shouldered him aside with a newly learned stomp-kick tactic, and happily launched the can. "C'mon," I shouted, "let's go!" Go where? Anywhere! The hand-tinted Lower East Side lay before us.

The Lower East Side was small and cramped and confined, even dinky, but to a child's eyes on summer afternoons the territory was boundless—well, nearly boundless. Two and a half short blocks south of Daddy's saloon was South Street, with its Pier 34 sitting at the edge of a slick gray-green East River. Resting between the saloon and the river sat tiny Cherry Park, where, when the fancy struck me, I could climb the silvery jungle gym and swing along hanging by my arms from the rungs of the horizontal ladder on top, making Tarzan yells.

The park, as I remember it, had two slim trees, each tree trunk enclosed within a stockade of ugly black iron javelins, points up, as if any East Side kid would rather climb a pindling tree than boost himself up the jungle gym. In the center of Cherry Park stood a small concrete mushroom-shaped drinking fountain around which, when the weather was right, a small group of men passed pint-sized bottles.

I knew, of course, what was in the bottles. Everyone knew. What they drank was called "smoke," and the men drinking it were called "smokies."

For a dime they bought a pint of wood alcohol from the paint store, poured half of it into an empty pint bottle, then filled both pints from the drinking fountain. The mixture became white and cloudy—smoke-colored. They then drank from one bottle and saved the other. Later, one of them would be found blind or dead, and an ambulance would come to pick him up. And that was fun to watch.

I've seen smokies up close—they made sounds but they didn't talk. Their eyes were glazed and they didn't walk as much as they flopped along. Their faces were scabby, their noses broken and snotty, their skin the color of dough, and they cried a lot. Sharkey called these smokies *real* bums—worse than the plain ordinary bums who regularly came to Daddy's saloon. But then, where else in the world could I find a jungle gym and smokies in the same park? (I sometimes wonder whether Yehudi Menuhin could possibly have benefited from such an enriching extra-musical experience.)

The park and the river were my southern limits. To the north, however, half a mile of glittering and crowded streets and alleys stretched before me, ending at Delancey Street, where the Williamsburg Bridge swung across to Brooklyn. As I walked or ran through the East Side, only north and south seemed safe, secure, comfortable, predictable, full of Jews. To the west, only one block—Pike Street —supporting the gray-black pylons of the Manhattan Bridge (all roads seemed to lead to Brooklyn) was safe; and to the east there remained only Jefferson and Clinton streets. Beyond that, on either side, east or west, lurked the dread goyim, waiting to castrate helpless Jewish aliens. Mama's nameless fears.

I had heard about a lovely spot called Corlears Hook Park, only six blocks east of Daddy's saloon, but I never saw it. I loved the sound of its name—Corlears Hook—but only a death-seeking Jewish boy would be caught in a place called Corlears Hook. Cherry, Monroe, Madison, Henry, East Broadway, and the half-dozen blocks from there to Delancey were the streets where I sought to learn about the world.

Tenements on both sides of the street rose boxlike, four, five, or six stories, their baroque cornices resting on bricks a thousand shades of dirty red and liver brown. Each block had its own special joys, its secrets, its dangers, its domesticities. Our own little street contained within its one block nearly all the necessities to sustain life, a little liberty, and occasional happiness.

(My grandmother Chana, who lived most of her life in our little Rutgers Street enclave, never learned to speak English, because there was no great need to. Along both sides of her street, and in the Monroe Street pushcart market around the corner, she could find anything her heart desired. She had her own shopping center only a few steps from her house. On heavy shopping days, before the Sabbath, I often carried her shopping bags as she moved up and down the street buying—in Yiddish, of course—at the local grocery store, the bakery, the remnant shop, the candy store, the newsstand, the drug store, the plumber's, the kosher butcher shop, the man who made and sold his own furniture polish, and a place where you bought herring and pickles and sauerkraut fresh from the barrels. And for such incidentals as eyeglasses, tableware, pots and pans, and bedsheets, these were only five or six blocks to the north, on the pushcarts and stalls of Hester Street and Orchard Street.)

Multiply the shops of Rutgers and Monroe streets a hundred times, with their stalls and stores and pushcarts aswarm with Jewish house-wives out shopping mornings and afternoons, pushing, shoving, and haggling, while children played their pushing, shoving, and haggling games morning to night; add to these shoppers and players those who collected rent, delivered ice and coal, picked up the garbage, swept the street, sharpened knives and scissors, begged and stole, sold *me-zuzahs* door to door, and perhaps you can look back and imagine the sum of what it was to live on Lower East Side streets.

Behind the tenements, in the back yards and alleys of my ter-ritory, lay fascinating sources of youthful delight. Here indeed was the hidden Lower East Side: the marks of its poverty, its hodgepodge images pleasing only to happy, uncomprehending children. Here I could study the capricious motion of gray towels and sheets and ragged shirts as they brushed against rusty fire escapes, their slight movement lightening the characteristic heaviness of the big-city slum. Here I could marvel at the wonderful dark tangle of lines and angles which crossed the yards behind tenements, watched over by cranky Gentile janitors (who I now know were as sick in spirit as many of their Jewish tenants were in body).

See there—the light-blue sky that shows between the socks and sheets as they swing from their clotheslines strung between weather-beaten poles like awkward mobiles. And watch that thin cloud of steam from the tailor's pressing machine as it climbs the back wall of the tenement to join the smog hanging over the rooftop. Down below, in the cracked stone and slate courtyards, lie rainbow puddles of stinking liquid (where could it have come from?) along the old wooden fences that bear the marks of rubber balls, knife gouges, FUCK YOU in faded letters, and where you can see the grain of the wood in the streaks of little-boy urine stains.

All these exciting explorations of backyard life waited for Petey and me as we ran headlong down Monroe Street and up Jefferson toward East Broadway. The back yards would have to wait. We knew where we were going. Words were not necessary—at our speed we were incapable of speech. Like the wolf in the story, we huffed and we puffed, and we blew past houses and street corners, running break-neck with one hope: to watch at least part of the largest Saturday-afternoon crap game on the East Side. Up a block, down another block, and here, bordering on East Broadway, one of the East Side's most spacious roadways, stood Seward Park, and now the colonnade deep inside the park appeared before our very eyes.

I can still see Seward Park, with its swings, slides, jungle gyms, grassy spots; old men playing chess, and young chippies lounging on benches, but none of these were for us; we came for the *game*. We stopped running and moved casually toward the curiously Greek stone building called the Pavilion. Once up the wide stone steps, we peered into its far open reaches (which we thought were like pictures of the Parthenon), sheltered from wind and rain and the cops. We hoped the game would still be there, with all that money scattered on the floor and all those big shots gambling like crazy.

And there it was—in the far corner where the huddled older boys and men, some on their knees, others hunched over, sang their Saturday blues. The big Sabbath crap game was on, and if we minded our own business and didn't get in the way, we would be permitted to listen to the shooters' cantor-chant, "Seven come eleven! Eighter from Decatur! Come on-n-n-n-n Fever! Snake Eyes!" Bug-eyed, we watched the dice fall, listened to the music of silver dropped on the floor, and watched the lovely crumpled green bills change hands. In seven million ways it beat practicing the fiddle in the back room of Daddy's saloon, seven million miles away.

That my fiddle playing had improved immeasurably under the critical eye of Mischa Hoffman, King of the Gypsies, was no question. My father had been much taken with Hoffmann's popularity at the American Casino, and he appeared to have little doubt that Hoffmann could help me. And he was right. Hoffmann's fingers inspired me. While I hated the daily back-room practicing, I enjoyed Hoffmann's lessons. He talked very little and instructed by example. His English had an exotic, mid-European accent, and I never learned where he came from. As I said, we talked little.

Hoffmann was not a large man, and (as he looked standing next to me as I went through my lesson) was rather pleasantly roly-poly. He usually wore a three-piece shabby gray suit and a splashy colorful tie, and in warm weather, beads of sweat seemed to drip down his forehead from his neatly parted brown hair. As I think back on it now, perhaps he wanted to look both artistic and businesslike, to maintain the East European virtuoso role reinforced nightly by his freshly pressed tuxedo (as the star performer in the American Casino), and to show the parents of his students that he was, indeed, a businessman. Sharkey's customers loved him, all right, because he played what touched them, and gave them the notion they were a fallen European nobility listening to the music of their native land; and the parents of his students were impressed with his suit, his tie, and, of course, his fiddle playing.

Hoffmann was a sort of great fiddler. He knew the literature that pleased the unschooled, and he knew how to satisfy his students' parents, which were more or less the same thing. That he was essentially a Gypsy fiddler bothered no one who mattered; no one he met complained of his distinctive Gypsy style. When, during my lessons, he demonstrated (for Daddy's benefit) how I was to play this or that passage or exercise, whatever he played—Gounod or Lully or Kreutzer—came out sounding vaguely Romanian, as if we were all gathered around a fireplace somewhere in Carpathia while the master fiddler played only to touch our hearts.

What Hoffmann played *was* Romanian, but to Daddy's and my inexperienced ears everything he played sounded wonderful. We were both entranced by his fiddle work and carried away by what he did best—playing with abandon, and sliding unpredictably into predictable cadences. Like all first-rate Gypsy fiddlers, he had incredible technical facility, and in allegro tempos he was a past master of those musical drolleries that give the impression the player is laughing at the world. In slow passages his creative improvisation could, as Daddy put it, tear your heart out. Stylistically, Hoffmann may not have been much with Bach or Beethoven or Tchaikovsky, but with "Dark Eyes," or "When a Gypsy Makes His Violin Cry," or "Play, Fiddle, Play," or an improvised *czardas*, he was unbeatable.

Hoffmann was not only a gifted Gypsy fiddle player, but he was a merchant of the first rank. Actually (as I discovered later), he was more like a robber baron. While the going rate for fiddle lessons ran between fifty cents (for the worst fiddle teacher) and a dollar (for the best), Hoffmann charged Daddy *three dollars*. Daddy paid Hoffmann's fee gladly, because Daddy strongly believed you got what you paid for. Hoffman believed you got what you charged. When he arrived to give me a lesson, he carried two violin cases, one of which carried the fiddle he played on and the other with enough fiddle-playing accouterments to fill a garage mechanic's toolbox.

The money Hoffmann received from giving lessons, and for playing nightly in Daddy's cabaret, made up a good part of his income. But there were interesting supplements. Take violins, for example. I was now the proud owner of *two* violins—a cheap three-quarter-sized pre-Hoffmann violin, and a new full-sized violin that Hoffmann arranged for Daddy to buy shortly after my lessons began. The new fiddle was a fair fiddle as fiddles go—Daddy paid Hoffmann one hundred dollars for it, heavy money in those days—but in Daddy's saloon that sort of money for a *fiddle* proved the astonishing degree of Daddy's financial commitment to his son's development.

"One hundred dollars for a piece of wood!" Daddy would say proudly, holding up my new instrument. "Who ever heard of such a thing! In my father's village so much money would feed a family for a year." And all the customers would nod wisely, with Hoffmann nodding *most* wisely.

Now consider the strings on a fiddle. Hardly a week passed without my breaking a string or two on my instruments. Like all of Hoffmann's beginners, I was without experience in replacing strings. I had, in fact, convinced myself that a broken string was *my* fault, brought about by something I was doing obviously wrong. The fragile wire E string never seemed to last the week, and when it broke I simply switched fiddles until Hoffmann's weekly arrival. He always carried a fat pack of strings in his fiddle case number two—the toolbox—and he was always delighted to replace the old string with a new string, and for his trouble he charged Daddy only an extra quarter. The string, I later learned, cost Hoffmann a nickel; and since it was necessary to restring one of my fiddles during my regular lesson time, he was, in effect, stealing time from my lesson to replace a string—and charged Daddy for both.

Mischa Hoffmann, King of the Gypsies or not, certainly knew how to deal with Daddy from all angles. Occasionally he decided the hair on my fiddle bow had to be replaced. He would look at my bow, shake his head in despair, and indicate to Daddy that the bow lacked what? Strength? He would then take my bow and lend me an extra bow he carried in his toolbox for just such emergencies; the following week he would return my old bow and collect from Daddy whatever he decided was a fair price for the rehairing, plus a little something extra for the one week's rental of his own bow.

He also sold rosin for the bow, and, when he figured circumstances warranted, he replaced or adjusted the fiddle bridge, the chin rest, or the string pegs—all involving very delicate and expensive rentals and adjustments and cost-plus calculations. A dollar for this, a quarter for that, a dime for something else. All good causes. Hoffmann's professional life was sensibly devoted to the sound proposition that there is no such thing as a straight three-dollar lesson.

Although these various fiddle adjustments, replacements, and repairs increased Hoffmann's income, the cash flow from these auxiliary enterprises was, apparently, not steady enough—too erratic, too inconstant. What he needed, in short, was a continuous day-in-day-out, watch-it-grow income that would go on long after his beginners had learned to put on their own strings (which, sooner or later, we all did). Hoffmann found his solution in the regular weekly sale of "pieces"—those two- or three-page standard, popular, public-domain arrangements of well-known "classical" tunes so dear to the hearts of doting parents—"Dark Eyes," "A Maiden's Prayer," "Anitra's Dance," "Air for the G String," and the like.

Students loved these pieces, and parents loved to hear their children play them; these were not exercises, études, and (as Sharkey put it) crap like that; these were real pieces—genuine music! When a child set out to play "Dark Eyes" what came out of his instrument was predictable, and could be judged by . . . well . . . by what it sounded like. Furthermore, every fiddle parent knew the basic psychological principle that Predictability Gives Rise to Security. Besides, a piece like "Dark Eyes" was something that could always be played for company.

Parents who felt it their duty to give their children music lessons (and Daddy was clearly no exception) judged each child's progress by the number of these "classical" pieces in the child's repertory. As a conscientious and dedicated pedagogue, Hoffmann was especially concerned with the progress of all his pupils, and no doubt he felt it was his *duty*, regularly, to provide all his students with as many of these new pieces as the child could absorb. No one, of course, ever wondered why he showed special partiality to those pieces published in a series called the Century Edition.

He sold each piece to Daddy for a dollar or a dollar and a half, depending on whether it was two or three pages long, including a piano accompaniment which was seldom, if ever, used. Nothing gave me greater pleasure, toward the end of my lesson, than to watch Hoffmann take a stack of Century Edition pieces from his toolbox and carefully select a new one for me to start learning. The pieces were not especially difficult, they were fun to play, and the comfortable rate at which I learned them gave Daddy and his favorite saloon customers a warm feeling of security. As for my own reaction—it made me feel I was at last getting somewhere.

(Many years later, when Hoffmann was no longer a part of my life, I was browsing in a music store when I came across the Century Edition publisher's catalogue. It was like Old Home Week. I ran a finger up and down the catalogue pages, checking the list against those pieces I had studied with Hoffmann. I was stunned to discover that most of the pieces Hoffmann had sold to Daddy were still available from the publisher at five cents each! One buffalo Indian-head nickel for "Dark Eyes," "Anitra's Dance," and even the great "Air for the G String." Hoffmann was indeed King of the Gypsies.)

CHAPTER FOUR

ALTHOUGH I continued to practice my violin in the back room of the saloon, my lessons with Hoffmann were in our new apartment—Mama's answer to the Great Depression. The crash of 1929 may have made a big noise on Wall Street, but for Daddy and Mama the crash was more like a tinkle of shot glasses. The end of Prohibition was still three years off, and Daddy's business was at its peak. Together with his brother Muttel, Daddy now owned two saloons, a restaurant, a resort in the Catskill Mountains, and, of course, Hoffmann's venue: the American Casino.

In the wake of Daddy's prosperity, we moved twenty-five feet across the street, from 55 Rutgers to 60, from three rooms to six rooms, from coal to steam heat, from no hot water to hot water, and, best of all, from a grimy hall toilet in 55 that served four families on our floor to two inside toilets at 60, one with its own bathtub. Number 60 was a new-style tenement conspicuous by its *covered* garbage cans placed neatly near an entrance with fake marble steps leading up to double entrance doors into a foyer with a wall of built-in mailboxes, and a busy janitor whom Mama called a "super."

"Number 60 was considered very hoity-toity," Mama told me years later. "The families of all the businessmen from the neighborhood lived there—Sawkin the saloonkeeper from Cherry Street, Dienstag the druggist, Lipschitz the plumber, Jake the grocer, and even some manufacturers who were in business uptown. All the cream lived at 60. And there were no rats in the walls, except maybe in the cellar."

When we moved into our new apartment, Mama was in her early thirties. Although she was five feet seven or eight, her dark brown hair pulled neatly into a bun and her proud bearing made her seem even taller. Whenever Mama's name came into the conversation, Daddy would sum up his own expansive view by saying, "I was lucky to find such a wonderful woman"—wonderful, of course, being Daddy's innocent exaggeration. Mama was moderately buxom, tall, with neat features, and fair—almost delicate—skin, big eyes, and a penchant for tam-o'-shanters. Her cap, at a severe angle, gave her an aspect at once youthful and imperious.

Mama was at her best, aesthetically speaking, when her eyes darkened, she lifted her chin, and her frown said she was capable of exploding in anger at the slightest challenge. Mama practiced this pose for years until it was perfect; she would look like an outraged governess, and my father would respond to this display of temper-barely-restrained with *his* practiced look of mock surprise. It was a game they played—he knew what Mama would disapprove of, and she knew he knew. When Daddy was ostentatiously extravagant in tipping entertainers (which he almost always was), or he quibbled with Zaida over a point not worth fussing about, or even if he remarked that Mama had cooked his meat too rare, Daddy expected—and received—Mama's *look*.

Daddy, of course, knew there was nothing hostile about Mama's fierce show of disapproval. It probably gave him a flash of guilt, but he recognized that her annoyance would soon be gone, and that the right sort of cheering words, the balancing rapprochement, would coax from her the exuberant laugh he loved to hear. Daddy, I'm sure, paid little attention to these squalls; he knew she loved and trusted him as he did her. I doubt that anyone but Mama would have looked at my father as if to say, "How could you do anything as *stupid* as that?"

When Daddy acted stupidly, as he frequently did, Mama simply stood fast with a quiet but consuming outrage, an emotion Daddy did not enjoy and found difficult to understand. And when he offered, evasively, what were supposed to be reasonable excuses for his actions, Mama laughed uproariously, and it was her unabashed laughter that made him realize just how silly his schemes were.

Mama's goal from the first was to turn Daddy's mind to her notions of safety, security, and American manners. She persuaded him to give up his job as bouncer at the Dump because she feared for his safety; she continued to remind him that hiding weapons even for his best customers was a dangerous act. She worked hard to reorder his thoughts, to quash his wild plans, his occasional dubious schemes. In a sea of confusion (she never let him forget) she was his anchor.

Daddy seldom needed reminding. Through the years, Mama's look of displeasure would bring him up short. When Daddy was in charge of his emotions, he surely understood his need for a cool head, controlled conduct, some respect for the law; and Mama provided the necessary clues for Daddy's decisions. She knew the sort of signals Daddy would accept and act upon, and if her suggestions to Daddy weren't always straightforward and respectable, neither were they downright crooked (perhaps a little *bent* is the right description). In any case, Mama's weapon (that angry look) kept Daddy reasonably free of his old-time recklessness, and securely tied him to his new life.

Outside of her participation in Daddy's work, I don't think Mama had any pleasures. She had the house to tend to, of course, and three children now twelve, ten, and two (years later Mama told me she chose to have three abortions over the years her four children were born), the usual day-to-day preparations for school, and the shopping and cooking. She worked hard to, as she put it, keep up a nice home. Her personal pleasure, however, came from keeping the saloon books, which she did mostly at night, and the part of her life that sustained her (I finally came to realize) was centered upon Daddy and the saloon. When Daddy was at home, she paid little attention to anyone else. "Be quiet," she'd say, "Daddy's taking a nap," or "Sit down at the table, Daddy's ready to eat," or "Put your homework away, I hear Daddy getting up." And so on.

The new apartment gave us more space. I now had my own bedroom, with a window that looked out on the brick wall of the adjoining tenement, and with several good places to hide books; my sister and baby brother shared a bedroom; and Mama and Daddy's bedroom, facing the street and adjoining the front room, seemed miles away. Mama furnished the small front room as a dining room (although that term was not in our vocabulary), with a decorative brass samovar on the long buffet, a china cabinet she called a credenza, a dining table big enough to seat twelve, and an assortment of chairs. No one actually walked through the front room, one simply bumped into one object after another. And while we could not boast a living room,

Mama designed our sixth room as a "music room." Altogether, a mansion!

In one corner of the music room Mama placed the Machine—Daddy's Victrola—and flanked it with two giant rubber plants, and in another corner my shiny steel music stand (ever ready for my weekly violin lesson), thus containing nearly all the family's musical activity in a single well-marked area. Dominating the music room, however, was Mama's favorite instrument.

Mama had always wanted her own piano. Music in Zaida's house had been treated as one of life's treasures, and even when money was scarce Grandma was able to slip out enough from the grocery money to buy a sturdy upright player piano, and while only one of the seven children—my Aunt Gussie, Mama's youngest sister—showed any interest in the piano, still, there the musical monster stood, filling up half their front room as a symbol of the immigrant family with cultural aspirations. And now, years later, Mama could own her own piano, if not for her own use then at least for her daughter Dorothy to study, and, of course, to maintain the all-important Lower East Side tradition.

Mama's piano was small, a mahogany baby grand with a sweet, full tone (and the rather unpretentious name of Braumuller), and though it did not deserve to be covered forever, it was, with a bright-green-and-gold Spanish shawl. Mama forbade the piano to be opened up wide, as a grand should be on occasion, because raising the lid rumpled the green-and-gold design and, unfortunately for exciting crescendoes, broke up the picture Mama had in mind.

The instrument was intended to be Dorothy's—in the same way the violin was mine. When, as it turned out, Dorothy took a few lessons and decided she hated all pianos, Mama wisely stopped her instruction. On the other hand, I became too fascinated with the piano for my own good. Every moment I spent noodling around with its attractive sounds caused Daddy no end of pain, and the situation became even worse on those days when I found reasons to miss part of my violin practicing.

"Why is the bum banging on that piano?" Daddy would ask Mama whenever I was foolish enough to explore the piano while Daddy was at home. "Why doesn't he practice the violin?"

I found it impossible to tell Daddy that while I hated the violin—*his* instrument—I enjoyed trying to play the piano; and the difference between his hatred and my enjoyment would forever stand between us. Besides, it was not the sort of message Daddy would have understood.

My love for the piano had its start in Zaida's front room, with the very piano Mama had grown up with. In my early years, when Daddy and Mama were working hard at making the saloon a going concern, they had little time to spare for me, and I spent several hours each day in my grandparents' flat four stories up, having lunch or dinner or simply passing the hours when the weather was inclement. I spent a good deal of time looking out the front-room window wishing I were down in the street, and when I wasn't doing that I was tinkling away at the upright player piano.

I loved the popular hits of the day as they came from this gigantic music box. Piled atop the piano were long boxes of piano rolls, and with a little instruction from my Aunt Gussie I soon learned to engage the rolls in their proper position and pump the pedals which turned them, and I would watch the tiny perforations as they rolled into and out of sight and the piano keys went up and down with a magic beyond my ken.

In addition to allowing me to produce music with my feet, this marvelous instrument had a "mandolin attachment." I flicked a lever, hidden inside the sliding music rack, and a supernatural force made the upper half of the keyboard sound vaguely like a clackety harpsichord, while the lower half retained its melodious piano sound. With the mandolin attachment moved to ON, I played by hand melodies chosen from a stack of sheet music brought home by Aunt Gussie, which were piled on the piano next to a sepia photograph of Zaida in full religious costume.

My violin training enabled me to read the piano scores' single melodic lines, and I reinforced my memory of the tunes by mouthing the sentimental lyrics of the twenties, and in this way I became familiar with such all-time Aunt Gussie favorites as "Makin' Whoopee" and "Barney Google—with his Goo-Goo-Googly Eyes." When Daddy heard me try these over on Mama's very own Braumuller, he shook his head in wonderment and said, "Where the hell did the bum pick up that crap?"

Mama pretended ignorance. I have an idea she enjoyed hearing any sort of musical sounds emanating from her music room when she wasn't in there; perhaps she had had her fill of sitting and listening respectfully to classical music. Given a choice, she remained in her kitchen, a space she had divided into *two* well-defined areas.

In one she prepared and cooked our meals, and in the other she put together a good part of the whiskey sold in Daddy's saloon. Because Mama's kitchen whiskey-making was nearly a daily occurrence, I remained in my early years completely indifferent to the intended purposes of Prohibition and the Eighteenth Amendment. Booze, as merchandise, was as much a part of my life as practicing scales and chords. Selling booze was the way Daddy made his living, and whatever was important to Daddy was important to all of us. To be surrounded by liquor and talk of liquor was, in Mama's household, a plain fact of daily life, to which we'll return in a moment.

Although the house was clearly Mama's house, my feeling was that she arranged it for Daddy; we children were incidental. Nothing was allowed to disturb him in the house, particularly in the early days when he left the saloon in the middle of the afternoon for a nap, and, later on, when we had regular family dinners. The table and chairs had to be arranged just so, the place settings according to his taste, the bottle of booze placed in the middle of the table alongside his favorite shot glass; books around the house were to be hidden, and homework was not to be spread over the dining-room table while Daddy was at home.

Mama watched Daddy as if he were a lighted firecracker. "When Daddy comes up to eat," she said one day, "I don't want any trouble. No talking before he eats. When he's finished eating, *then* I'll show him where you tore your new jacket." For me that always meant still another beating—after he ate, of course.

Mama saw herself as Daddy's intelligence officer. While their private late-night discussions provided her with saloon news she would otherwise never have heard, Daddy counted on Mama for all the news from outside the saloon. She was responsible for important newspaper stories, neighborhood gossip, and family matters. My own indiscreet actions were, of course, important family matters, and if before a meal Sharkey heard any news directly from me or from my sister that required quick punishment, he punished us immediately and invariably left the house without eating.

Mama's game was for me to avoid punishment until, at the very least, Daddy had finished the main course. She had worked her fingers to the bone to prepare the sort of dinner he could find nowhere else, and for him to leave without eating, his appetite now gone because he had had to punish me, enraged Mama. Mama never struck me, but she scolded me mercilessly. She would wait, of course, until Daddy left the house before I received her tongue-lashing. I was told I had spoiled Daddy's appetite, I had ruined a good dinner, I would just as soon lie as tell the truth, and it would be a miracle if Daddy didn't throw me out of the house. Pretty rough stuff for a crying twelve-year-old.

Mama was a good talker; I don't mean she was an orator, but for a woman born and raised on the East Side, her English was as good as anyone's. When she and Daddy discussed serious questions—shall we buy another saloon? shall we open a bank account under a new name? shall we lend Jack five hundred dollars?—Daddy trusted Mama's English as if she were a distinguished lawyer. It was one of Mama's best roles. When it came to talking with Daddy, she knew what she could control and what she had to give way on. Mama explained (in English) what was important for Daddy to know, Daddy added one or two necessary points, and the case was closed. In these circumstances, Mama controlled Daddy's love, his sympathy, his goodwill, his self-assurance, and—if she should need to—his physical strength.

In his white bartender's apron and an expensive short-sleeved sports shirt that allowed his biceps free play, Sharkey dispensed drink, advice, and his special brand of justice. Which meant that in Sharkey's saloon you did what Sharkey suggested or you got knocked on your ass; Sharkey's etiquette was uncomplicated, and everyone understood it. He was busy now pouring boilermakers, but not as busy as he would be later this evening.

Saturday was always a good day—the ordinary bums and the blue-collar workers drank on and off all day, and the Yidlach took over in the evening, and Sharkey could expect to sell a lot of schnapps, including a few bottles like the one in my briefcase. When Sharkey said "Have a schnapps on me," you had better know he was talking about bourbon. In Sharkey's saloon schnapps was the comprehensive name for *all* booze. I never heard anyone ask for scotch or bourbon; and cocktails were some sort of uptown drink for ladies and suspect men.

Furthermore, as Sharkey would have been the first to tell you, no real drinker ever drank his drink mixed—he drank it straight, neat, with a water or seltzer or beer chaser. Only a complete stranger, or a complete fool, would ask him for a mixed drink. Sharkey did not suffer fools lightly: you ordered and drank the specialties of his house or you took your trade elsewhere, ya crummy bastard.

Sharkey's house specialties included two kinds of schnapps—the twenty-cent "ball" I mentioned, and the fifty-cent bonded stuff. Water and carbonated chasers—ginger ale, lithiated water (what I thought of as "lemon soda"), and seltzer—were free, and bottles of these were kept in an ice chest under the bar, alongside the washtub-sink with its secret whiskey slots. No one was ever offered ice to mix with his drink. "Who ever hoid of ice?" Sharkey asked, as if this were a legitimate question. "If you want ice, I can stick a bag on top of your head." And so no one asked for ice. The beer, though, was as cold as one could wish, and a twelve-ounce glass sold for ten cents.

Where Sharkey bought his beer was a mystery—from a friend, perhaps. Several times each week a truck pulled up in front of the saloon and two drivers lowered barrels of legal "near beer," with its 0.5-percent of alcohol, down to the cellar. Sharkey then "needled" the beer (brought it up to 5 or 6 percent of alcohol) and made it, in his eyes (and in the eyes of his serious beer drinkers), fit for human consumption. A couple of balls, chased with a glass or two of Sharkey's needled beer—the original boilermaker—made an ordinary bum feel that life might, after all, still hold one wonderful pleasure.

Some pleasures, however, were not available in Sharkey's saloon—wine, for instance. Why this was so I can only guess; other saloons sold wine and there was good profit in it. Perhaps the lack of wine had something to do with Zaida. As we know, Zaida was a religious man, and wine drinking for him was a sacrament, a holy act.

Sharkey may not have been much moved by Zaida's drinking notions, but Daddy would have considered Zaida's view with respect, that is, that the consumption of wine was no joking matter. One drank wine to toast life (*l'chaim*), and one drank to life before one broke bread on the holidays and on the Sabbath—but not in a saloon!

Even the goyim in Washington who, as Daddy put it, made up those *meshugeneh* laws, recognized that the Jews had a special relation to wine. Otherwise, why would they permit Jews to buy five gallons of real wine each year? Not grape juice, but real wine. Legal. For practicing Jews the real seller of wine was their rabbi and leader of their synagogue, whom the Prohibition goyim permitted to sell wine to bona fide members of his congregation. And if there were a few rabbis who were crooked, or a few crooks who pretended to be rabbis, who showed up at the Prohibition office with fake lists of members of fake synagogues so they could buy wine and sell it even to goyim, did their unholy crookedness make the wine less holy? Of course not, which is why—I think—Daddy could not bring himself to sell wine.

By the time I was twelve, eavesdropping while Mama and Daddy discussed such matters as why he didn't sell wine, taking a pinch, bribing the police, paying off revenue agents, avoiding conviction, copping a plea, cutting the goods (*vahre*—lowering the alcoholic proof), meant listening to what was for me their unremarkable daily conversation. From their talk I suspected that every time Daddy sold a customer a drink he was in danger of being arrested. Moreover, I had heard Zaida say to my grandmother, many times, that a person who ran a saloon was no better than a common thief. Daddy wasn't my favorite person when I was twelve, but I wouldn't have believed he was no better than a *thief*.

People bought whiskey and drank it, Mama explained, because they liked it, or because they were stupid. They bought it, and if you have a buyer, you have to have a seller. Daddy was no thief, he was a seller! In fact, we *helped* him. I could only think, therefore, that for Mama and Daddy to ask me to carry a bottle of Old Grand-Dad, in my violin case, from the kitchen to the saloon just across the street showed how much faith they put in my good sense. As I said, the task was, to me, routine.

While other kids on the Lower East Side enjoyed themselves

searching for treasures, say, in rat-infested tenement cellars, or looking in on back-alley gambling games, I was required to help Mama make whiskey in the kitchen, thus enabling me to participate, firsthand, in the family's entrepreneurial system. I suppose there was some room for complaint, but it was not my habit to complain about small things. After all, a boy who agrees to help his mother make whiskey can expect to be asked to help his daddy by carrying a bottle of whiskey in his violin case. Even if it was Old Grand Dad.

Mama and I made two kinds of whiskey—cheap whiskey from scratch, and expensive whiskey by cutting other expensive whiskey. Mama and the corner druggist, a sleazy chap with a Groucho Marx mustache, had worked out an arrangement that was so simple it must have been elegant, which I suppose is the best kind if you're doing this sort of business. Groucho bought pure grain alcohol from the government, supposedly for pharmaceutical purposes; he then sold the alcohol to Mama in five-gallon cans several times a week, which must have made the local Prohibition Bureau wonder how many thousands of Lower East Side men, women, and children were either incurably sick or constantly drunk.

Our booze-making process always began when Mama told me to bar the front door of our kitchen (which led to the outside hallway) to prevent any unauthorized, surprise entrance. I slipped the door bolt into its slot and turned to help Mama. We picked up a five-gallon can together, and poured some of the alcohol into a medium-sized metal pot, after which I drew some water from the kitchen faucet and added it to the alcohol. Mama, meanwhile, held a hydrometer in the mixture, and when she was satisfied that I had added enough water to match the proof she had in mind, she yelled, "Stop!"

Part two. She now gathered together the appropriate flavoring, coloring, and beading ingredients (oil of rye, burnt sugar, and glycerin—all bought by me in Groucho's drug store), added a dash of this, a spot of that, and the job of manufacturing was about done. The whiskey now had to be bottled, corked, and labeled. Sometimes Mama would allow me to pretend to drink through the thin rubber hose, the siphon that transferred the whiskey from the metal vessel to the empty bottles lined neatly on the kitchen table. The trick was to draw fast on the hose, and then drop its free end into a bottle without tasting even a smidgin of the whiskey. Once done, we corked the bottles and pasted on labels that announced our brand as REWCO (God only knows what that meant). The whiskey was now ready to be transported down three flights of stairs and across the street into Daddy's saloon, where it would be judged before the bar.

Sharkey sold most of Mama's homemade whiskey to the saloon regulars—bums, dockhands, and blue-collar workers. He served a drink, called a ball, in a narrow three-ounce glass, and in 1930 a ball sold for twenty cents. They talked, drank, listened, talked, waited, tapped the brass rail, used the brass spittoons—sometimes with accuracy—clinked their glasses, toasted each other, sang, smoked, drank, argued, and sometimes fought. They were At Home, and Sharkey was often called upon to remind them of this fact. "Listen, you punk," he would say, "if you spit on the floor at home, then you can spit on the floor here." Sharkey's expression and the bulge of his muscles somehow dried up his customers' juices. Then, what the hell (another would say), let's have another round.

His good customers, those in the money, drank the better brand of booze, the kind Mama called bonded whiskey. These drinks for Sharkey's peers were served in standard shot glasses from authentic bottles of whiskey with such well-known labels as Old Grand-Dad, Sharkey's favorite brand.

These bottles of whiskey came originally from government-bonded warehouses which sold their liquor to wholesalers who sold it to druggists like Groucho, who sold the booze to anyone with a doctor's prescription. Groucho, as Mama related years later, not only *accepted* forged prescriptions, but he *sold* forged prescriptions. Apparently he would not sell bonded whiskey *without* a prescription.

Mama was quite put out when she discovered that Groucho, intent upon satisfying all his customers—those with genuine prescriptions as well as those with fake ones—had been cutting the bonded whiskey with water. "He was one of the worst chiselers on Rutgers Street," Mama said. She made her discovery one day when she tried her own hand at cutting the "bottled in bond." "Daddy used to charge our good customers sixty cents a shot for Old Grand-Dad, but then he decided it would be easier for him to make change if he charged only fifty cents a shot. That gave me the idea to cut the Old Grand-

Dad, and that's when I found out that the proof on the bottle was a lie. The druggist had already cut it. Daddy walked over to the drugstore and had a little talk with the druggist, and after that we got the Old Grand-Dad uncut. I fixed it up and Daddy was then able to charge fifty cents a drink."

Sharkey's great strength at this time was his self-confidence. He believed, for example, that he could distinguish on sight anyone who represented the law from anyone who did not. Cops, detectives, agents, prohibition men, and other law enforcers. Sharkey could not articulate his way of knowing, but he believed he *knew*. He was confident that he could guess something from the cut of your clothes, the angle of your hat, the sound of your voice, the knot in your tie, the shine on your shoes. The configuration of these various personal details, along with things that Sharkey knew from the pattern of his own experiences, made up a message that said *cop!* This gift was indispensable, because Sharkey's business life depended on his ability to recognize a prohibition agent in the wink of an eye—whether he was obviously a federal agent or a disguised one.

That Sharkey's judgment was not always correct occasionally led to difficulties, the greatest of which was the unscheduled pinch, during which federal agents disguised as workingmen entered his saloon and tried to persuade him to pour them a drink. If they could make him do that, they could arrest him, and that arrest (and its follow-up) would cause grave disruption in the saloon's operation.

Sharkey had a cold understanding of the meaning of search, seizure, arrest, conviction, and other aspects of the Noble Experiment; he was satisfied, however, as long as the game was played properly. Playing properly, according to Sharkey, meant playing by the rules. I often heard Sharkey and Mama discuss an upcoming "legitimate" pinch (all saloonkeepers were expected to "take" one or two pinches each month, for the local police record, but they also expected to be told when each arrest would take place).

To take care of the scheduled pinches, Sharkey sent a bundle of cash each week to the precinct commander, with extra dividends to the cop on the beat. Sharkey wished to cooperate with those in charge because when local forces were pressured by higher forces, he knew that pinches had to be made, if only for the record. An open bottle of booze was left on the bar, where even a blind agent could see it, and when the feds arrived at the prescribed time, there it was for everyone to see. There was no necessity for the agents to rip open closet doors to find the required evidence, or to break apart plumbing fixtures and act like firemen putting out a three-alarm blaze.

You made it easy for them; you played along; you didn't resist. With the whiskey in hand, the revenue agents, pleased as Punch, escorted you downtown, where you pleaded guilty, and where a stern but tolerant judge fined you twenty-five or fifty dollars. And shortly after, you were once more behind the bar laughing, joking, serving drinks, discussing what life was like downtown, secure in the knowledge that you wouldn't have to take a pinch for perhaps another thirty days.

The unscheduled pinch was another matter. Sharkey was well aware that there were crooked federal agents who arrived in a saloon unannounced, ostensibly to make an unscheduled pinch, who were personally on the take. Sharkey handled such perfidious agents with dispatch and a bit of loose money. On the other hand, there was always the chance that they were not on the take, that the fix was *not* in. The precinct chief had not been alerted, the cop on the beat had not been alerted, and therefore Sharkey had not been alerted. Thus there would be no leverage with the agents, the court, the judge, the whole *megillah*. Incalculable distress, and a circumstance that frequently led to a padlock procedure—a padlock hung on the front door of the saloon, to accompany a sign that said, "Closed for One Year for Violation of the National Prohibition Act."

The thought of an unscheduled pinch was therefore never far removed from Sharkey's mind, because it had happened to others and it could happen to him. An especially good idea was not to keep more whiskey in the saloon than you could quickly pour down the drain once a suspicious stranger made his way in. Sooner or later, of course, one would.

Sharkey's gravest fear, an unscheduled raid—the situation he could not control—took place one summer Saturday afternoon. I had just finished a midafternoon snack in our kitchen and told Mama I was going out to play in the street. "Be a good boy," she said. "Take your violin and go down to the store and practice now." I made a face. "If you don't practice now," she said, in warning, "later will be too late, and Daddy will have to murder you. Don't give him the satisfaction. Practice first."

Mama's words hit me in the belly and ruined what would have been a happy afternoon. I knew I had to practice; there was no way, short of suicide, that I could get out of it. I just didn't like to be reminded of my inescapable and vexing fiddle duties when my mind was engaged with plans for fun.

I picked up my violin case and my small music briefcase and, promising I would kill myself someday (*then* they would all be sorry), moved dejectedly toward the kitchen door. "Here," Mama said, taking a pint of Old Grand-Dad from the broom closet, "put this in your briefcase. It should hold Daddy until tonight."

Maintaining my pensive manner, I opened the briefcase and slipped the bottle down among the sheet music. Mama's request was routine, and I had no reason to believe that carrying this particular bottle of booze across the street, and handing it over to Daddy unobserved, was to be on this lovely afternoon anything more than the simple chore I had completed dozens of times in the past.

As I went through the swinging door, I could see Daddy pouring drinks and beer chasers for several customers gathered at the bar. I knew the faces of these men—they all worked on the waterfront, and I could see a small stack of money laid out in front of them. They were in a celebratory mood. They sat on bar stools, forearms on the edge of the bar, heads bowed, shoulders hunched forward in an attitude of prayer.

Meanwhile, at the moment, Sharkey was too busy working to pay much attention to his whiskey-carrying son waiting patiently to catch his attention. Sharkey had three boilermaker drinkers to take care of while he prepared for the evening ahead. By the time I finished practicing, the sun would have gone down, Pietro the bartender would have come on, and the evening regulars would appear. The bar would be nearly full.

I waited as Sharkey mopped the bar with a bar mop, washed and rinsed glasses, emptied ashtrays, turned the radio dial yet again in an attempt to screen out some of the crap (no program remained unchanged for more than five minutes), checked the cash in the cash register against the register tape (in seven years, Mama said, the two did not coincide once), and sent Gus the Bum to buy him a pack of cigarettes or a sack of sawdust or the *Daily News* or a hot pastrami on club with a cherry pepper and a touch of sauerkraut. The main thing, Daddy often remarked, was to keep busy and ring the cash register a lot, and in that way you wouldn't notice that some of the customers didn't smell so good.

Later in the afternoon Mama would no doubt drop in carrying an extra bottle or two of whiskey in her black oilcloth shopping bag to help Daddy through the night. And during the peak of the evening's activities Daddy, too, would have motioned to his favorite bum, Gus, who ran all of Daddy's errands and slept in the rear of the saloon for his room and board and free drinks, to go up to our apartment and return in a few minutes with two fresh bottles of whiskey. The saloon schedule was a tough one—five-thirty in the morning to midnight— and although Daddy employed two part-time bartenders for early morning and late evening, he expected his family to help wherever they could, and smuggling in booze in bits and pieces was an essential activity.

As Daddy finished pouring a round of drinks, I tried to catch his eye and draw him to the back room where I could safely remove the Old Grand-Dad from my briefcase and hand it to him. Now Daddy was talking. He was *explaining*. He was discoursing upon the special qualities of men who drank boilermakers and why they were more masculine than ladies who drank pink ladies or pansies who drank Manhattans. "Gimme a boilermaker drinker every time," he said, with heart and soul and body and mind. Which meant, of course, that it was impossible for him to know I was alive.

I jerked my head toward the back room, and he finally saw me. I raised my briefcase a bit, and he received my message. Gesturing with his head, he said, "*Shpetter, shpetter!*"—Later, later. No doubt he meant Sharkey was busy (and that fool kid should see that). Second, it was my duty to make my way to the back room and start practicing, and when he had time (and that fool kid should know that) he would come to the back room and pick up the Old Grand-Dad. And, finally, when would I ever learn that in Sharkey's saloon the customer *always* came first? If I'd been asked I would have liked to say, "Never, Daddy, never." But no one did.

I walked to the back room, shifted my briefcase so I could open the door, and entered for my hour of solitude. I removed my fiddle and rosined the bow, taking lots of time. The longer I fooled around with the preliminaries the less time I would actually have to practice. One hour of fiddle-dee-dee and I could be out on the street again, where perhaps one of the gang would let me ride down the hill on his pushmobile.

I opened my briefcase, taking out my hated exercise books and uncovering the Old Grand-Dad. I arranged the sheet music on the wooden stand Daddy had built for me—ungainly, heavy, a deep, dark brown like my own mood—and flipped the pages looking for something intense, something on the G string, something slow. I scraped the strings several times, tuning up loudly enough so Daddy would know I was now officially started. I looked at the alarm clock Daddy had positioned on my music table—only fifty-five minutes more.

Hell, I thought, I might as well get it over with. I started an adagio on the G string, and the noise of the saloon faded to jumbled background. Only when I stopped to turn a page or replay a phrase was I aware that there was life outside the back room. I enjoyed in those few moments the tinkle of glasses, the sound of the cash register, the somewhat muffled laughter of serious drinkers. If only Daddy kept busy at the bar, I might even be able to leave the back room several minutes early, with no serious repercussions.

Today, though, I remembered that nothing would work because I couldn't leave until my master came for the whiskey in my briefcase. And so once more I dug deeply into the fiddle with little hope of relief from my certain disappointment. Daddy, I petitioned silently, come and get your goddam Old Grand-Dad.

I had now finished practicing my assigned pieces; the clock showed five more minutes, but that was easily taken care of by packing up my fiddle, my bow, my rosin, my music, and moping my way *largo* toward the swinging door. I cocked my head, listening for the muffled voices, the scraping of chairs, the ring of the cash register, but there seemed to be a lack of sound—perhaps on account of the closed door.

Earlier—was it during my G-string lament?—I had thought I heard the usual noises, but now it was quiet. I planned to stop at the end of the bar, motion to Daddy, hand him my briefcase so he could remove the bottle and slide it into the secret compartment below the washtub-sink. Then perhaps I'd be able to go out into the street and play. That, at least, was my plan.

I opened the door and stepped into the barroom, and I didn't like what I saw. My first reaction was to return to the back room. To hide there. To hide someplace. Anyplace. But I was a moment too late; I had just been observed by an outsider. And now Mama's and Daddy's late-night words came to me in a flash: revenue men, conviction, pinch, federal men, padlock, Prohibition.

I looked toward Daddy. He stood at one end of the bar, his back to me, and watched a man working to pry open the cabinet doors below the cash register. Another man, the one who saw me emerge from the back room, stood between the bar and the swinging door, watching Daddy as his partner searched the cabinets. In this startled moment I recognized the affinity between this observer and the searcher. They both carried that look Daddy talked about, that downtown, City Hall, Wall Street look of strangeness, that unique, non-customer, non-Jewish look that was the sole property of cops, detectives, federal agents, and your favorite district attorney. I had seen that look in the movies, and I now knew what Daddy meant when he said, "I can smell a cop a mile away." These were cops, all right; but I didn't know at the moment who I feared most—the cops or Sharkey.

I walked slowly toward the bar, and Daddy turned and saw me. The weight of my briefcase was now beyond belief, as I watched the man down on his knees continue his searching. He may have heard me moving, for he, too, looked over at me, and I paused. "That's my kid," Daddy said to him. Then, speaking to me gruffly, he said, "*Gay a haym*"—Go home. His voice was heavier than usual, his expression was wary, but his tone was significantly urgent. *Beat it!*

I nodded and moved down the bar slowly. I would have given anything to be able to run. Or at least to disappear, to be out in the street, up on the roof, away, any place but in Daddy's saloon. I continued moving toward the swinging door. The man down on his knees stood up and called over to me. "What have you got there, kid?"

"Where?" I asked blankly. All I could see was a stranger in a business suit.

He gestured toward my hand. "In that *case*," he said. He smiled and spoke to Daddy. "What's in the case, Sharkey, a machine gun?"

I looked back at Daddy, who smiled at the cop as I pleaded silently for advice. "No," he said, "it's only a violin. I'm givin' the kid violin lessons."

The man studied me for a moment, and I remained frozen—as if I had to go to the toilet and I couldn't. "Was that you playing back there just now?" he asked.

I nodded—it was easier than talking. I was afraid to talk. I was afraid to say anything. I nodded again, and waited. When in God's name would they let me *out* of here?

The man behind the bar seemed neither crushed nor overjoyed. So far his search had been in vain. He had missed the secret compartment under the sink, which was easy to do, but all he had to do was ask me for my briefcase and Daddy's saloon would go up in smoke. And all my fault. What flashed through my confused head was whether I should keep moving toward the door or whether I should wait until someone ordered me to do something.

He acted as if I didn't exist. He gestured toward the back room. "What have you got back there, Sharkey?"

"Nuttin'," Sharkey answered. "It's just a back room—where the kid practices."

He looked at Daddy, doubtfully. To his partner: "I'd better take a look back there," and he moved toward the rear.

I stood there, glued to the sawdust, the violin case in one wet hand and the briefcase in the other, as I waited for my world to collapse. Waiting, waiting. Finally, the man standing only two or three feet from me and my briefcase jerked his head toward the swinging door and said, "Okay, beat it, kid!"

I nodded my gratitude, swallowed hard, and moved off, my legs delighted to find they could still *move*. I now felt marvelously free. I wanted to run, to shout, to gather all the kids around me, to have them sit at my Keds while I took the Old Grand-Dad out of my briefcase and passed it around for them to heft; I wanted to tell them how, in the face of the most terrifying, unusual danger, I, and I alone—clever, intrepid, cool beyond imagining—had conned two of the shrewdest, most fearsome representatives of the U.S. Federal Government; how I had just saved the day, saved Sharkey's saloon, saved his life, saved him from—who knows?—maybe the electric chair!

I pushed against the swinging door and flowed right through it onto the sidewalk. Rutgers Street seemed strangely quiet. Nobody skipped rope, bounced a ball, played hopscotch, or kicked a can. Across the street, bunched together in front of Number 60, a group of neighbor women were gathered on our stoop, watching me closely.

I saw Mama's head above the crowd, and I started across the street toward her. She shook her head vigorously, and I paused. Why was she denying me? And then I understood immediately. I was not to go near our tenement building. I was less than safe until I was completely out of the sight of the two federal agents. Mama's message was clear: I was being watched and I was to avoid going near our apartment.

Nervously, I turned aside, and tried strolling down the street toward Cherry Park, away from Mama's stricken face and the scene inside the saloon. I worried about Mama's concern, Daddy's frustration, the whiskey in my briefcase, and the whiskey hidden upstairs in our broom closet only until I turned the corner and started down Cherry Street, my fiddle case swinging gently along. When I reached Jefferson, a long block away, and noticed no stranger following me, I was at once happy and at peace with the world. My world.

A block ahead I saw a kid scooting along on his pushmobile, the skate wheels whirring and gritting against the pavement, and the fantasy world of saloons and padlocks and Old Grand-Dad nestling between protective sheets of music disappeared. The crisis was over, and I decided I would just take a long walk. To the Williamsburg Bridge on Delancey Street and back. I was no longer wet with fear, and I was no longer scared shitless. I was free. Mama and Daddy, I was certain, could take care of themselves.

Later in the day I returned to Rutgers Street, to the saloon and home. I could have been away for days; without my father's usual admonishments to plague me, the hours took on a life of their own. But now, as I walked down the street across from the saloon, I knew I was back in town. The saloon, I could see, was once more in action. The sleepy bums had returned to sit at their small tables up front, secure in their once again established territory; Pietro was behind the bar working his shift. And now I could make out Mama and Daddy sitting together at the end of the bar waiting—I hoped—for their conquering hero.

I entered the barroom, and as they saw me their smiles gave me a soft and pleasant warmth, a comfortable nearness I hadn't felt for years, and as I think back on that marvelous episode I still relish the moment. As I walked toward them, I could feel this glorious closeness, the intimacy of shared fear and danger overcome. Mama and Daddy had no secrets from me today, no special looks between them, no no-child's land. I was a valued member of the family; I was, at least for the moment, a partner. We *shared* something.

I told them, with a wide grin, how I had recognized Mama's signal, how I had escaped our enemies, where I had walked, and, once I had realized that the coast was clear, how I had made my way home. I handed Mama the guilty briefcase, and listened as Daddy told *his* story.

Two strangers, he said, got out of a taxi on the corner of Monroe and Rutgers, where they were seen by Gus the Bum, who had been lounging outside the front door. As they started down the street, Gus, suspecting they were agents, rushed into the saloon to alert Sharkey, who whisked all the glasses from the bar into the sink, told all his customers to get out quickly, checked to be sure the secret compartment was properly sealed, and was nonchalantly mopping the bar when the agents came in.

By then it was too late for Sharkey to remember that I was still in the back room with a bottle of Old Grand-Dad in my briefcase. Sharkey greeted the agents politely, asked on whose orders they were there, and tried dropping a couple of names for them to think about. When the agents sneered at Sharkey's attempts at subornation, he knew the game was up. "That's when I knew I was in the middle of a goddam search and seizure," Sharkey said angrily, "and if the bastards had their way, I'd wind up with a pinch and then a padlock."

Mama now took over. "Yes," she said, "we could've lost the store." Gus the Bum had run up the stairs to tell her that a pinch was in the making. She hurried down to stand on the stoop where she could see with her own eyes whether Daddy in fact was to be taken downtown, God forbid, in which case she would immediately have to call her brother Mike the politician. When Gus told her I was still practicing in the back room, she was undone. Mama now looked at me, tears in her eyes. "So you can imagine how I felt," she said, turning to Daddy, "when I saw him come out of the store safe and sound. I tell you, I gained ten years of my life."

Daddy put his arm around her shoulders. "It's okay," he said. "It's all over."

Mama dried her tears. "Yes," she said, "we're *very* lucky."

I listened as they talked. I felt great. Cozy and contented. It was nice to be part of a family.

CHAPTER FIVE

WHILE THE SALOON was nominally Daddy's—his character and physical strength carried it from one hour to the next—it was, in its way, a family affair. I was in and out several times a day, often having lunch there on schooldays (I was crazy for the clam chowder Daddy made on Friday, and the baked herring and potatoes he made most any day) and stopping in for a bottle of lemon soda when the weather was right, and, of course, there was my endless practicing in the back room.

Mama was—as few people realized—the saloon's administrative maven. Daddy made no saloon decisions of any consequence without Mama's approval. I can't say with certainty that Daddy *welcomed* Mama's approval; he probably had no other choice. Mama's role as administrator may have been (partly, anyway) a cover-up of Daddy's inability to read and write English.

Like a child able to guess at words accompanied by pictures but unable to recognize words standing alone, Daddy was able to fool most of the people around him. Mama, of course, was aware of Daddy's handicap and tried hard first to have him acknowledge his deficiency and then to help him get over it.

Daddy, as you may have guessed, was a hard man to convince. When he sent one of the saloon bums who could read to buy him a copy of the *Daily News* or *Mirror*, he'd ask him offhandedly what the front-page headlines said; and during the rest of the day, whenever it seemed fitting, he'd pick up the paper, "read" the headline, and ask a customer for pertinent comments. Because Daddy, with practice, became a pretty skilled deceiver, his patrons had no idea he couldn't read. Reading the headlines and guessing at what the reporters said, he managed to acquire a fair amount of daily information.

He was also able to make change, although Mama said the cash register never tallied at the end of the day. Daddy claimed the bartenders were stealing him blind, but Mama was clearly working with hard information. Another of Daddy's devices which made it appear he knew what he was doing was to have Mama make up the daily checks he used to pay for, say, six cases of lithiated soda or a dozen cases of seltzer. Mama would complete the checks, leave them unsigned, and put them into the drawer of the cash register—"Millie, the top one is for the soda, the second one is for the beer, and the third one is for the seltzer"—and at the proper time Daddy would select the appropriate check, sign it for all to see, and pass it on to a grateful vendor.

Occasionally, of course, Daddy's trick didn't work, as, for example, the day he signed and handed out several misdirected checks. His ability to write English, as he well knew but admitted with reluctance, was nearly zero; to write checks, as Mama told him over and over, one had to, well . . . one had to learn to *write*.

I can still see Daddy hunched over our kitchen table late at night trying repeatedly to write his name with a giant orange Waterman fountain pen, laboriously filling the lines of yellow foolscap necessary to Daddy's nocturnal drill. After what must have been untold nights of agony, he eventually wrote something that looked like his name in a stiff straight-up-and-down script that carried a lot of authority.

Daddy was rightly proud of this exercise, and at the outset, he wrote his name everywhere. Practice, practice, practice. He now insisted that Mama save everything that required signing, so he could acquire the precise motion for quickly representing himself on receipts, bills, documents, and even my report cards. But learning to write something besides his name was nearly impossible. He tried hard; I saw him try. Mama actually pushed him into writing out Dry Dock 1401, our home telephone number; inevitably, when his efforts to write anything beyond that failed, his discouragement was too great and the lessons ended.

Daddy of course lost for good whatever motivation he had had, and he soon found sufficiently logical reasons to avoid becoming involved in any circumstance in which he could be required to write. One night, toward the end of his writing career, I heard him make his pitch to Mama: writing, in general, he rationalized, and writing checks especially, was no work for a man as busy as he was. At some length he enumerated the details of running a successful saloon. Writing, he went on, was woman's work, and no self-respecting saloonkeeper should have to spend half his time learning how to make out a check.

Tapping a keg of beer—*that* was a man's work. Besides, he said, *one* writer in the family—Mama—was enough. He was through practicing writing, and there was nothing more to discuss. "What's the use of having the only wife in the neighborhood who can write good English," he asked, "if you don't let her write good English? Right?" And so Mama went back to writing all the checks—and signing them. She was delighted.

Daddy loved his saloon, and no one knew it better than Mama. The secret to running a successful East Side saloon was no mystery to Mama—she was Daddy's confidante and confessor; she knew all about his hopes, his dreams, his hatred and fear of the law, his streaks of sentimentality, his lack of plain common sense, and his impregnable belief that he could solve most of life's problems with his ruthless brute strength. Any encounter involving Sharkey that could rise to violence—Mama knew his savage temper—frightened her. His fearlessness was a constant worry. I had no judgment on this at the time, but I now know that all Mama ever wanted in those years was to keep Daddy out of jail. How she managed to do so is beyond me.

Sharkey's smart-money customers—drawn from his netherworld milieu—expected him to be more than an ordinary saloonkeeper. This was, after all, Big Jack Zelig's friend. As a saloonkeeper he was called upon to be discreet, act as a go-between, provide a safe mail drop, maintain a safekeeping depository, and sometimes act as a pawnbroker. He had no objection. He saw these favors as relatively innocent—acts that helped his customers while he remained inculpable; acts that increased his business and, at the same time, kept him inside the law. (That the very selling of whiskey was something *outside* the law remained, in his rather strange social philosophy, not so much his problem but a problem for federal agents.)

When Sharkey entered the saloon business he believed he had left his brief East Side contact with the underworld behind him. This is not to say that Sharkey had joined the Chamber of Commerce—far from it. His plan (with Mama's support and encouragement) was to avoid all underworld relationships. He intended to stay clear of close business relationships with known gangsters, to remain personally uninvolved in the day-to-day life of East Side gangs, and, finally, to arrange his life so that whatever work he did would benefit essentially himself and his family.

And so Sharkey, the vicarious gangster, stood on the underworld fringe, a not quite passive observer, nearly objective, acting (or not acting) as much as his indulgent conscience would permit. He had learned he could be affected by what was right or wrong for him. If a customer was accused of a crime, Sharkey pretended the police had caught the wrong man, but he would never suggest he knew the *right* man. If a prime customer asked him to "hold" a package for an indeterminate time, Sharkey would say, "Don't tell me what's in it. I don't wanna know." And if the customer insisted on divulging the contents of the package, Sharkey said, "You told me nothing—understand?"

His curious sense of honor thus enabled him to make fine distinctions between what was illegal and what was stupid, and in making these distinctions he leaned heavily on his own criteria, his personal interpretation of the law. And because his lively street sense always jibed with the minds of those he was intent on protecting, and his actions usually reflected the underworld's own code of honor, Sharkey acquired the reputation of being trustworthy, tough, and just—the underworld's model of a right guy.

Sharkey's house rules were strict but fair, and were intended to appeal to all reasonable and circumspect saloon patrons—even the bums. Swearing, cursing, and mouthing of vulgarities were permitted provided they were delivered in a normal tone of voice and were directed to no one in particular. (If, on occasion, Mama happened to be in the saloon, the rule was suspended—crude and indecent expressions were forbidden within her hearing, on penalty of a shot in the jaw from Sharkey's iron fist.)

As in any hospital zone, the level of noise in the saloon required special control. Sharkey's "Hey you! Shut ya mout'!" rang true and clear to noisemakers who questioned Sharkey's explications. When Sharkey commented on a fact of life, he expected to see heads nod approvingly. He had little patience with moodbreakers. When he said that Dempsey had it all over Tunney, or that Jimmy Walker was the best mayor the city ever had, or that Moishe Oysher sang a helluva lot better than John McCormack, his word was law. To question Sharkey's authority was to question his honesty, his integrity, and the honor of his intention—and that was worth, as he put it, a sock in the kisser.

Questioning Sharkey's authority was the crowning insult begging to be avenged, and in his merciless quick way he made no distinction between an insulting Jew or Gentile—although Gentiles, on an average, were more likely to suffer Sharkey's wrath. Gentiles, once in their cups, often expressed disapproval of Jews in general, or the "Jewishness" of a specific Jew (saying bad things about the light heavyweight champ Maxie Rosenbloom, perhaps, or the lightweight champ Al Singer). Such a Gentile became in Sharkey's estimation a goy—a foolish, unaware, insensitive, stupid lout who unfortunately had lost track (if he ever had it) of the heavy freight, the ambiguous meaning the word "Jew" carried at Sharkey's. And so the culprit left the saloon feet first, wondering what hit him.

Daddy was tolerant, and would most times rather toss off a good line than a good punch. Sharkey, however, was easily irritated and physically impulsive, and few things ignited him as quickly as a noisemaker or cheat. A saloon is an easy establishment to cheat—especially when the wrongdoers are irregular customers—and no doubt cheating was quite common. My father, however, never knowingly cheated a customer, and he could not understand why anyone would try to cheat *him*.

One time I heard him tell Mama how he handled a typical pair of cheats. "There was a coupla punks," Sharkey told her, "who worked on the docks—I never saw them before—and they came in after work with some of the regular guys and they paid for a coupla drinks, then they ordered a coupla more, and then I saw there was no money on the bar, and I said, 'Where's the money?' and one a the punks said he paid me. 'What do I look like?' I said to this punk. 'Like I'm stupid

or something?' He said he paid me. I said, 'Pay up, ya sonofabitch!'
So the other one sticks his two cents in and says, 'He paid ya. I saw
him.' Can you beat *that*! One sonofabitch lies and the other swears
to it! So I took off my apron and stepped around the front a the bar.
How could I let those two punks pull a fast one? So I gave the first
one a *zetz*, and when his friend t'rew a punch I hada give him a
knockout too. Who needs punks like that in *my* saloon?"

His late-night discussions with Mama, during which he gleefully
recounted the day's adventures, seldom failed to include a description
of how he was forced to give this guy a *zetz*, or that punk a *bukh-cheh*
or a *khhamalyeh* or a *trahsk*. I read somewhere that Eskimos have forty
or more words for snow, presumably because snow is an integral factor
in the Eskimo's daily life. When snow is that important, perhaps even
forty ways to say "snow" are not enough, or, as in Sharkey's case,
forty different ways couldn't describe the degrees of his daily physical
violence. To hit someone was one of the clearest ways to display power
in Sharkey's world—and certainly more important than the accident
of *being* hit.

My father's descriptions of how he struck an opponent provided
me with an early understanding of Yiddish as a language with scope.
His conversations taught me, for example, implications of and subtle
differences and gradations of meaning between *zetz*, say, and *bukh-
cheh*. I learned that although both words described a blow, Sharkey
would no more say *zetz* when he meant *bukh-cheh* than a prizefighter
would say jab when he meant hook.

Zetz and *bukh-cheh* are particular blows to the *head* (as are *hock,
shuss, knahk, schmeiss, klop*, and others). When Sharkey said *zetz*, he
meant one punch, generally a roundhouse right directed to the side
of the head, invariably resulting in a knockout; a *bukh-cheh*, on the
other hand, was a short hook to the head thrown with either hand
—a blow that required following up: another *klop* or two, say, and
then a rapid *shuss* (out like a light!).

Where an outsider would be forced to guess at the meaning of
one of Sharkey's words—*potch*, for example—Mama and I, upon hearing the word, understood the need for considering such clues as voice
inflection and the look on Sharkey's face as he told the story, as well
as his crisply executed hand and arm motions. A *potch* is a slap, and

may be found in any Yiddish dictionary. But Mama and I knew that Sharkey did not use *potch* lightly.

When he said, "So I had to give the punk a *potch*," we knew the circumstances under which one was potched, the sort of punk he would potch, whether the situation was serious or funny, whether the punk would return to the saloon or Sharkey had banished him forever, and, of course, the duration of the potching conflict. The Answers: the punk was an itinerant bum who had committed a minor infraction of a house rule of thumb, and he would no doubt return to the saloon on the morrow. Duration of the conflict? Five seconds.

It wasn't long before the neighborhood kids recognized that I was a physical coward, and this despite my father's reputation as a *shtarker*. In the gang's long hours together, verbal spats and physical confrontations were frequent. Whenever I was picked on by kids smaller than I was, after a couple of blows I nearly always withdrew. My withdrawal stopped the punches, a result I wished I had been able to achieve with my father. Invariably, a swift attack, the gang came to know, forced me into a quick retreat, and I came to have the reputation of being a coward, which was better (in my eyes, anyway) than standing up to a beating.

Moreover, all through the twenties I was too tall for my age, the kids made my eyeglasses objects of mockery along with my fiddle playing, my clothes were newer and more expensive than their hand-me-downs, and I almost always had more money than any of them.

For the Rutgers Street gang, cash was hard to come by. Few received anything that might be called an allowance. A penny or two for a growing boy to spend in the local candy store was considered by most East Side parents an ample reward for a job well done. But the gang had its accustomed way of picking up extra pennies. One source was answering the corner drugstore's three pay phones that served perhaps a thousand neighboring families who didn't have telephones; answering a public telephone and running up several flights of stairs to deliver a message was always good for a penny or two.

We could count on another chance to make money during the winemaking season. Small trucks or wagons loaded with lovely purple-black grapes would pull up in front of a tenement, and any of the gang who were on the street would carry, on their shoulders, boxes of grapes weighing fifteen pounds or more, up one, two, or three flights to the winemaker's flat. (The larger, stronger kids could carry *two* boxes at once.) The winemaker, who waited in his flat, would show us where to stack the boxes, and paid out his pennies immediately upon delivery. An hour's work was worth as much as a dime.

I took part in such efforts only when I was certain Daddy was likely to be busy elsewhere and would never find out what I was doing. In Daddy's view, running to deliver phone messages and carrying boxes of grapes were jobs for children of peasants; *his* son, the violinist, had more useful things to do. Besides, people in the neighborhood might get the notion that Sharkey's son actually *needed* the money, and was therefore as poor as the rest of the street Arabs. What my father did not understand was that I *wanted* to be a poor street Arab, even though the gang members themselves only reluctantly let me hang around. They didn't like me because I didn't look or act as if I belonged. But they tolerated my presence because I usually had more money than they did, and I was always willing to join their gambling games, and I always left as the big loser.

The Rutgers Street gang had eight or ten members between the ages of eleven and fourteen, all of whom lived a block or two from the saloon, with headquarters just outside the drugstore on the corner of Rutgers and Monroe. From this spot all trouble sprang, all schemes for petty thefts, all arrangements for picking up extra money, and all strategies for gaming and swindling.

The gang's leader was known simply as Muttsie, a tiny older boy, perhaps fourteen or fifteen, with a doughy face and a pink knob about the size of a Ping-Pong ball over each eyebrow, stringy blond hair, and a fierceness—to my childish eyes—second only to Sharkey's. Muttsie took a tiny boy's pleasure in pushing me around and poking fun at my size, my glasses, and my frequent inability to join the gang in one of their more distant escapades. I could never explain to his satisfaction that I was required to show myself to my father several times a day (unlike those lucky stiffs who could disappear forever with no explanation), and while I was deadly afraid of Muttsie, I was much more afraid of Sharkey.

As far as I knew, the rest of the gang, like Muttsie, had no surnames and most had no American first names. The names that served them on the street were no different from what they were called at home. Even at this distance, I can still vividly recall Little Moshe, Duvid, Faivel, Chaim, Hershey, Butch, Yushkeh, Sollie, and, of course, Leroy, also known by Muttsie at various times as Blinder (the blind one), Shitface, and the Big Schmuck (nowadays "schmuck" is a mild expletive on both coasts, but on the East Side, schmuck had only *one* meaning—the penis).

Muttsie's gang had a repertory large enough to keep them as busy as they wished. Weekdays we could steal fruit from pushcarts on Hester Street, or late in the evening we could amble down to South Street and the waterfront and lush bums (today it's called mugging). Muttsie would find a staggering drunk and punch him silly while two of the gang went through his pockets as the others watched for cops. And when a drunk refused to pass out gracefully, Muttsie helped him along with his homemade cosh. When I first saw Muttsie blackjack a bum I had the feeling I was finally in a *real* gang.

On weekends and during the summertime, the gang's most important daily activity was gambling. When there was nothing else to do Muttsie would work up a game—any sort of game, depending on the number of players available—a game that would guarantee that whatever money I had would pass from my pocket to his.

Small amounts of money came to me quite easily. When Mama sent me out to buy fruit or vegetables from a pushcart around the corner on Monroe Street, I always added a penny or two to the cost of the merchandise. This made my errand worth an extra nickel. On Saturday and Sunday nights I took my little sister Dorothy out to dinner at the delicatessen called Manufacturer's or to the Chinese restaurant on Canal Street we called the Chink's. Mama gave me fifty cents for both our dinners at the deli, of which I seldom spent more than thirty-five cents—a nice profit. The Chink's, however, was a bonanza, because Mama gave me a dollar. I would order for each of us the special dinner—egg-drop soup, chow mein, rice, an almond cake, and tea—at twenty-five cents apiece, that left me a big half-dollar, which would eventually find its way into Muttsie's welcoming hands.

If there were no other solvent pigeons available, Muttsie and I played cards. It kept me in his good graces. He taught me how to play a Muttsie-dominated knock rummy, a game called casino, a childish game called bankers and brokers in which extra players could drop in and out at will, and a strange little Italian game called seven-and-a-half which in later years I discovered was a kind of blackjack (with the eights, nines, and tens removed and each face card worth half a point). I can't remember ever winning. Muttsie was either too good a player or too good with his hands—a first-rate cheat. Now, as I write this, I can say that at the time it didn't matter; I felt honored to be asked to play cards with Muttsie.

Muttsie was also a master at pitching pennies. We chose an agreed-upon line in the cement sidewalk and, from a given distance, took turns pitching pennies at the line, with the penny closest to the line winning the pot. I always came close—I practiced a lot—but Muttsie was a born "liner." He could hit the line as if his penny had eyes. His best game, however, was dice. He was so consistently lucky at shooting craps that it took me perhaps ten years to discover what he had known right along: a safe place to buy crooked dice—what were then called shapes, markers, or loaded dice—was better than being lucky. I had little reason to suspect I was being cheated, and I don't know what I would have done had I been told about it. Nothing, probably.

The only gambling game I was any good at was selling punches from a punchboard—mainly because it did not involve Muttsie. I could sell punches to anyone, even without his knowledge. When I was about twelve years old, punchboards were in. All the kids bought them for a dime a board at Cheap Haber's on Essex Street, a general kids' store that sold pencils, magic tricks, secondhand pulp magazines, and, of course, punchboards.

Each board, about one and a half times the size of a playing card, the kind that fit my pocket easily, had a hundred sealed holes and a puncher, and was devoted to football, boxing, baseball, movies, and other favorite pastimes. Hotshot salesmen, like myself, sold chances at a penny a punch to kids who seldom saw a dime all at once. A rapid calculation showed that the sale of a hundred punches brought in a dollar, from which you deducted the cost of the winning punches, and the heavy percentage of profit was at least as good as that from an average Wall Street stock.

The profit, as everyone knew, was supposed to be fifty cents—provided, of course, you sold all your punches. Each board included a number of winners (the odds were usually two to one), with some depending on the significance of the punched-out, accordion-folded words or names—in football the big winner was marked TOUCHDOWN: in baseball it was BABE RUTH. In a boxing punchboard, for example, the name Jack Sharkey paid three to one, Max Schmeling five to one, and Dempsey—the big winner—ten to one. I'd once owned such a board and was forced to throw it away while it still had about a dozen punches left after the main winners had already been punched out. Still, it was fun to approach neighborhood kids, flash your board, and say, "Take a punch? It's only a penny!" It made me feel I was a true resident and a member of the gang on Rutgers Street.

My one unfortunate punchboard experience took place one afternoon as I made my way out of the saloon. I had finished my practicing and, according to Mama's instructions, I was to pass on to Daddy some sort of domestic intelligence before I returned to the house to deposit my violin. Daddy was busy talking and serving a group at one end of the bar, and I stopped for a moment across from the cash register, where on his return he would be forced to acknowledge my existence. While I stood there waiting, I reached into my pants pocket and slipped out my latest board, still relatively unpunched, so I could study the names of the Big Winners.

Sitting quietly at the bar was one of Daddy's good customers, a small gray-haired chap with a rosy face and sharp features, and dressed as if he was going to a party. He must have known I was Sharkey's son (fiddle case under my arm), but we had never been formally introduced. I knew, of course, who he was; I had heard Daddy refer to him several times, late at night. Like the kids in Muttsie's gang, he had no surname. Daddy called him Izzy der Grinner—meaning Izzy the immigrant (presumably to distinguish him from all of the East Side's other Izzys).

Izzy sat at the bar smoking, sipping his Old Grand-Dad, waiting—I guessed—for Sharkey to join him, or for a friend or a business companion. Sharkey had characterized Izzy as a "racket guy." I had no idea of what racket guys actually did, but from Izzy's confident slouch at the bar and his obviously expensive clothes, he had long since given up being an immigrant. He saw me with the punchboard in my hand, and he smiled.

"What kinda punchboard you got?" Izzy asked me.

I handed him my board. Up to that moment I had sold punches only to my friends Joey and Petey and Faivel; three cents' worth. Izzy seemed delighted to find that the board dealt with racehorses. He studied the top of the board and presumably read the names of those horses among the top winners: Sir Barton was certainly among them, and there were Dan Patch, and a horse with the wonderful-sounding name of Zev. The big, big, overwhelming winner was Man o' War, shown in bold letters at the top of the punchboard, with the legend "10 to 1"—odds I still remember after fifty years. The rest of the punches, the losers, contained the lovely inscription "Left at Post."

Holding my board in one hand, and apparently satisfied with what he saw, Izzy picked up a dollar from a pile of bills on the bar and handed it to me. "Here," he said, "I'll take four."

I hesitated. It seemed ridiculous to tell him that a punch was only a penny. Nevertheless, a dollar was a dollar, and if he wanted to be nice to me that was *his* business. Furthermore, Sharkey had come back to the cash register and now stood in front of us, in an inquiring manner. I was, for the moment, not at my happiest, because I knew my father did not like to have me stand at the bar. "Your boy," Izzy said to him, "is gonna be a real businessman. You'll have *nachis* from him."

My father smiled, but I could tell he was uncomfortable with this interruption of the normal rhythm of saloon activity, and even more so with Izzy's idea of how I would grow up. A businessman indeed.

Izzy turned the board over in his hand, removed the metal punch from its slot in the back, smiled at Sharkey, then at me, chose his first hole, and then punched out four holes one after the other, as he whispered, "A quarter a punch!"

I stood there with the dollar bill in my hand as Izzy laid the punchboard down on the bar and then proceeded to unfold the paper strips, while he read his findings aloud: "Left at Post, Left at Post,

Man o' War, Left at Post." He picked up the punchboard and once again studied the printed odds, and then he grinned. "Man o' War! Ten to one, boychik!" he said. "That's two and a half bucks." He held out his hand. "Pay me!"

I stared blankly. Besides Izzy's dollar I had about fourteen cents in my pocket. I had heard what happened to guys who welched on bets, and now I was about to find out the hard way. "A punch," I whimpered, "is really only a penny. I didn't know you were gonna take a punch for a *quarter*."

Izzy smiled and handed me my punchboard. "That's two and a half bucks, boychik," he said. "Who's gonna pay, you, or"—he nodded toward Sharkey—"the house?"

Sharkey gave me a look that said, "You'll hear from me later," turned to the cash register, withdrew two dollars and a fifty-cent piece, and with a bitter smile, laid it on the bar in front of Izzy.

"Thanks, Sharkey," Izzy said. "Have a drink on me!"

Sharkey was indeed unhappy; he looked at me balefully. "Gimme that goddam punchboard," he said. I handed him the punchboard, gingerly, and watched him toss it into the slop bucket behind the bar. "If I ever ketch you again with a punchboard," he said, his chin thrust forward, "I'll break every bone in your body. Now beat it!"

I moved away from the bar, toward the swinging door, my feet leaden, my heart pounding, my sweaty fist tightly clutching Izzy's dollar bill. Sharkey had forgotten the dollar bill, and while I could expect to receive his full reckoning in the next day or two, my introduction to Izzy der Grinner was not a total loss after all.

My father's good customers—the sharp guys, the big-money boys and their compatriots—never showed much interest in me. Sure, they paid attention to Sharkey's stories of his son's musical development, and on occasion there would be some joshing in my presence about my growing physical or mental stature. But none looked upon me as a *person* (in the saloon I was, after all, just a child). If there were any saloon people who acted toward me as if I actually walked, talked, and sometimes had thoughts of my own, they were invariably among the fluid group of men often characterized, in other social contexts, as unemployed, unschooled, unskilled, hangers-on, drifters, and panhandlers. In a word, bums—perhaps too harsh a label, but a saloon term hallowed by usage.

My father was ambivalent about bums. He was fond of some—as fond as he could be. But he had strong views about others. What he disliked was a bum with pretensions, a bum who refused by his action or his language or his style of life to admit he was a bum. I can remember when it was quite common for East Siders (particularly those who had little to do with bums) to relate how this or that bum had once been a successful doctor or lawyer or actor or best-selling author or millionaire stockbroker. Whenever he heard this, Sharkey would make his terse ruling: "That's a lotta crap!"

After a dozen years of saloonkeeping amid a constant stream of bums, my father told me, after I had grown up, that he'd never met a bum who hadn't come from the bottom of the lower classes. "I have seen some a them with a book under his arm," he said, "trying to look like he's educated. One rumdum I knew said he was writing a book. I told him toilet paper would be easier to read. And one bum —a punk named John—used to tell people he was a lawyer, and one time I asked him to look at a lease I was supposed to sign and I found the sonoafabitch couldn't even read. So don't try to tell me about bums! They were *all* no fuckin' good!"

The bums I knew spent a good deal of time in Daddy's saloon. They were all broken men, each in his particular way, but as I came to know them during their brief periods of sobriety, they had a curious and touching sadness, and innocence. The saloon was a second home for those I knew—some stayed a day or a week, and some stayed for years. The best of them were treated by Sharkey as members of his saloon family. He clothed, fed, housed, trusted, and rewarded them when they were good, and punished them (as he did me) when they were bad.

I have warm memories of Gus the Bum (who sometimes served as a baby-sitter when Mama had to travel downtown to see her politician brother Mike); Eddie the Bum (who walked me to Public School No. 2, carefully holding my hand as we crossed dangerous Madison Street, a principal bus route); and Charlie the Bum, not the most colorful bum, but close to the seediest, who, when he was sober, carried Mama's bundles and packages between the dairy and the fish market and the poultry market and the grocery and the laundry, standing sentrylike outside each shop, his red nose constantly dripping into his sandy mustache, waiting for Mama to make her last stop and hand him the final package, so he could hurry back to the saloon, where in two fast gulps he would knock down a three-ounce ball of bar whiskey that might (just might, mind you) stop his nose from forever running down into his mustache.

For a true bum the day's basic requirements were seven balls, or twenty-one ounces of bar whiskey. The cost was a dollar and forty cents, to be begged, borrowed, stolen, or, if necessary, even earned. Working for Sharkey provided at the very least a free eye-opener and a free nightcap. That was two balls out of the way. Life was simple, a journey, and each hour brought one closer to the next map reference. Each day's task was to move unsteadily from one ball to another. To miss even one ball muddled the serious bum's thoughts, his judgment, made his life more difficult and risky. Without proper sustenance, at the end of the street lay the smoky. If by four or five o'clock the bum had not cadged enough, if he'd had only four balls instead of the six balls he had to have, he was through, and he began to stagger along the street until he stumbled and fell. Literally.

When Gus and Eddie and Charlie were sober, they recognized each other for what they were—not bums, but fierce competitors for food, drink, handouts, a space in the home territory, and, above all, Sharkey's goodwill. When they were drunk they tolerated the world, tolerated Sharkey, and even tolerated each other.

To drink a ball in two, three, or four quick swallows, to feel the first warmth, the first flush of excitation, the shifting into high, the acceleration of heart and mind, to feel the warmth, the comfort of being home, to know the meaning of self-confidence, self-importance, self-awareness, to feel the ever present fright diminish and the belli-cosity rise, to be king of the hill, to know that rain or shine it's *always* fair weather, to play with one's moods (now be calm, now be merry, now be poised, now be terrible), to move quickly to the fore, walk on air, be immune to words, to people, to a punch in the nose, a kick in the shin, a kick in the balls, well . . . that was the life, I guess, of good bums like Charlie, Eddie, and Gus.

I can remember some of the bums because they had names.

Itinerant bums had no names—not for me. They never stayed around the saloon long enough for me to learn whether they really had any names. One bum's name, however, still sticks in my mind. I remember Mary Shikker Bum, the generic name for an itinerant female bum. Shikker meant "drunk," of course, and these old, used-up female bums staggered into the neighborhood from their usual sleeping places among the waterfront warehouses to panhandle a nickel or a dime, to work as scrubwomen or cleaning ladies wherever they were welcome. And if the circumstances were right and a bum with an extra quarter could be found, the ladies were always ready for a fast, nervous romp in the nearest available back hallway.

Female bums were not welcome in Sharkey's saloon. When a female bum lunged against the swinging door and hesitatingly stepped onto the sawdust-covered floor, Sharkey directed Gus or Eddie, or another steady bum, to "take the bum for a walk." Later, the couple weaved their way down Rutgers Street, now escorted by jeering kids attracted to the poor drab like flies to manure. "Mary Shikker Bum, Mary Shikker Bum," they shouted gaily. Mary was not always completely insensitive. "Get away from me, you little Jew bastards," she countered sweetly. And the kids responded by spitting at her. An East Side human comedy.

The bum I remember best, the bum in my life, was Gus. Daddy and Mama called him Gus the Bum, but to me he was plain Gus. Somewhere Gus had managed to become both a drunk and a religious fanatic (the order escapes me, if I ever knew it). One day he arrived at the saloon (he never told us where he had come from) and soon proved to Daddy that, unlike other itinerant bums, he was an unusually quiet drinker, kept his mouth shut when sober, and, when asked to run errands, was reliable and trustworthy.

Gus became Daddy's chief lackey, potwasher, sometime bouncer, and night watchman. Daddy set up a cot and mattress in the back room, facing the yard, so Gus could sleep there at night. I peeked into the room, but I never saw any evidence that Gus had moved in; his cot looked untouched, there was nothing to show that the room was inhabited, but Daddy told Mama that Gus slept there every night.

Gus struck me as a mysterious man. When called upon, he shopped for Daddy, washed windows for Mama, and, when necessary, ran up and down the stairs picking up and delivering Mama's home-made booze. Gus seldom laughed, or even smiled, and his sour look discouraged strangers. He talked rather infrequently, and when he did his sentences were unusually short and never anything but declarative. As I discovered early on, Gus believed himself to be a Christian, and I gathered this because he spoke a great deal about Jesus—no, that's not right; he used Jesus' *name* a great deal.

"Hey, Gus," I once said, because he seemed to know all about boats, "where didja learn all that stuff about boats?"

"Jesus taught me," Gus said, matter-of-factly.

Another time, when Daddy asked Gus to hustle an especially unruly bum through the swinging door, Gus grabbed the bum by his collar and, lifting him off the floor, said, "Jesus help me."

When I first met Gus I thought he was an Indian. I had no idea what a real Indian looked like, and I was going mainly on those Indians I had seen in westerns at the Dump. Gus looked the way I thought a real-life Indian *should* look. Although his skin was sallow, not red, it was wrinkled and leathery; his hair was thick and black; his eyes were big and dark and deep and teary; he had a broken nose, and his chin was hard and square; mostly he wore an old gray peaked cap, and a rusty black jacket over a worn-out khaki army sweater. Altogether, he looked quite a bit like Buster Keaton made up to look like an aging Indian.

I never thought about Gus's age, but Mama once told me he was about forty. Nobody really knew where he came from, but I guessed he had been to sea. He was a great hand at making knots, and we once spent an interesting session during which he taught me to make an unusual tie in my shoelaces, a tie I still use. (One time after a shoe salesman had watched me tie my shoes, he shook his head unbeliev-ingly, and asked me where I had learned to make that kind of knot; he had never seen one quite like it. I was tempted to say, "Jesus taught me," but I didn't.)

Gus gave Sharkey a good day's work and still managed to drink his daily requirement without dropping unconscious. He drank as much as any bum—the usual eye-opener, five balls during the day, and a nightcap—but he held his liquor as well as Sharkey did, and I never saw either of them falling-down drunk. Gus went about his duties slowly, deliberately, and always with economy. Where other bums were obsequious, subservient, Gus was stolid. Where others used the name of Jesus as a verbal crutch, Gus sought only His blessing. Where others regularly crapped in their pants and stank even at a distance, Gus, fortunately, exuded only the smell of cheap booze.

Sharkey saw Gus as a special sort of Bum among Bums. "He was a First-Class Bum," Sharkey said, and in a crescendo of commendation, added, "and he was better than a lotta crummy Jews I knew." High praise from Sharkey, indeed. When much later I asked him what Gus used to do around the saloon, he said, "He woiked like a horse." No bum who worked for Daddy, before or after Gus, worked with such dedication. "Gus," Daddy recalled, "was a *zhlub*, a peasant, made of iron. He worked from morning to night. He never got tired. If you ask me, he didn' even sleep. In the morning, at five-thirty, he was already up, waiting for me to give him his eye-opener. Then he was ready for woik."

Gus swept up, tossed fresh sawdust on the floor, emptied and washed the spittoons, washed glasses and pots and pans and dishes and the cheap steel knives and forks laid out alongside the free-lunch counter at the end of the bar, cleared tables, washed the front window, ran up the street for the morning newspaper, and, when he returned, set out to keep the back-room toilet clean.

I smiled as Daddy enumerated this last of Gus's duties. "Then why," I asked, "was there *always* piss on the floor?"

"The bums pissed on the floor," Daddy said impatiently, "and Gus was supposed to clean it up; he did his best. Wadja want him to do? *Live* there?"

I said I was sorry, and Daddy went on to relate how, in the winter, Gus shoveled the sidewalk in front of the saloon clear of snow, and in the summer lugged cakes of ice for the beer cooler from the ice cellar just up the street, and, no matter what time of year it was, Gus did his work without complaint. No job was too boring, too demeaning, too distasteful. But Gus had one duty which deserves more than passing mention, because it was the death of him.

Late on Saturday nights, when the saloon was full of dockworkers, seamen, con men, big money men, and other regulars, all of them flushed and half seas over, Sharkey would pass the word along the bar, which propelled all interested parties into the back room, where any who wished could gamble on the cat-and-rat fight which took place in the wire cage Sharkey had built himself, for that purpose. You could bet on the cat or you could bet on the rat; the contest was not for those with queasy stomachs.

The alleys and backyards were full of lean, hungry, mean stray cats. The saloon cellar—damp, dark, and just a hop-skip-and-jump from the waterfront—had its good-sized share of water rats. It was Gus's job to find the most suitable, the meanest cat-and-rat opponents, and he made even this job seem easy. Gus caught the street cats by tossing a burlap bag over their heads, and he trapped the rats in an oversized "live" trap.

With cat and rat in hand, as it were, and at Sharkey's signal that all bets were down, Gus would toss, throw, shove, push, fling, or in some other way release the animals into the cage. During one of these set-tos, Gus received a rat bite on his forearm. Daddy pressed him to go to the emergency ward at Gouverneur Hospital—a fifteen-minute walk from the saloon—to have the bite looked at. Gus could not be made to take the rat bite seriously; instead he mumbled something about Jesus. The next day Daddy continued to urge him to go to the hospital. Gus shook his head and said softly, "Jesus'll take care of it." Two days later Daddy found him on his cot, dead of blood poisoning. Full of trust to the end. As Daddy put it, "He was the best bum we ever had."

When Daddy discovered Gus's body in the back room, according to stories Mama told me years later, his immediate problem was to have Gus removed without involving either the saloon or himself. What he needed was a "downtown" friend—someone to make the necessary arrangements to remove the body discreetly, and to assure a high degree of personal security for himself. To do this, he had Mama telephone her brother Mike.

Uncle Mike was the family politician, and in short order he arrived at the saloon, directed two bums to carry Gus's body through a side door leading into the narrow tenement hallway, which gave on to the backyard, and set Gus up against a wall of the now defunct old backyard toilet; called a friend at the local police station who called the morgue; and before the wrong sort of Prohibition people could discover what had happened, Gus was picked up and safely put away where he could forever rest in peace.

Uncle Mike was a tidy, mild-mannered man, with thinning sandy hair and myopia, and although he was only thirty-eight in 1930, he seemed much older. He had a short, thin, sharp nose, and wore pince-nez glasses like Woodrow Wilson's, which gave him immediate distinction and came in handy when he seemed to be weighing his answer to a question very carefully and took them off and polished them with a small pink cloth. Uncle Mike smoked cigars, and on the Lower East Side a man with pince-nez glasses who also smoked cigars and regularly wore a three-piece suit *and* a tie (as Uncle Mike did) was a big shot indeed.

That Uncle Mike had pull was no question. He worked for the Board of Education, which meant, of course, the City of New York! Furthermore, he was the only person we knew who was on speaking terms with a *judge*. It was also rumored in the family that Uncle Mike was close to Mayor Jimmy Walker and Tammany Hall; and some rumormongers, perhaps at Uncle Mike's instigation, did not hesitate to mention, *sotto voce*, the magic name of Governor Alfred E. Smith, a possible candidate for next President of the United States.

The important thing for Daddy (and for other neighborhood immigrants and ignorants—good citizens and lawbreakers alike) was that Uncle Mike had enough power to keep his constituents in a state of mixed gratification and terror. How much weight he carried in the upper echelons of city government is beyond my knowledge, but his connections with the local Tammany Hall club gave him the political clout that brought results down in the lowest depths of city government, where, of course, East Side Jews needed him most.

For truck drivers, taxi drivers, and citizens who owned cars, he fixed tickets; for local businessmen he straightened out violations of the fire code and the sanitation code; for the very poor he arranged for Tammany's distribution of free wood and coal in winter and food packages for Christmas, Thanksgiving, and Passover; and he acted as go-between for Jews who couldn't speak English, introduced them to young lawyers and an understanding judiciary. But above all, he earned his keep because at election time he could guarantee Tammany Hall a fair amount of the neighborhood vote.

While there had always been a handful of Jews, and Catholics who weren't Irish, at the periphery of the city's Tammany leadership, the Irish Catholics, working hand in hand with Lower East Side immigrants, quickly climbed to the top. The Democratic Party became the party of the Irish, supported by Jews who could see no good reason for not voting a straight Democratic ticket. Irish leaders, moreover, were not averse to rewarding those who were willing to help the party, and Uncle Mike discovered early on how the system could benefit him.

Once a constituent believed he owed Uncle Mike a favor, Mike explained the benefits of American citizenship and the all-important business of voting correctly. And while he made more than a little money from his various business transactions, his principal responsibility to the Lower East Side political establishment was to deliver the Democratic vote. To do this, he expected, of course, help from his brother-in-law Sharkey. And they pitched in to help each other.

Daddy helped Mike by arranging for him to meet with anyone who complained of trouble. On Rutgers Street it was common knowledge that the saloon was the place to start, and that Sharkey was the principal liaison between Uncle Mike and the oppressed. The understanding was that Uncle Mike would find a way to help, and on election day the saloon would become the headquarters from which thankful voters (as well as regular saloon hangers-on) would be transported from one polling place to the next, voting according to Uncle Mike's instructions. And, as the Democratic party record shows, for many years the scheme worked successfully.

When Sharkey himself encountered serious trouble—like what to do with Gus's dead body—the sort of trouble he couldn't handle with his fists, Uncle Mike stood by, always ready to help. As Mama told me, Uncle Mike paid off clerks, bailiffs, and, when necessary, an important city official. He helped Daddy by guaranteeing that every bribe he made was an *honest* bribe—when Mike worked for Daddy, he gave up all personal gain. Every penny of the money Daddy gave him he tucked into the right pockets.

Uncle Mike found out, for example, why the city's sanitation department okayed the toilet in a saloon around the corner and claimed that Daddy's toilet was in violation of the sanitation code when *both* toilets had piss all over the floor. Why? Well, the answer was simple: during the previous month the other saloon was in violation, and therefore this month it was Sharkey's turn. Mike arranged to pay ten bucks to the clerk in charge of the rotation file. "And the clerk," Uncle Mike reported to Mama, "promised he won't bother you for the next six months."

Uncle Mike could fix anything. Given proper notice he supplied the right sort of bail bondsman, a crooked lawyer, a crooked judge, a clerk in the Prohibition Bureau, a blind probation officer, a deaf police lieutenant, or several smartly dressed Irish cops from New York's finest platoon. All it took was a little of Uncle Mike's time, and a bundle of money. It was a game open to everyone, and on most occasions the players included Sharkey's collection of his favorite Irish customers.

The local Irishmen liked Mike, they liked his snappy three-piece suits, his cigar, his important glasses, and, of course, his clear connection with Tammany Hall—their very own political party. Whenever Mike—who lived in Brooklyn—found himself in the saloon on business he never failed to buy the local Irishmen a drink, and they were indeed grateful. Ordinary Jews did not buy Irish customers drinks.

Uncle Mike and Sharkey were their idea of what Jews ought to be. The regulars, who lived on Monroe Street a few blocks from the saloon, were to my eyes overwhelmingly Irish, strong, pugnosed, and full of good spirits. They liked Mike and Sharkey—perhaps "admired" is a better word—because they were both "good" Jews. Like the Irish, Mike and Sharkey feared no one, had the right connections, and could be trusted to drink and laugh and shoot the breeze with the best of 'em.

The Monroe Street Irish were headed up by a fellow named Jim Nooney, a powerful, red-faced giant who had put together a social-political group more or less associated with Tammany Hall, rented an empty store on Monroe Street, and called the group the Monroe Pleasure Club. During election sessions they worked helping Mike and Daddy accumulate voters and hustled them from one polling place to

126

another, thus ensuring the East Side's well-known and expected Democratic plurality (I was twenty-eight years old before I was on speaking terms with a known Republican).

In the off season, the Monroe Pleasure Club ran card parties, lotteries, and the occasional open house, mainly for Catholics who weren't Irish. Someone—perhaps Jim Nooney himself—once conned Daddy into joining the organization, and he became a paid-up, prominent (if nonattending) member of the Monroe Pleasure Club. "I was the *only* Jew-boy," Daddy stated proudly.

Daddy catered to the Irish because he liked their swagger, their toughness, their sentimentality, and their magnificent inability to hold their liquor. Besides, they were good customers. They weren't in the same spending class as his Jewish buddies, some of whom could have bought and sold them, but the Irishmen spent their money to the limit of their means and often beyond. In turn, Daddy made them laugh, bolstered their egos, supported their social and political enterprises, and—best of all—every Friday gave them all the clam chowder they could eat, free.

The Irishmen good-naturedly teased Sharkey because he would not eat the chowder. Sharkey laughed and said such crap was good enough for Irishmen to eat, but not for Jews. He had his own rules of *kassruth*: he would, for example, just as soon eat roast pork as he would chopped liver; but he would rather be caught dead than be seen eating any sort of shellfish. As he understood Jewish dietary laws, what a sometime Jew ate was all a matter of interpretation, and clam chowder was out!

In time, however, the members of the Monroe Pleasure Club (and their families) were forced to agree that Sharkey's interpretation of what was fit or not fit to eat was also, for Sharkey, a matter of great pride. Each summer the club hired a couple of buses, loaded them with wives and kids and food and beer, and traveled to a distant park to eat and drink and play games on a spacious green that reminded the grownups of home. The Monroe Pleasure Club annual picnic.

One gloriously lovely day Mama and I joined Daddy (and his two kegs of beer) and together with former residents of counties Down, Tipperary, Kildare, Cork, Kerry, Mayo, and Sligo, took off for a day in the country. The pleasure of that day has never left me. I can't remember which park we visited, but it was a large one—Prospect Park in Brooklyn, perhaps, or Van Cortlandt Park in the Bronx. I remember wide-open fields, gentle hills I could roll down without being warned I might kill myself, a raft of boys and girls—one of whom called me Roy and treated me as if I were just another member's son—and a child's version of *haute cuisine*: all the hot dogs, fried chicken, pies, and slabs of cold watermelon I could eat. It was a perfect day—Daddy and Mama had no idea of where I was or what I was up to.

We children gamboled, romped, played tag, and raced each other; the women gathered around long tables, discussing the lovely weather and the proper time to eat, and uncovering and laying out the day-in-the-country's comestibles; the men sat on the ground in small groups talking, laughing, drinking beer, and waiting for the women in their bright yellow, pink, and green summer dresses to tell them it was time to eat. Afterward, some of the men took turns batting a softball, but Daddy, I noticed, lay on his back on the ground away from the others, and practiced springing straight up and landing square on his toes.

Late in the day, President Jim Nooney announced that the last event was now about to begin. Sitting atop one of the tables was a wooden crate from which I could hear grunting noises. The crate, Jim announced, held a heavily greased pig. Jim planned to put the crate on the ground, lift the lid and release the pig, give the pig a fair start across the fields, and then whoever caught the pig could take him home.

The pig, smeared over with what looked like a couple of pounds of Crisco, was let go and ran for his life, and at Jim's cry of "Go!" every man and child ran after the frightened animal. Several men took turns grabbing at the pig, but there was no easy way they could hold on. The Criscoed pig simply squirmed away. Finally, in competition with a screaming mob of boozed-up, pig-hungry sons of the Emerald Isle, Daddy, the *only* Jew-boy, caught the greased pig.

Holding the squealing pig tight against his chest, tucked into his Crisco-covered sport shirt, Daddy marched down the field, as happy as if he had just knocked out the middleweight champion of the world. As he approached the crowd waiting with Jim Nooney, who was holding open the wooden crate, someone shouted, "Hey, Sharkey, you're not allowed to eat that stuff—it's pork!"

Sharkey stopped at the crate, paused to catch his breath, and in full view of all the lads and lassies smiled and said breathlessly, "Here, Jim. I'm givin' you a present. Shove it up your ass!" And the crowd laughed to beat the band.

That day, among the Irish, Sharkey did more for the Lower East Side Jews than Rabbi Stephen Samuel Wise, founder of New York's Free Synagogue.

CHAPTER SIX

When at the end of the Monroe Pleasure Club annual picnic Daddy presented Jim Nooney with his greased pig, I think Daddy couldn't help himself. He always gave things away—free drinks, loans he could never recover, excessive tips, and now even a greased pig.

Not only was he extravagant, but also, as Mama said a thousand times, when it came to *counting* money Daddy was a flop. He was slow and deliberate and somewhat abashed—at the cash register particularly—and the change he returned to his customers was occasionally right. It was not as if Daddy set out to be wrong. He just made his habitual mistakes; his ability to add, subtract, divide, and multiply had always been somewhat less than perfect.

Daddy was fast with his fists or a snappy put-down, but when it came to numbers he was close to helpless. He had never mastered the logic of arithmetic. When he stood in front of his cash register preparing to make change, he pondered in fuzzy deliberation, and became hopelessly confused and embarrassed when he discovered that the change he was about to give the customer wasn't correct.

Incorrect change was not unusual. Some saloon customers, remember, especially itinerant drunks, cheated bartenders when they could. Many East Side saloonkeepers were also famous for cheating anyone who looked a little tipsy; for these saloonkeepers, shortchanging was the way they did business. My father, too, did his fair share of shortchanging, but in all innocence, and he was probably better at it by mistake than he would have been on purpose.

Daddy's difficulty was that he could think only in coin numbers, which was one of the reasons Mama changed the price of Old Grand-Dad from sixty cents to fifty cents. Half the change he calculated in

English, half in Yiddish, and half in an East European lingo. (That three halves could equal a whole would not have surprised Daddy at all.) When he picked up a customer's money from the bar, he stood before the cash register, his eyes on the geometric designs in the pressed-metal ceiling, and counted softly: "Ten 'n' twenty is *dreissig* . . . and *dreissig* fum a *hundert* is *siebsig* . . ."

After he had gone through what he thought was the proper calculation, he pressed the cash register keys as if he had just begun a piano concerto, watched the drawer shoot open, removed what he hoped was the proper change, and spread the coins on the register's narrow marble ledge. Like a numismatist, he would scrutinize the coins, mumble a bit, push them around with his large fingers as if to guarantee their denomination, mumble once more, and then, satisfied that the change was close enough not to be embarrassing, he would slide the coins briskly off the ledge into the palm of one hand. The coins, now hidden in his big fist, were slapped flat onto the bar, and with an eloquent flourish he slid them toward the customer's drink.

As the customer watched Daddy's performance, his graceful coin-sliding technique, his *style*, it would probably not have occurred to him that he was being shortchanged. And if it turned out that he was, well . . . my father smiled and paid him the difference. He was better at making restitution than he was at making change.

Daddy also had difficulty knowing what to do with the extra money good customers sometimes left on the bar. Was it for the bartender? Was it a mistake? Was it a genuine tip? Daddy couldn't believe a real friend would intentionally leave him a tip. Who ever heard of anyone tipping a guy like Daddy? In Daddy's world *he* did the tipping. Mama called him a maven on tipping—maybe the best.

Daddy never left his saloon without a baseball-sized bankroll of cash in his pants pocket, so that during the course of the evening he could dig down, pull out his roll of bills, and peel off big tips. All his life he enjoyed giving away money. Next to being a boxing champ or the father of a virtuoso violinist, he wanted most to be known as a Big Spender. Mama tried to control this obsessiveness, but Daddy was resolute. He enjoyed his reputation, and while he generally took Mama's advice on other money matters, when it came to tipping he refused to knuckle under.

When Daddy was ready to tip, Mama would invariably wince and whisper, "Please, please, don't try to be a big shot!"

Daddy would shake his head, exasperated. Henpecked. "My dear wifie," he would say, "when are you gonna stop stickin' your nose into my business?"

"So *be* a big shot," Mama would say—she knew she had lost again. Mama's cold-water approach to the art of tipping left Daddy temporarily despondent; but a moment later, after he'd had the joy of overtipping everyone in sight, things for him were once more looking up.

My father lived in a world of cash. And cash to him meant green bills. Checks were not money. Money was money only when he could see it and feel it and count it and hand it out. Money was green and came in ones, twos, fives, tens, twenties, fifties, and hundreds. He wanted his cash where he could *feel* it, hold it, and pat it—which is why I never saw Daddy with a wallet. His cash was all there in his right-hand pants pocket. And if he ever carried any loose change, I don't remember it.

For anything that cost less than a dollar, Daddy paid a dollar; for anything over two dollars, he was likely to pay five—with a single bill. When, on occasion, he bought us all tickets to the movies and received his change, he tipped the cashier, as if tipping movie cashiers were an everyday affair. For thirty-five-cent haircuts he paid a dollar; dollar-and-a-quarter taxi fares were two dollars; and a twelve-dollar restaurant tab was easily twenty dollars—I went to restaurants with Daddy and Mama where, by the time we were ready to leave, Daddy had tipped the headwaiter, the table waiter, the busboy, the hatcheck girl, and the cashier, and had gone back to the kitchen to tip the cook.

Mama's most strenuous objections arose over Daddy's indiscriminate tipping in already overly expensive restaurants, speakeasies, and cabarets populated mainly by the East Side's best-dressed rabble. I think she really understood the rationale for Daddy's tipping habits —a tipping system that clearly separated the winners from the losers, the handlers of the long green from the nickel-and-dimers.

She wanted Daddy to make his mark, but not here, not in the midst of the East Side's unsavory nightlife milieu, surrounded by the very people who had admired and embraced the likes of Big Jack Zelig. Still, it was precisely here that Sharkey actively sought the respect, admiration, loyalty, and support of waiters, bartenders, entertainers, and, in some instances, the most dangerous sort of night people. Mama must have known these were his favorite people, the true inhabitants of his not very secret world.

But in Sharkey's night world, where a waiter was satisfied with a tip of two dollars, or a girl singer five, Sharkey tipped the waiter five dollars and the girl singer ten. He was not to be confused with the cabaret's looped, staggering, nameless tippers. Lushes often dispensed money as freely as Sharkey did, but he knew that night people distinguished between those who tip when they are drunk and those who tip when they are sober. Sharkey's reputation was founded on sobriety. Everyone *knew* he was sober.

One weekend night as I lay in my bed reading, I heard Daddy and Mama return from one of their cabaret evenings out. Mama was furious. She had no doubt tried her famous look, this time without result, and now that they were alone she reminded him that he was not as sober as he pretended to be. He had been foolish enough to heavily tip a female singer before Mama's very own eyes.

"Shameful!" Mama said bitterly. "Only a drunk would give that whorish singer—that *koorveh*—a ten-dollar bill!"

Daddy laughed good-naturedly. "The way that girl sang 'Romania, Romania,' " he explained patiently, as he paused to hum a few measures, "she was worth every nickel." He paused for a moment, and I could imagine him shaking his head in pity. "Besides," he added, "somebody told me that she supported a very sick mother. So the ten dollars was for her *mother*, right?"

"All right," Mama said with finality, "when we go to the poorhouse, we'll see who'll give *you* ten dollars!"

(Like the faithful horse player, Daddy died nearly broke. Even so, I imagine as he went through the gate, he managed to slip Saint Peter a twenty.)

In all these early years I am not certain that my connection with money made any more sense to me than Daddy's made for Mama. Whether I was aware of it or not, Daddy's easy use of money was passed on to me as clearly as if I had been formally instructed. Day after day, as I practiced my fiddle, I heard the saloon's cash register ring, and without understanding the economic principle, I knew the sound made Daddy happy. And later, when Daddy emptied the register and gave Mama the money, it made Mama happy. And anything that made them happy made me happy.

The register provided us with the best the East Side had to offer. Money took care of my fiddle lessons, set us up in a new apartment, paid for our eating out, for the movies, for my white flannels, for Daddy's flashy apparel, enabled Mama to buy the best meat for Daddy's dinner, and made Daddy a Big Shot. And money, as I slowly grew to learn, counted for more (among my peers) than muscle. Being tough and strong and fearless brought money *in*; but those who already had money needed little else—in fact, those with money could seek out the support and friendship of the tough, the strong, the fearless.

I learned these facts informally, and innocently, until I was about six; from seven to thirteen I received my basic training in the handling of money by sly observation (with Daddy's childish openhandedness as a living example); and by the time I reached thirteen my understanding of East Side money was such that I could not be trusted to carry a fifty-cent piece around the block without my claiming I had lost it along the way. In short, Daddy's excesses had become my own.

While it is no doubt true that Daddy's excesses were heightened by his early admiration for Zelig and his mobsters, much of Daddy's mental gyrations were certainly initiated by his earliest male influence, his brother Muttel. My earliest influence derived from Muttel's wife, Annie.

According to Mama, Annie was indeed a rough customer, and it was worth your life to stay out of her mouth. She was a big, overpowering woman, a Slavic beauty with big dark eyes and a brand of Yiddish-English that in her mouth seemed to become a new language. She spoke with such verve, such confidence, such chutzpah, such unconcern with whether she was in fact relaying any message at all, that she created a language form I can only think of as pidgin Yiddish. And she was at her best, of course, in dealing with the tiny group on the East Side who didn't speak Yiddish.

Annie lived a few blocks from us and often offered to look after me when Mama had to help Daddy in the saloon. Mama was not overjoyed with Annie's endeavor to help, because, as Mama put it, "It was better not to owe Annie *anything*." Still, I suppose any watchdog was better than none, and Mama handed me over.

I was five at the time, obviously too young to fend for myself, and I enjoyed Aunt Annie keeping her big eyes on me, treating me like a son (she was childless): buying me thick malteds and Tootsie Rolls; buying me a pair of Dr. Posner shoes; teaching me the proper way to deal with bakers who leave flies in bread, and milkmen whose horses have no manners, and other such important facts of East Side life.

Upon returning me to the safety of Mama's arms one day early in September, Annie explained to Mama that she had heard of a public school on Madison Street, only two blocks from the saloon, where parents could send their children every day without having to worry about their safety. "You could leave him there all day," Annie said, "and he'll be safe. My *diamonds* should be so safe. Fum oyside the school looks like a prism!"

Mama pointed out that I was too young. To go to school in America, she explained to Russian-born, unschooled Annie, you had to be six. Because I was born in January, I was about five and a half and I was not eligible to enter the first grade until *next* September. On the record, I was only five. Annie, who had less concern for the law than apparently Mama did, accepted Mama's challenge. "So I'll tell 'em ehr is zex," she said. "For my own nephew I shouldn't lie?"

A few mornings later Annie took me to school and managed to persuade whoever was in charge not only that I was six and a half, but that they were lucky to get me. Schools all over the nation were *dying* to have me as a pupil, and the Madison Street establishment could thank its lucky stars that she had chosen it because it was so close to home.

In later years, she laughed uproariously at her lies. "I showed them real boith-papers with doctors' names fum the Board of Helt. I told them I was your *real* mama. So what was for them not to believe?" (She really did show up with documents; Muttel, as a famous Bowery figure, had the necessary downtown connections for Annie's small-time but successful con game.)

Annie's gentle swindle put me at least a year ahead of myself, and (as I discovered later) made little difference in my intellectual development. When I finished the sixth grade, for reasons best known to New York sociologists and progressive educationists, I was moved into a "Rapid Advancement" program—a program designed to move "RA" kids through the seventh and eighth grades in one semester *each*, instead of the usual two years. I was enrolled in what was called RA-one (the seventh grade) at age eleven; and in 1930, at the age of twelve, fiddle case tucked under my arm, I entered the ninth grade, fully qualified to be an emotional misfit.

My moving on to a new school—Charles Sumner Junior High —had as much effect on Daddy as if I had switched from lemon soda to orange crush. School was school, and how I did at school (as long as what I accomplished did not involve the police) was, for Daddy, just another test of my ability I would have to do on my own; the development of my intellect was beyond his competence. Overseeing my emotional maturity was, of course, his forte, and he handled this responsibility by his careful oversight and manipulation of my fiddle-playing career.

It wasn't enough that I must take lessons and practice. The occasions Sharkey called me out of the back room to display my latest technical achievements before favorite saloon customers were certainly my most onerous duties.

While Sharkey was not particularly adept at recalling the names of these pieces (except for the Monti *Czardas*), his descriptions were sufficient to let me know what he had in mind. Sometimes he hummed or sang a bar or two, or he'd say, "Play the piece where the bow is going fast, up and down, like *this*," then he'd jiggle his arm in a way that clearly indicated he meant the flashy Kreutzer *spiccato* exercise. His gestures weren't always precise, but his signals were clear. To play a piece of music for his personal satisfaction was important to me, if only to help cut down on his usual brutality. But when he called me into the barroom to play something for one of his good customers, the choice of selection became more difficult.

I soon discovered the unpleasant fact that what pleased and impressed Sharkey did not always impress his customers. Objective where Sharkey was all subjective pride, they listened to (or perhaps tolerated is the right word) the praise he gave my inconsistent but flamboyant noodling, and waited to hear the magic I could draw, as he put it, from a piece of wood. I remember one frightening afternoon when Sharkey called me out of the back room to face a snappily dressed, fierce-looking man named Joe Levine, who, I had heard, was a big-shot gambler. Beaming at Joe Levine, Sharkey said to me, simply, "Play something!"

I played "La Cinquantaine", one of Daddy's favorites. It was a simple, melodious piece in the approved Yiddish minor, but long before I was through I could sense (and I could tell Daddy sensed) that Joe Levine was not overwhelmed—what he had heard didn't match Daddy's rococo introduction. I finished playing, Joe Levine said he thought it was a nice piece played by a nice Jewish boy, and he picked up a dollar from his change on the bar and handed it to me. "A nice piece," Joe Levine said.

Sharkey looked at me and frowned, but would not speak. Clearly, I had let him down. His promise to Joe Levine was broken—and who could be blamed but me? He had promised Joe Levine a special treat, a surprise, and my effort (Sharkey could tell from Joe Levine's manner) was nothing, a piece of music that was brittle and dry, like a piece of wood.

I put Joe Levine's dollar into my pocket and set out to win him over. I lifted the violin to my chin and moved intensely into "Oytchi Chornya" ("Dark Eyes"), the favorite of "Russian" Jewish cabaret goers the world over, and Joe Levine, my tiny bit of savoir faire told me, was one of them. Daddy hummed the tune frequently, I had heard it on the radio, and it was the piece Hoffmann, King of the Gypsies, had presented to me in a Century Edition months before. The words were in my heart, the tune in my fingers, and a voice from heaven told me this was an *echt* Joe Levine tune.

As I glided into my second chorus, in my best Hoffmannesque style, Joe Levine smiled and nodded as if to affirm my sensitivity, my impeccable taste, my unquestionable talent. His eyes left me and met Sharkey's, and affirmed Sharkey's good taste, his pride of ownership, his prodigious and unparalleled good fortune in having this talented son, this young genius! Where else anywhere could one hear music as good as this except in the best cabarets? "I've heard plenty of fiddle-shpilling in my life," Joe Levine said, admiringly, "and what I just heard—you can't beat it! His fingers should only remain healthy." And he handed me another dollar.

Daddy smiled. He looked at me, approval in his eyes. "I didn't even know he knew that song," he said, with what passed for modesty. But pride was in his voice. I had redeemed him. I had saved his day. I had proved to Joe Levine that Sharkey knew what he was doing. And I was two dollars richer.

I think of my musical life to this point as my Gypsy Period. My years with Hoffmann marked my style of fiddle playing for life, and I am now free to state unequivocally that I have always loved, I still love, and I will always love Gypsy music—even when it is fake Gypsy music. Under Hoffmann's spell I may have been born again as a Gypsy—who knows? Gypsy music helped sustain my back-room life, and, thank God, there were at least two pieces of "Gypsy" music that I could practice to my heart's content: the Monti Czardas and Sarasate's Gypsy Airs. Because I was allowed to work on these pieces, there were moments in the back room which I enjoyed.

Of the two, the Czardas was the easier and, in the end, offered no real challenge; I had given it up, except as a show-off piece for Sharkey's friends and customers. Gypsy Airs was different. There was, of course, the Heifetz recording that went constantly around on Daddy's Machine, available to overconfident neophytes like me who wished to hear how a virtuoso piece ought to be played—a piece constantly staring me in the ears, as it were. Over and over I listened to the incredibly brilliant Heifetz performance, overwhelmed by its speed, its flash, its dazzling technique, its—well, its superhuman quality. (In those years I thought Heifetz was possessed by the devil; I still do.)

As my own technical facility grew, I had tried imitating Heifetz, but with little success. Much of his performance of Gypsy Airs flew by so fast I was unable to fathom the technique—the fingering, the bowing, or even what strings he played on—and along the way I picked up the notion that Gypsy Airs was indeed a Heifetz improvisation, that he was making it up as he went along, much as jazz musicians do. No composer, I assumed, would bother to write down *that* many notes.

I was therefore stunned one day when Mama's Aunt Mary, who lived next door to us and who had no doubt suffered from the Heifetz recording as much as I had, presented me with a piece of printed music that said *Zigeunerweisen* (Gypsy Airs) by Pablo Martín Sarasate y Navascues, known for short as Sarasate. She told me she knew how much I loved that piece, and because she knew I was a good boy, she had gone to a music store uptown and bought it for me. Now, all I had to do was play it for her—once would be enough—and that would be her thanks.

I couldn't believe it. Here, in my very own hands, on a few sheets of paper, was treasure. In black and white. I couldn't see anything like the Heifetz fire, the schmaltz, the bravura, but I could see the *notes*. My heart pounded, my fingers came alive. I could hardly wait to take it into the back room and try my hand. The pages were black with precipitate arpeggios, runs, trills, harmonics, slow and fast piz-zicatos, mountains and valleys. Never before had I seen a graphic representation of what was written to sound like an improvisation.

I took the piece to the back room and turned the pages in awe. On the title page (I have the music before me at this moment— frustration revisited), I read, "It is hardly possible to prescribe any set of rules as to the exact manner in which this composition is to be played. It should be interpreted with absolute freedom, in order to resemble as closely as possible the character and style of improvised Gypsy music." Whoever wrote that knew his onions. Except for the brief, slow, poignant middle section, *Gypsy Airs* was likely to break my spirit.

Daddy soon learned that Aunt Mary had bought me the music, and he was quite gracious in accepting it as an appropriate back-room practice piece—what was good enough for Heifetz ought to be good enough for me. My intention was to learn it from the top, one line at a time, working each line over and over, thousands of times if necessary, until I owned each line separately. Then I would present the work *in toto*, an astounding performance that would knock the world of Sharkey's saloon on its ass. That was my general idea. But Sharkey's world really had nothing to worry about.

With considerable faking and stumbling (can fingers stumble?) I ran through the piece once, the sound of Heifetz ringing in my ears. The result was lamentable. After a short introduction and brief piano interlude, I was called upon to rip out, with brute strength, several measures on the G string that demanded a certain dark brilliance. Then, winging in with a magnificent vibrato, I was supposed to shoot up in a jetlike ascent through a Hungarian scale that started in the bowels of the earth and ended up on another planet, in a passage calculated to show in two seconds whether you should be practicing *Gypsy Airs* or driving a truck. And that was only the *first line*.

Well, I went to work on this first line. I was determined, driven; I practiced the first line before, after, and between my regular assignments. I tried it slow, fast, sideways, upside down, and inside out. For the speedy run up, I exhausted seventeen fingerings before I found a pattern that almost worked. I shifted fingers, shifted positions, and every day I owned a bit more of it. And one day, weeks and weeks after I had started, just when I had Line One on the ropes and my fingers were beginning to feel something less than sandbagged, I counted all the lines and, *mirabile dictu*, there were forty!

A rapid calculation showed it would take six years and eight months before I could present *Gypsy Airs* in public, or, for that matter, anywhere else. Images of playing my piece on the radio, in the movies, in the main room of the saloon for Joe Levine, faded. Still, for one crazy moment—for Daddy's sake especially—the task seemed almost worth trying. But six years and eight months was a long time for a twelve-year-old would-be virtuoso, and my heart wasn't in it; I had lost my ambition. And so, *poco à poco*, I stopped working on Line One, and after my two-month foray into the land of true virtuosity, I was finally forced to return to the more pedestrian *Czardas*; but at least, by now, I could play the *Czardas* all the way through. Daddy was satisfied, and that was *always* important.

From time to appropriate time he listened to me play while he freshened customers' drinks and rang up the register, and once in a while when the fancy struck him, he would make those small alterations to my musical life that, he hoped, would bring us closer to his goal. It was in this context that he had placed me with my first violin teacher, and then with Hoffmann. Now, as I heard him explain to Mama one night, there was something about Hoffmann that was beginning to bother him.

That very day Daddy had heard my bizarre, sliding, Gypsy-like rendition of the "Air for the G String," and it came to him like a flash of lightning from the blue that I was coming to sound more and more like Hoffmann (Daddy was not, after all, stone deaf). And while he had been listening carefully, perhaps even objectively, contemplating my musical future, he decided on the spur of the moment that he would have to initiate some sort of action that would result in my sounding less like Hoffmann and more like Ricci or Menuhin or Elman or Heifetz or some other bona fide virtuoso violinist. As he said to Mama, "It's enough Gypsy already!"

How my father managed to arrange my life with the next series of events has always been a mystery to me. When I think of who his close friends and colleagues were then, it seems inconceivable that one day shortly after his conversation with Mama, I found myself, fiddle case under arm, following him into the Forward Building on East Broadway four blocks from the saloon, where the *Jewish Daily Forward* was edited and published.

Without my knowledge Daddy had earlier met the newspaper's music critic—whose name I never knew—and now we were on our way to meet with him. I was to play not only for the critic, but (as I later discovered) for a famous violinist named Toscha Seidel, a minor virtuoso who had studied at the St. Petersburg Conservatory with Leopold Auer, teacher of the greatest violinists in the world. What Toscha Seidel was doing at the *Forward* will forever be a deep secret. But according to Daddy, we were on our way up to see him, and dazzle him with my fiddle magic.

For years I have wondered how Daddy ever managed the whole business of convincing the critic and Toscha Seidel that I was worth their trouble. Daddy wasn't famous for his persuasive verbal powers, and my Gypsy style of fiddle playing would have been, to any serious musician, an insurmountable handicap. Still, Daddy *had* brought it off. As we made our way toward my interrogators, I began to become aware of his determination to take me out of Hoffmann's hands and move me up some sort of musical ladder; but more important, I was beginning to understand the meaning of his boast to Mama that he would find me an important teacher if he had to, as he put it, turn the world upside down.

I always had the feeling that Mama would have been much happier if someone in her house played the piano properly. The violin may have been Daddy's instrument (and even mine), but it was not Mama's instrument. At no time, to my knowledge, had she ever indicated to Daddy that she shared his ambition for me. In fact, I have thought through the years that Mama merely tolerated the fiddle—Daddy wanted me to play the violin and that was okay with her; she never did anything to help me except when she told me it was time to practice, but that was as much on Daddy's account as it was on mine. She simply wished to avoid unnecessary conflicts. She told me later how surprised she was to learn that Daddy was unhappy with Hoffmann. She thought Hoffmann was perfect, and certainly good enough for me.

Considering Daddy's parochial East Side connections, Mama believed that with Hoffmann Daddy had gone about as far as he could toward providing my musical education, that with Hoffmann Daddy had exhausted all his resources. Mama thought Daddy was content with Hoffmann's handiwork. As for her own view, she enjoyed watching my development, but then she had never taken it seriously, not in the sense Daddy did. And when she learned Daddy was determined to find a new teacher for me—someone outside the limits of the East Side—she tried to dissuade him by laughing at his efforts. A big mistake.

"The boy is learning to play the fiddle," she said in Yiddish, "so let him *play*. Don't be a fool."

Only Mama could say that to Daddy and walk away. When she wished to impress him with the importance of something she thought he wouldn't understand, she spoke to him in Yiddish. He knew that. She had suggested if his new venture, his new idea, was unsuccessful, *others* might see him as a *nar*, a fool. Daddy's reaction apparently was to treat Mama's advice not as making good sense, but, rather, as a challenge. Nobody was going to tell *him* what to do.

He began his search, in secret, by somehow reaching the foremost Yiddish daily's music critic, who, perhaps impressed with Daddy's earnest presentation, agreed to help him provided Daddy could give him a list of the musical compositions I was currently working on. Daddy agreed, and a few days later when I entered the saloon for my usual practice session Daddy handed me a page from the big yellow pad he used when he practiced writing his name and asked me to make a list of all the pieces I had played for Hoffmann and all the music books he'd laid out good money to buy, and to print the names of these ("Don't scribble") so a person could easily read them.

At the time, I had no idea why he wanted me to do this, but the prospect of killing half an hour writing instead of practicing the fiddle had a certain appeal, and an hour later ("Printing takes a *long* time, Daddy") I gave him the list. He studied the yellow sheet for a moment, as if he could read. He then asked me to read the page-long list aloud, listening intently as I pronounced the titles of the pieces and the names of their composers; he then carefully folded the page, rang up the NO SALE sign on the cash register, and tucked the list under the cash-register drawer. I suppose this same list was then delivered to the music critic.

What I remember best about our meeting with Toscha Seidel is that he was dressed in a suit. I had no idea, of course, he had studied with Auer—the teacher of Mischa Elman, Efrem Zimbalist, and Jascha Heifetz—and was himself a virtuoso. He was a serious-looking young man (I now know he was about thirty), and I sensed he was the maven in the room. Another man, older and *without* a jacket, greeted my father, and I assumed he was the go-between. Clearly, I was here to play for the maven.

My father, speaking in Yiddish, introduced me. Someone asked me how old I was, and I replied, wisely I thought, in Yiddish. Seidel, who was now looking at the yellow sheet containing my repertoire, asked me how long I had been studying, and I answered that question correctly. The critic said something about how he and my father had talked earlier, and how my father believed I was ready to move on to a more suitable teacher. "Very good," Seidel said, "now let's hear him play."

I looked at my father, and he nodded. I moved a few steps to the corner of the room where I had left my violin, took it out of the case, tightened the hair of my bow, and tuned up a bit. With the fiddle under my chin, I asked Seidel, who continued to study the yellow sheet, what he would like me to play. He studied the list but didn't seem to find anything especially attractive. "Play whatever you feel like," he said.

I thought about playing one of my Mazas exercises, the one that Daddy once said I played a mile a minute, but I changed my mind, and began with the Monti Czardas because I thought it sounded more like a piece instead of an exercise. I did a pretty fair job of the opening slow section, full of my special rubatos and Romany slides, I paused a second before I broke into the rapid, rollicking Hungarian dance movement, and then as I prepared to return to the gentler, slower, contrasting section, Seidel held up his hand and said, "Good, good." I stopped, and he continued, "What he needs is to study seriously."

I stood there, fiddle under chin, wondering whether I ought to go on. Seidel and the critic began to discuss certain aspects of my playing as if neither Daddy nor I were in the room. I looked at Daddy, and he nodded again, which seemed a clear signal to put the fiddle back in its case, and I walked to the corner to do so, wondering whether Seidel (or anyone else) could know anything from what I thought was an extraordinarily short audition. If I had known my time was limited I would have played the Mazas étude—at least I would have got through the whole piece.

Seidel now picked up the telephone from the critic's desk, and in a moment I heard him speaking to someone in Russian. (It sounded much like my friend Petey's parents talking to each other, and I knew that sound.) The conversation went on for several minutes, and I gathered from the tone of Seidel's voice that the conclusion was a satisfactory one. He hung up the phone, jotted down some words on a slip of paper, and handed the note to my father as he spoke.

The message came to me as a shock: I was to have a new teacher. My playing was stylish but not precise. The list of pieces on the yellow sheet lacked scope. He had just talked to a classmate of his from the

St. Petersburg Conservatory and he had agreed to teach me. His name was Michael Cores, and he played viola in the New York Philharmonic. Seidel had told Cores I would be a difficult but apt pupil, and Cores had agreed to take me sight unseen and sound unheard. My father was to call Cores and they would make all the necessary arrangements. Cores lived on Riverside Drive and was a first-rate teacher, and I was lucky he had the time. My playing needed considerable work, and Cores would see that I got it. This may not be the order of Seidel's message, but it is the substance.

We left the critic's office, Daddy all smiles and thank-yous, aglow with the success of his ingenious maneuver—whatever that may have been. He had managed to provide me with a first-rate teacher recommended by someone who should know, and, above all, he was now on his way to disclose to his loving but skeptical wife the power of his influential connections. He would show her he was a long ways from the *nar* she had imagined. When she heard the good news she would be forced to acknowledge he had indeed carried the day.

My own feelings were somewhat different. The fact is, I was worried and unsettled at Seidel's news. I thought I had learned to satisfy Daddy's needs, Hoffmann's needs, and therefore my own, and I did not enjoy the prospect of exposing my weaknesses to a new, untried, unpredictable fiddle teacher, the viola player Michael Cores. During our short walk back to the saloon, Daddy recognized my lack of enthusiasm, and it angered him. Later, after he saw Mama and had explained the result of our afternoon's activity, his anger subsided before he decided to beat me.

"No matter how much I try to do for the bum," he said to Mama, in my presence, "it's *still* not enough. I ought to break the fiddle on his goddam head!"

Later, once I had started my lessons with Cores, I knew my fears were accurate. At the beginning, however, there was some excitement, because for the first time in my life I was able to hear from Cores, firsthand, up close, impeccable fiddle playing. But the excitement was short-lived; frustration and depression settled in. I discovered that everything Daddy, Hoffmann, and everyone at the saloon had admired in my playing, had *loved* in my playing, was exactly the sort of thing Cores despised!

* * *

Daddy was sold on Michael Cores, not because Cores was a good teacher or a good performer (he was both of these), but because he admired Cores's hardnosed business ways. Until Cores came along, Daddy had little respect for fiddle teachers; he had, of course, great respect for famous fiddle *players*; but fiddle teachers . . . well, what can you expect from someone who comes to your house for three dollars a lesson?

Daddy liked Cores's business style, which, summed up, meant that Cores charged five dollars a lesson—at *his* house. For weeks, this fact was Daddy's favorite conversational opening; and when that intelligence had been received by his good customers and properly assimilated, Daddy followed through with his punch line: Cores not only charged five dollars for the lesson but he required payment every four weeks of twenty dollars—in advance.

And now Daddy grew ecstatic—imagine! His eyes flashing, his arms opened wide as if to embrace a beer barrel, with the zeal of a faith healer he extolled the financial ingenuity of this Russian-born fiddle teacher. ("A *grinner*. Just off the boat. His English, I swear, ain't better than mine.") And now came the last straw: "And if my son misses a lesson, even if he's sick or in the hospital, or dying, it counts just the same as if he *took* the lesson. You hear? Twenty dollars every four weeks come hell or high water. Now, *that's* a racket!" But Daddy believed Cores was worth it; if Toscha Seidel picked him he was worth it.

And that wasn't all. There was the business with Smack, who lived around the corner from the saloon and drove a taxi. Daddy arranged to have Smack deliver me on Saturday mornings to Cores's Riverside Drive apartment, wait for me to take my lesson, and then drive me back to the saloon. I don't know how much Daddy paid him, but Smack was apparently satisfied. As I remember Smack, he was middle-aged, tall and thin, and wore a pepper-and-salt peaked cap. We hardly spoke to each other for the six miles up the west side of Manhattan Island, and said even less on the way back. I imagine we both knew we were simply doing a job of work for Daddy.

During these trips to my lesson, I looked out the window a lot as soon as we got clear of the Lower East Side, and by the time we were on Riverside Drive it seemed to me we were in a different city. Grownups—dressed like rich people in the movies—were walking dogs who often wore little sweaters of their own; the apartment houses looked massive and dignified and clean—no garbage cans on the sidewalks; occasional trees; no one sitting on stoops; no kids playing stickball; no street market. To tell you the truth, I thought it must be pretty dull living there.

In the beginning I enjoyed sitting in the back seat of the taxi, wondering when we stopped for a light what the pedestrians in the crosswalk might be thinking about this rich young man with the genuine alligator fiddle case propped between his knees. But after the first few weeks even this game palled. Everything palled. I was unhappy with Cores and his lessons, with my musical progress (or, better, the lack of it), and the lies I had to tell Daddy because I wanted to placate him, tell him what he wanted to hear, namely, that I was on the move, traveling down the right road.

In fact I was going nowhere except to Riverside Drive and back once a week. I realize now that Cores was the best musician I had known. He tried to make a passable violinist out of a cabaret fiddler, and after a few months he must surely have known his efforts were in vain. Either that, or he needed the money. In 1930 five dollars was quite a bit. Daddy had no idea how I felt about my lessons, because after our initial meeting with Cores he was forced to take his cues from my little white lies. I wanted Daddy to believe his confidence —not so much in me as in himself—was not without justification. And so I lied.

"How was your lesson?" he'd ask upon my return.

Why, I'd reply, Cores said I would soon be ready to play in public. Cores said I was one of his best pupils. Cores's wife gave piano lessons. Cores had a daughter who also played piano, and once she accompanied me. Cores talked funny but he liked me. Cores was a warm, decent, wonderful person and my playing was improving with every lesson. To see Daddy flash his smile and say "I'll make a fiddle-player out of you yet!" made all those lies seem worthwhile.

I wish Cores had liked me better, but the truth is I irritated the hell out of him. In fact, he may have despised me. He must have been a masochist—I can't believe he put up with me merely for the five dollars per lesson; there had to be a better reason. After the first several sessions I realized his name was not Michael Cores at all; his first name was "Scales," and his last name was "Position."

Unfortunately, my weekly performance of this basic drill of fiddle playing was never up to his hopes or expectations. He actually expected me to spend all my waking hours in my back-room hellhole holding the fiddle in its proper position while I practiced scales. I prayed he would someday abandon that hope, because his chance of succeeding was indeed small. While I now know that his expectations were based on a solid pedagogical foundation, I also know that psychologically I still had no motivation. The reason my playing was never up to snuff was clear: Daddy didn't think playing scales had anything to do with playing music, and neither did I. Neither of us knew any better.

Cores gave me mostly exercises to practice, a piece by Vivaldi, and another by Saint-Saëns; instead I practiced my old pieces. Daddy was convinced they sounded better now than they had under Hoffmann's instruction. Anything that made Daddy happy made me feel a little more secure, and sometimes weeks went by without so much as a bruise on my backside. Choosing between Daddy's approval six days a week and Cores's approval one hour a week, I chose Daddy's. He believed "Position" was the secret of my success. He had my word that my supposed improvement was a direct result of Cores's concern for "Position"—a concern I believed at the time to be an idiot's obsession.

It was Cores's thesis that unless you knew the proper way to hold the violin and the bow, you ought never to be allowed to draw the bow across a string. First things first. You had to be com-*fort*-a-bull! One grasped the bow at the frog with thumb and index finger, elbow pressed firmly into ribs, and as you moved the bow up, your wrist arched between eye and chin, smoothly, smoothly, making yourself (as Cores said in his special English) com-*fort*-a-bull! My elbow would swivel out a little. "Make yourself com- *fort*-a-bull!" Cores would shout, and when I did he rapped me on the elbow with his bow.

I didn't know what the hell he was talking about. My lessons were all the same, in the same pattern. Cores had an idea, and it was probably a good one, that what was good enough for the St. Petersburg, Petrograd, or Leningrad Conservatory, by God, ought to be good enough on Riverside Drive. "When you hold violin in left hand," he said patiently, "you should see elbow. And when you push bow *up* the string, wrist should come up to nose. Make yourself com-*fort*-a-bull!" And when he finished manipulating my right hand and forearm so that my entire right side was acutely uncomfortable, he transferred his beady attention to that incredible left hand of mine—fingers I used to be able to move a mile a minute through scales, arpeggios, Gypsy trills and flutterings—fingers now barely able to move, with all the flexibility of a poker.

"You must learn hammer strokes!" he said. "You understand hammer strokes?" I nodded. The fingers must drop onto the fingerboard like a hammer on an anvil. I tried. Bang! Bang! Cores: "That's a *hammer*?" I tried again. I *knew* I could do it if he would just allow me to move my left elbow out a bit. I swiveled my arm. Bang! Bang! Cores's bow rapped against my left elbow. "Keep your elbow *under* violin. Do again! Make yourself com-*fort*-a-bull!" I tried hard. My arms and wrists ached trying to satisfy that . . . that Russian viola player's idea of "position." Surely, I thought, there must be some other way of playing the goddam fiddle.

Then one day my public school music teacher took a group of us to see the great violinist Joseph Szigeti, who was playing at a local settlement house. I couldn't believe what I saw. According to all the rules in Cores's book on "Position!" Szigeti should not have been able to play the fiddle at all. He stood on stage all hunched up, all arms and wrists, and a 100 percent genuine failure in "Position!" But what came out of his glorious instrument was lovely. Szigeti played with incredible technical facility, and his legato was smooth as butter.

At my next lesson, when I mentioned to Cores that I had seen Szigeti play and that he didn't do what he, Cores, was asking me to do, he said, "When you can play like Szigeti you can hold violin like Szigeti—com-*fort*-a-bull!"

My junior high school music teacher and conductor of our small symphony orchestra was Mrs. Rothstein, a stocky, full-bodied woman in her early thirties, with glorious rich auburn hair piled up in braids around her head and in a bun at the back. She was abundantly chesty, and since I was fast approaching puberty, this weighed heavily in her favor. It may have been the principal reason I agreed to play in her orchestra. Mrs. Rothstein conducting, and her bosom now bounding, now jiggling, now rising, now falling, now quiescent, was a marvelous sight to behold. Especially in the reprise of "The Stars and Stripes Forever."

Unlike Cores, Mrs. Rothstein liked me. She liked me because she needed me. I was the best fiddle player in the Charles Sumner Junior High School and I was her concertmaster. I was a wizard sight-reader among my junior high contemporaries, my fiddle stayed in tune most of the time, and everyone had to take his A from me because we had no oboe player and no one else could be trusted. The orchestra consisted of four violins, two cellos, a few woodwinds, and a few brasses, and exemplified the worst aspects of a beginners' marching band and a junior high school orchestra. It is my recollection that I was the only student whose playing did not embarrass Mrs. Rothstein. As I said, she liked me.

Daddy was happy with my participation in the school orchestra because, as he put it, "You're loining to meet the public," which of course was nonsense. Mrs. Rothstein's orchestra played for special school assemblies, graduation, and the usual spring concert, and the public I was "loining to meet" could be found roaming the streets any day after three, playing stickball, shooting craps, stealing fruit off pushcarts, and ganging up on kids they thought wouldn't fight back. In short, very few Carnegie Hall types. Just the same, anything that made Daddy happy made me happy.

One day Mrs. Rothstein called me to her office. She told me she had just received a notice that there was to be a city-wide contest for junior high school violin players, and she wanted me to represent Our School. The competition was set for a Sunday afternoon several weeks off, and would take place at a hotel called the Barbizon Plaza. Earlier in the term, at her insistence, I had played a part of Saint-Saëns's *Introduction and Rondo Capriccioso* during a school assembly (a piece Cores thought I might learn to play but on which he had given up), and from that performance, which she had accompanied, she thought I had a good chance of winning. She said if I agreed she'd call my father and give him the necessary information so he could take me to the hotel at the proper time.

I didn't know what to say. Her proposal was at once interesting and frightening. The contest sounded exciting, but the Barbizon Plaza sounded like a pirate's cove. Still, it was something to think about. I think the reason I didn't refuse was that all during the months I had spent sitting at Mrs. Rothstein's feet, my eyes on the same level as the hem of her dress, she was my favorite time-beater, my personal metronome. I have a vague recollection of being in love with her; I say this because there had to be an extra-musical reason for my playing in Mrs. Rothstein's orchestra. I agreed to participate in the contest.

When Daddy heard the news he acted like a poker player holding all four aces. I was now, in his imagination, definitely on my way; I was chosen to play against every other young violinist in the city—or so he told his best customers. On the Sunday afternoon of the auditions, Daddy had other business to attend to, so he put me in Smack's taxi, told Smack where to go, and reminded me I was to take a regular taxi back home after the contest, and Smack sped me to the Barbizon Plaza.

I had never been in a hotel before, and the name—Barbizon Plaza—frightened the pants off me. Nonetheless, I found my way in, signed in at the table in the lobby, took the elevator up several floors, and found myself in a hall lined with chairs occupied by serious-looking kids grasping their shiny instruments. An elderly woman took my entry card and showed me to the last vacant chair. I had no sooner sat down than all the kids got up and moved one seat closer to the door of what was clearly the auditioning room. The room of horrors. What, I wondered, had I got myself into? I moved down with the rest, hurriedly removed my fiddle from its case, and waited for the next dreadful move.

As I sat there last in line, silently fingering the *Rondo Capriccioso* I had been practicing assiduously (and on my own) for the past six months, I could now hear faint sounds from the room with the closed door. As each auditioned kid came out and a new one entered, and we all moved down one seat, I began to hear the hauntingly lovely music coming through more clearly, and I couldn't believe what I was plainly hearing. The whole idea of my being there was suddenly nuts and all crazy-like. Holy God, those kids were good!

After what seemed hours later, the contestants had all had their turn going in and out of the judges' room except me and the two kids ahead of me—a blonde girl who looked scrubbed and Gentile, and a fat, round-faced boy with the air of a whiz kid. Now, as the fat kid got up to take his turn, the girl moved into his seat and I slid into hers.

The door to the judges' room had been left ajar, and I could hear people conversing, but not clearly. I could hear the fat kid tune up, and then he started playing. It made me sick; I wished I had never heard it. He came on like Daddy's recording of Heifetz, and the depth of his sound made me tremble. And as I listened to the best live *Gypsy Airs* I ever had the misfortune to hear, the palms of my hands ran with sweat.

After an eternity he came out, fat and red-faced, and the little blonde girl was ushered in. I don't remember moving into her chair, but I must have. The partly opened door was now closed properly, but my hands were still sweaty. I was sitting so close to the door I could hear the blonde far better than I cared to. She started with a piece I later learned was a Paganini caprice—a Paganini caprice!—and I knew at once she could play rings around me and the fat kid and all the other would-be fiddlers. God, I wished I were at home with my head under the blanket. What in the hell was I doing waiting on Barbizon Plaza death row? I looked up and down the hotel corridor. Empty. I got up quickly, put my violin back into its case, tucked it under my arm, and tiptoed down the corridor, and as I opened the door to the fire exit (who could wait for the elevator?) I could still hear the clarity of her up-bow staccato. I nearly vomited.

There was a taxi waiting outside the hotel, and, wet with fear, I plopped myself into the back seat. I arrived at the saloon, all my lies clearly in mind, and told Daddy that the competition was incredibly difficult, I managed to play my piece but not too well ("I was really nervous, Daddy"), and I didn't think I had won. Our music teachers, I told him, would be notified who the winners were, and until that happened all we could do was wait. (I was ready to wait forever, if necessary.)

In school on Monday, Mrs. Rothstein (who had apparently received notice of my absence from the competition) wanted to know why I hadn't shown up to play. The quickest lie I could think of was to say that at the last moment my father had decided he didn't want me to compete. Now, I thought, all I had to do was to return home and tell my father that I had lost the contest and the danger would be past. But Mrs. Rothstein fooled me.

Without my knowing it, she called my father on the phone, I suppose to complain about his lack of support. Thus, when I came home from school that afternoon and walked into my room, Daddy was right behind me. "Why did you lie to me?" he asked, as he removed his black leather belt. And before I could think up still another lie, the beating began. I screamed even more loudly than usual, but the stinging smashes never stopped. And if I think about them long enough now, I can still feel them.

CHAPTER SEVEN

It's NOT EASY to say, but by the time I was old enough to enroll in one of the East Side's better junior high schools, I must have been thoroughly unlikable. I was alternately despondent and happy (both with a certain gracelessness). I was despondent because I was unable to recognize what Daddy had in mind for me as I stumbled behind him up the trail of his ambition. Moreover, I had little notion of what my music teacher, Mrs. Rothstein, had had in mind for me, either, when she sent me to the Barbizon Plaza. As for the rest of my school-work, I displayed irrelevant skills in nearly every class, impressing no one.

While my despondency carried the day, I did have moments of happiness. Sitting in the concertmaster's position and being asked to take a bow for a small solo moved me (at least for a moment); having my English teacher read a good sentence aloud from one of my papers, without mentioning my name, but looking clearly at me when she had finished so that the class knew the sentence was mine, all mine; that, too, provided a wisp of joy. But my greatest happiness came on those days when, with two or three other kids, we wandered the city's streets while students in schools we passed paced back and forth between classrooms like animals in a cage.

I would like to believe that at twelve I was just an ordinary East Side misfit. As I think back to those days, however, and realize the number and variety of people I rubbed the wrong way—Daddy, Mama, my sister, the neighborhood gang, my teachers—I was (as Daddy put it) a no-good bum, and (as I would now put it) the model of misfitness.

I was not only underage emotionally and oversized physically, but I had no comprehension of anyone's motives or purposes except my own. I was too quick where quickness counted for little (in my algebra class I would entertain myself with arithmetic—adding long columns of numbers almost instantaneously), and I was so inattentive that I never understood that the value of x had to be *discovered*. In my civics class I drew Betty Boop, Mickey Mouse, and Dick Tracy, and had trouble remembering that "Staten Island" was the name of a New York City borough. In a classroom full of sharp-eyed tough kids I was myopic; boys half my size practiced lascivious glances at the girls and shooting each other with the evil eye, but I wore glasses ("Hey! Four-Eyes!"), and even if I'd tried, no one looking straight at me could have seen what I was up to.

No doubt I read too much, and all the wrong books and magazines. I comforted myself with trivia without knowing the meaning of the word. I was too smart-ass uppity to get along anywhere socially, and too dumb to understand why I was forced to lead a life of unrelenting persecution. Then, too, I would have been happier named Jacob or David or Philip, instead of the giggle-provoking Leeeee-roy. My East Side school life was, plainly, unhappy. Let me illustrate my frustrations and confusions with pictures drawn from an exhibition of memories born sixty years ago and still nurtured. Let me count the ways.

1. It is a beautiful September morning and the sun shines brightly on a New Beginning: it is the first day of school. I am full of high spirits—this year *has* to be different, and, more important, I'll be out of my father's sight for five or six hours a day. I skip down the steps, scamper across the now lovely sunlit cobblestones, and push my way into Daddy's saloon. It is too early for the morning sun to enter, and the atmosphere is beer-gloomy. I am here because Mama said, "Daddy wants to look you over before you go to school," and I now stand before the mahogany bar, ready for Daddy's inspection.

Daddy is perched atop his stool, arms folded across his chest, ready for battle. He examines me and I wait impatiently for his usual belittling remarks. He studies me carefully, moving his head and shoulders as if he were coming out for the first round. I am there so Daddy can see what his paragon looks like before I join the bedraggled masses who will also be on their way to school.

He observes the new briefcase I am holding. Since he presented it to me a week ago I have been told at least several times that it was made of genuine cowhide—"so the teachers won't think you're just another bum." I hold the tobacco-brown case lightly in my hand, its heavy brass fittings a close match for the spittoons lined up along the base of the bar. Outwardly I am calm, but my nerves are ragged. I want to get *out* of here. By the end of the schoolday my briefcase will have books in it for me to carry home, and that prospect makes me happy. But the other kids will carry their books with worn leather belts or lengths of graying clothesline, sling their books over their shoulders or toss them into the air, because the newly acquired books are now something to play with. Later, I will ask Mama if I can have one of Daddy's old belts to wrap around my books. Mama will shake her head. "You carry a briefcase, you're *somebody*."

I don't understand why it is so important to be *somebody*. Why is there no place for me in the crowd of poor, among my exuberant peers? Soon after school they will congregate in Cheap Haber's, their principal school-supply house, and come away with brilliantly enameled pencils and penholders in red, blue, green, and royal purple, all for a penny apiece. Why can't I buy my *own* school supplies? My school supply center is Uncle Mike, who borrows unopened boxes of pens and pencils from the Board of Education and gives them to Mama who, in turn, supplies me.

Lemon-yellow Ticonderoga pencils, walnut-colored Eberhard Faber penholders, and sticky Falcon penpoints (their brand names will burn in my memory forever), and when I lay out my yellow and brown writing tools in the groove of my inkstained school desk for all my classmates to see, the impact of this assortment of "somebody" merchandise is intended to shame the tasteless reds, greens, blues, and royal purples of my underprivileged peers, but it doesn't. It shames me.

2. The morning sun still shines outdoors, the saloon air is still melancholic, and I await Daddy's approval of my back-to-school apparel. I'm all dressed up fit to kill but I don't know who it is I'm supposed to kill. This Monday morning I sport a pair of gray made-to-order knickers and a chocolate-brown genuine leather jacket like those made popular by World War I flying aces. Both the pants and the jacket were chosen by Daddy so I would look like "somebody"—

so I would have school clothes worthy of my genuine cowhide briefcase. Daddy studies his winning combination and nods approvingly.

Before the week is out I will have lost that approval. On a mild afternoon as I return home from school I will manage to bury my Lindy-style jacket in a tenement garbage can and report to Daddy that someone at school stole it. Daddy will be furious but helpless, and if I am lucky he will be forced to believe my story—the jacket is, after all, gone, and perhaps Mama can be persuaded to buy me an orange-and-green or a red-and-blue plaid woolen lumberjack like those all the other kids wear.

(Later, when the cold weather sets in, Mama will provide me with a pair of leather fur-lined gloves and a leather aviator's helmet, and these too will be "stolen," so they can be replaced, I hope, with a pair of shoddy mittens and a cloth cap with earmuffs.)

There is nothing, however, I can do about my shoes. The most expensive children's shoes my mother knows of are called Dr. Posner's. They are, I suppose, hygienically sound, and are made of real leather, and I am now wearing them. My schoolroom contemporaries mostly wear sneakers. I often wish I could swap Dr. Posner's for their Keds, but I don't think my parents would recognize the fairness of the exchange.

The change from sun to snow will pick up my spirits. As the winter draws closer, I won't have to wear the pongee shirt Daddy bought me last summer. The shirt looks as if it were put together in an East Side sweatshop, but it is actually from Hong Kong—it says so right on the label—and is only one small result of Daddy's idea of a shopping spree (he wished to buy himself some clothes, and took me along for company).

As a reward for being his son and as a way of sharing his joy in assembling exotica, he bought me the pongee shirt, a pair of white flannel trousers, a double-breasted navy-blue jacket with brass buttons, a lavender straw hat made in Panama, and a pair of brown-and-white shoes. My summer outfit. Clothes to parade in through the East Side's colorful alleys and spiffy byways, clothes to shoot craps in, clothes for summer weddings, dances, and Bar Mitzvahs. Luckily, I am not required to wear my warm-weather clothes to school, even though the sight of the Panama hat—*especially* the Panama hat—fills Daddy with pride. I wish it fit him.

3. My fingers clutch the sturdy rolled-leather handle of my genuine-leather briefcase, and if you look closely you will see I am wearing a gold ring. Daddy is certain the ring is gold; the jeweler told Daddy the ring is gold, he told him the ring came from Japan and it's called Japanese gold. But it has a dull, unburnished look; it is not, to my amateur eyes, the color of *real* gold. The ring is in the form of a coiled dragon, and the dragon's head bears my initials, in an oriental style borrowed from Fu Manchu movie posters. In the dragon's eye is a small shiny object that Daddy believes is a tiny Hope diamond.

I am not much taken with my Japanese ring. My friend Joey wears a ring he made by rubbing a peach pit against the concrete water fountain in Cherry Park, and it is very becoming indeed. And my friend Petey, who is dedicated to masculinity, says only girls wear rings. When I am fifteen I will sell Daddy's Japanese ring for two dollars during a crap game, to a fellow who will throw five straight passes.

I also own a wristwatch—a Bulova. Daddy gave it to me so I could be home by eight o'clock, my evening curfew. Having a watch makes it more difficult for me to lie and to frustrate Daddy's schedule. When I am miles from the saloon and the hour grows late, I can study my timepiece and run a series of five-minute miles, arriving home with time to spare, thus avoiding my usual licking. Now I have no excuses.

At school, Mrs. Follmer, my history teacher, notices my wristwatch and, during short quizzes, says, "Tell me when the ten minutes are up." My watchless classmates ask me to lie to Mrs. Follmer so they can have an extra minute or two or else they will wait for me in the schoolyard. I wish Mrs. Follmer would ask someone else to keep time for her, but nobody else has a Bulova wristwatch. The Bulova is more valuable than my Japanese ring, because I will pawn the wristwatch for five dollars and then sell the pawn ticket for two dollars more.

4. Daddy is a great present-giver. He gives presents the way others say "Thank you." That is the reason Daddy is such a heavy tipper—a tip is, after all, a present. But you can't give everyone a tip, because a tip is money, and Daddy knows you can't give just *anyone* money —a gift of money may be misunderstood, but who can doubt the intention of a present? There are those who think Daddy's presents are not presents at all; these insensitive people do not understand Daddy's intentions and call his presents "bribes." The East Side is full of such people.

The difference between a present and a bribe is a matter of openness: a present is a gift, but a bribe is a *shmeer*—a smear with grease for easy access. A present is open and aboveboard; a shmeer takes place under the table. Still, there are some people who pretend there is no difference. Mrs. Follmer, my history teacher, a severe, no-nonsense Irishwoman whose small round face and severely cut black hair scare the hell out of me, is one of them.

Mrs. Follmer doesn't like me. She likes to use my Bulova watch, perhaps to show there is something about me that is trustworthy, but she grades my history papers from zero all the way up to 50. Perhaps that is all my papers are worth, but that is no reason for pounding the palms of my hands with her steel-edged ruler for what she has labeled my insubordination (caught talking too loud when she enters the classroom). I'll be glad to be promoted out of her class into the next class—if she'll let me go. In Mrs. Follmer's class, grades for deportment weigh heavily.

My midterm report card (which I have in front of me at this very moment) is a scaly horror—music, 70; biology, 47; English, 75; civics, 40; French, 80; history, 35. I am supposed to bring the report home and show it to Mama for her signature. I am afraid she will read it to Daddy (*after* he finishes his dinner) and he will offer to kill me, but then I have been killed before. This time, after dinner, Daddy surprises me. Instead of chasing me through the crowded front room, strap held high, he wants to talk about it; he wants to discuss my report card rationally; he does not understand the meaning of the grades (except that Mama told him they are low) and he wants me to explain why a boy who has his nose in a book alla time should have such a bad report card.

I tell Daddy that Mrs. Follmer, who is responsible for my report card, doesn't like me. I don't know why. Maybe I'm too tall, or too outspoken, or maybe she just doesn't like Jews—the look on Daddy's face tells me I just hit the jackpot. In the East Side's public schools, teachers who don't like Jews are not exactly unknown, and my new-born thesis is something Daddy can cope with, something he can understand. Furthermore, it is a situation Daddy is sure he knows how to control. A goyishe teacher is no better than a goyisher cop, and with a goyisher cop you shmeer—grease for easy access. If a teacher doesn't like you, Daddy tells Mama, there are ways to change her mind, to *make* her like you.

I listen as Daddy and Mama explore various courses of action and finally arrive at a decision. "Ask your teacher what size silk stockings she wears," Daddy says, "and then give it to Mama." Daddy's simple request sounds nuts. He actually intends giving Mrs. Follmer a *present*. I suggest that there is no proper way for me to ask this Irish witch—who has already *proved* she doesn't like Jews—such an intimate question. Daddy, speaking to his astonished, helplessly innocent son, goes over his strategy once again, and since it temporarily checks the big black strap, I join in the game.

I am now standing in front of Mrs. Follmer's heavy oak desk. She is busy writing. I shake with fear in these several moments of desperation after my history class leaves the room and before the new class wanders in. I whisper Daddy's magic words to Mrs. Follmer and they stick in my throat. "My *mother* wants to know what size . . ." and I croak out the rest.

Mrs. Follmer stops filling out her attendance sheet, stares at me curiously, and, apparently assured that my question is a serious one, picks up a scrap of paper, writes a few words, and pushes the paper toward me without asking what right I have to this odd information. I slide the paper off her desk, deposit it in my briefcase, and hurry out of the classroom as quickly as I can. I suddenly have to go to the toilet. I don't know why I feel queasy, but I do.

Once at home, I give Mama Mrs. Follmer's slip of paper, and a few days later I am given a long, thin, neatly packaged box of stockings to deliver to my mentor. In the morning I come to class early, remove the box from my briefcase, and place it in the middle of Mrs. Follmer's desk, covering it with some sheets of paper. I receive no acknowledgment of this shmeer until I receive my next report card—which is even worse than the first.

With a strong conviction of righteousness I deliver my latest piece of bad news for Mama's signature. Mama studies my low marks, and is confused and, justifiably, she must think, outraged. "Three beautiful pairs of stockings," she bemoans, "pure silk, the best! And like thrown into the garbage can!" Daddy hears the bad news and seems to dismiss this failure. He has made a deal and it hasn't worked. "Who knows," he says temperately, "maybe the stockings didn't fit her." Let the briber beware.

But my life with Mrs. Follmer has, for now, a happy ending. At the end of the semester I am promoted along with all those who *didn't* give Mrs. Follmer three beautiful pairs of silk stockings. Still, the experience is important to my development—to know that a strict teacher like Mrs. Follmer could be shmeered by the parents of an obviously failing student brings me a degree of worldliness I might not have acquired for years to come. This experience also makes me believe Daddy is a pretty good judge of people, even when he doesn't know them personally.

By the end of the ninth grade, my futile groping, my early ridiculous underachieving, my disdain for and disgust with the New York junior high school system, all bore fruit. Instead of being promoted to the tenth grade, I was left back. Left back: the East Side household term for the worst possible academic failure, pronounced "*left*back." To be left back was to be planted inside a barbed-wire enclosure inhabited by weedy kids raised by indifferent grown-ups, by bum kids with bad eyes and no glasses, and by young punks who were too street-smart or too dumb, or clearly headed for the electric chair.

A pimply-faced kid who liked to read, wore glasses, played in the school orchestra, and wore white flannel pants and a lavender Panama hat in the summertime was seldom left back. Daddy was appalled that *I* had been left back, and what that might do to his neighborhood reputation God only knew. Nonetheless, he and Mama were forced to accept the fact that I would have to return to Charles Sumner Junior High School with my not-so-new cowhide briefcase and, no doubt, a fresh batch of Ticonderoga pencils.

Mama was not looking forward to the prospect of explaining my Fall to her nosy neighbors (who would have heard about it from their kids anyway). And I was angry because the powers-that-be hadn't kicked me out of school altogether. I believed I deserved it. In my up-and-down academic existence since Mrs. Follmer and the silk stocking charade, I had become snotty, willful, unscrupulous, and nearly incorrigible. I was undoubtedly a product of my environment—I couldn't escape myself.

My school transcript (as I now look at it) shows that I scored in the 47th percentile in my biology final, received a 33 in geometry, and (as one of the fastest street runners my age) somehow managed to flunk physical training. There is, however, a clue to my consistency at failure, and it's shown under the heading "Days Present" on my transcript for that year: in a semester containing ninety-five school days, I showed up fifty-five times, which works out to less than three days a week. Apparently I went to school whenever I felt like it.

Still, I was not without some means of educating myself. For one thing, I read a lot—a habit I picked up from Mrs. Ehrhart's English class. Mrs. Ehrhart, a blond, middle-aged, pretty woman with carefully rouged cheeks, seemed to care about my work. Her comments on the papers I wrote for her were always favorable, or at least encouraging. I was not particularly interested in the daily class work—bits and pieces from *Julius Caesar* or *Silas Marner*—alongside bums who favored the pornographic comic books we passed among ourselves. I had finished all the required reading I was interested in, and when Mrs. Ehrhart discovered this she gave me a list of books I could borrow from the public library. (I loved her then, and I still do.)

Mrs. Ehrhart may have been a good English teacher, but I am afraid her efforts were mostly unproductive. Nearly all of her languid students were raised in immigrant-style households where basic Yiddish or Italian was the first language and fractured English the second. She tried hard to teach us the language of, say, Winston Churchill, but most of us never listened—we were too busy studying the symmetry of her rouge or shooting broken paper clips at each other.

I remember when she tried to teach us the parts of speech and how to parse sentences. That, I thought, was a flop—who needs grammar? I had no cogent reason to follow Mrs. Ehrhart's grammatical explications and (like another would-be gentleman) I was past thirty before I discovered I'd been speaking and writing prose for years.

I did have one verbal gift, however, and that was spelling. (I must have read enough junk to have seen lots of words.) Thus, one day when Mrs. Ehrhart selected a spelling team for the all-school spelling bee, I was her first pick. Then she added two of my classmates who always got to erase the blackboard, Mrs. Ehrhart's award for good conduct and one I had never received. I didn't think much of my teammates—a quiet boy who had a *Saturday Evening Post* route ("A Curtis Junior Salesman") and perfect attendance, and a snippy, plump girl with long curls. The best I can say of them is they were steady, reliable, and industrious.

But nothing could spoil my pleasure at being selected by Mrs. Ehrhart. In the event, I did win the spelling bee, with "monocotyledonous" (I'd seen it in my biology book), and my prize was an Inkograph fountain pen. It leaked. The victory, though, made me feel wonderful—I knew I had pleased Mrs. Ehrhart, and that was important.

If "monocotyledonous" had appeared in the mysteries of S. S. Van Dine, in Street and Smith's *Detective Story Magazine*, in the Broadway-Hollywood gossip columns of Mark Hellinger, Walter Winchell, Sid Skolsky, in the vigorous, six-words-to-the-sentence prose of the New York *Daily News* or the *Daily Mirror* (*Daily Mirra*, as we called it), and the *Forward* (for the city's Yiddish-speaking mavens), then I would have read it many times over.

A list of what I recall reading at this stage shows, surprisingly, that some good stuff slipped in among the cascade of junk. I discovered, for example, *Liberty*—a magazine where the reading time for each item was boldly stated, and gave the reader something to match himself against; the weekly page of jokes and light verse in *The Saturday Evening Post*; and the cartoons and short essays in *Judge*.

At Cheap Haber's—that wonderful Essex Street hodgepodge of school supplies, magic tricks, and pocket warmers—I came across back issues of such eye-popping magazines as *Breezy Stories* and *Hot Dog!* and the penny-a-word prose of *Flynn's Detective Fiction Weekly*, *Amazing Stories*, and *Astounding Stories*. The prices of these back issues ran from three for a nickel (*Flynn's Weekly*) to a dime apiece (*Captain Billy's Whiz Bang* and *Hot Dog!*), and over time, depending on my finances, I sampled them all. Later, to help round out my education, I accumulated most of *The Adventures of Sherlock Holmes*; and still later, working on what I will have to call poetry, I memorized the words of 385 popular songs, more or less, from the stacks of sheet music piled on Zaida's piano.

The formal school assignments included *Julius Caesar* and *The Merchant of Venice* and *Hiawatha* and *Rip Van Winkle*, and I even memorized "Trees" (". . . a nest of robins in her hair"), but these were not my favorites. Before Mrs. Ehrhart gave us her suggested reading list, I spent my time mostly with short stories—stories that were realistic and closed with a snappy ending, which is why one of my most coveted magazines was entitled, simply, *Snappy Stories* (same price as *Hot Dog!*). I may have chosen to read short stories instead of longer works because Daddy insisted he would rather I practiced the fiddle instead of "killing time" reading.

"Why has he always got his nose in a book?" he complained to Mama.

"It's not a book," I would say, "it's a magazine!"

But Daddy saw no distinction. "Who cares what it's called? Go and *practice*. What am I paying money for? You can read books in school!" (During World War Two, barracks buddies would say to me, "Ya got any books?" They meant "books" in the same sense Daddy had—comic books mostly—but other "books" included *Reader's Digest*, *True Detective*, *Argosy*, and *Popular Mechanics*.) Daddy's obsession, of course, forced me to do my home reading in short bursts, and on the sneak if I wished to avoid his wrath and a bang on the head.

Reading books in my father's mansion was easy if you were an acrobat. Lying in bed in the dark—no bedlamp, no night light—with nothing to read by except an inch-and-a-half of light from the kitchen which shone through the gap at the bottom of my bedroom door required a special kind of night vision and the ability to read while crouching on my knees. All I lacked was books.

As I pointed out, there were neither books nor magazines in my father's mansion, not even a Bible. Oh, from day to day there were fresh copies of the *Daily News*, which Daddy brought home from the saloon; and occasionally I would look at pages from the *Forward* or

The Day or the *Morning Freiheit*—Yiddish dailies Mama brought home wrapped around dill pickles or soup greens or schmaltz herrings. They were at least something to read.

Mama's solution to the book problem was straightforward: she saw to it there were no books, and she gave up reading them. What she did best was *hide* stray books. Meanwhile, as I received my new schoolbooks each semester, or acquired a small stack of magazines, I brought them home and stashed them in the two drawers at the bottom of my bedroom wardrobe. Out of Daddy's sight. By this time, even *I* could tell he didn't like to see books lying around. I suppose he had a right to avoid even the sight of them; the house was, after all, *his*.

And so for several years I read mostly pulp magazines. In addition to magazines I bought regularly at Cheap Haber's, I acquired stacks of others by swapping and gambling with like-minded kids. We favored the Italian card game *sette mezzo* (seven-and-a-half), in which a gambler could either bet a magazine or use real money; the cash value of the magazines was whatever Cheap Haber's unfluctuating stock quotation said it was. *Detective Fiction Weekly*, for example, was worth two cents in a seven-and-a-half game, and that agreement made me feel I had a better chance to win than the others.

I was a rapid reader, and besides, I spent considerably more time actually reading than my fellow gamblers. Once I finished reading a magazine it no longer had any value to me; therefore each night, in the secrecy of my badly lighted bedroom, I read myself half blind, secure in the knowledge that the next day's seven-and-a-half game would enable me to bet my now worthless magazines against some of real value. How could I lose?

And then Mrs. Ehrhart's reading list changed my scheme: it brought me to the nearest public library—five blocks from the saloon—on the corner of East Broadway and Jefferson Street. On a cold day (I know it was cold because I remember wearing a heavy coat), I walked up the steps of an official-looking gray stone building and entered my first public library, my head full of ancient dreams and faraway places, only to discover that the books, watched over by a grim, gray wardress, were divided, like my life, into a Children's Section and an Adult Section.

I soon learned that my age limited me to the Children's Section, from which I could borrow only one or two books at a time (depending on the librarian's state of mind), and then for only seven days. I thought the system was rather demeaning; I wasn't interested in the so-called children's books, and after I received my library card I resented being held down to only one or two books a week. I considered myself a fast reader. Who could go to the library every *day*?

One day, while wandering through the stacks in the Adult Section, I saw a book whose size and color and title I fancied. Painfully aware that the wicked Queen would not allow me to borrow that book, I quickly checked to see whether I was under observation. The librarian was busy stamping someone's books, and as soon as I was certain no one else was watching me, I thrust the book inside my coat, tucked firmly under my arm, buttoned my coat, and leisurely moved past the busy librarian, who was still stamping books at the checkout counter.

What puzzles me most is that I don't remember feeling any fear. What might have happened had I been stopped and searched and found guilty never occurred to me. Why wasn't I intensely excited and nervous and all sweaty—like the criminals in *Detective Fiction Weekly*? I suppose I was too stupid and thoughtless to think of the consequences.

I walked out into the street, looked left and right as if I were making up my mind which way to go, and still no one came in pursuit. I took the book home, read it, stuck it in the bottom drawer of the wardrobe along with my magazines and an old pair of galoshes, and waited. Still nothing happened. Perhaps the lack of swift retribution wasn't in my best interests, and society and I would have been better served if I had been caught red-handed the first time around. As it happened, I had just launched a new career and, to put it in gambling terms, I was off and flying.

Inside of six months the galoshes had been moved to the top of the wardrobe, I was curator of a couple of dozen unchecked-out New York Public Library holdings, and I now had the pleasure of handling (and reading) more stolen books from the Adult Section of the East Broadway branch of the New York Public Library than you could shake a nightstick at.

By now I knew the library inside out. Starting slowly, I worked my way through all the available Conan Doyle, Arthur Train,

O. Henry, and Mark Twain (it seems to me some of these should have been in the Children's Section); then, by careful digging through the stacks, I came across, and stole, works by Agatha Christie, S. S. Van Dine, and Sax Rohmer. Titles I remember falling in love with were *Vanity Fair*, *Paradise Lost*, *Is Sex Necessary?*, *Barnaby Rudge*, and something called *The Amenities of Life* ("amenities," of course, meant nothing to me, I simply liked its noble sound).

I was reading like one possessed. The combination of "free" books chosen with no outside control, the pleasure I derived from outsmarting the librarian, the thrill in cheating members of the New York Police Department, and, above all, the joy of secretly frustrating Daddy's high-minded ambition for his misfit son made all the risks worthwhile. And what I stole from the library mixed nicely with a mess of five- and ten-cent dreadfuls I picked up God only knows where—*Nick Carter*, *Nick the Newsboy*, *Phil the Fiddler*, Haldemann-Julius little "Blue Books," and my own personal five-inch shelf of *Italian Jokes*, *Darkie Jokes*, *Irish Jokes*, and *Hebrew Jokes*, (Teacher: "Abie, give me a sentence with the word 'formaldehyde.' " Abie: "Formaldehyding places came dee Indians!").

Reading, mostly in half-light, did my eyes little good. My poor eyesight may have been genetic, but nobody else in the family wore glasses, and nobody else was called cockeyed. Daddy's observation on this small matter provided as good a warning against reading as any I've heard. With his usual authority he said I'd be sitting on the corner selling pencils from an old tin cup if I didn't stop having my "nose inna book alla time." His regard for my welfare was touching indeed.

Mountains of library books were now piling up in the drawers of my wardrobe, and I was forced to stow new books *inside* the wardrobe closet, and although there was little reason for Daddy to rummage around in there, still, he might. And if he did, the result would be a back-room caterwauling better left unheard. I may have been a fool to steal those books, but I wasn't so warped that the accumulation of them didn't worry me. I had occasional thoughts of taking the books back to the library and simply leaving them on the steps for somebody to find (the days of book drops were still to come). But I never did so. I finally decided the books wouldn't be missed; after all, the library had so many that who would miss "my" books?

By now, the books in my closet were stacked in three rows two feet high, stolen by a gangly thirteen-year-old thief with glasses, who might (with a little prodding) turn from books to hard cash. Why not? The whole thing was something out of the movies anyway: violin virtuoso steals rare books, moves on to money, and then—who knows?—the Hope Diamond? What would Mama say when she visited me in Sing Sing? And what if Daddy ever found out what his firstborn was doing? I'd be an inch away from being drawn and quartered.

I know it's easy—at a remove of sixty years—to sentimentalize my predicament, but a growing heap of brightly colored stolen books hidden in a dark bedroom closet where an innocent bystander— Daddy, for example—might accidentally stumble over them caused me considerable anxiety, when I thought about it. In my own aimless way, I suppose, I was asking someone, anyone, for help, for a way out, for an exit sign.

Help eventually came. It came either through the hand of God, the virtuoso performer of miracles, or through Muttsie, the gang leader who was exceptionally adept at dealing seven-and-a-half. One afternoon, during our long, ongoing game (which meant I was a consistent loser), Muttsie was struck with an idea born from winning my small pile of magazines. He offered to exchange ten of them for the interesting-looking book tucked under my arm.

"Just to keep the game going," he said.

I think Muttsie saw such an exchange as a loan of ten magazines with the book as collateral. He was merely lending me the equivalent of twenty cents on a book he could see I'd borrowed from the library. When I paid him twenty cents in cash (paid off my ten-magazine mortgage, so to speak) he would return my book. Muttsie's deal saved me. He not only exchanged my "borrowed" library book for honest magazines, but changed my occasional closet nightmares to carefree sleep and increased my readable gambling capital.

And soon, by judicious use of the free-enterprise system and certain banking principles (ten magazines equals one book), titles like *Vanity Fair, Paradise Lost,* and *Barnaby Rudge* came to be circulated among the gang's seven-and-a-half players like good news. God in his heaven smiled, our seven-and-a-half games continued to flourish, and the neighborhood juvenile economy hotted up. It would be nice to report that some of the books were read. It would be nice, but unlikely. Exchanging ten back issues of *Detective Fiction Weekly* for one bound copy of *Paradise Lost* was extraordinary enough.

One of my greatest difficulties at Charles Sumner Junior High School grew out of my relationship with Jimmy Wong, my Chinese classmate and friend. Jimmy was older than I was. How much older is hard to say, but he looked older than the rest of our class, and I would guess he was fifteen to my thirteen. Jimmy's father, the story went, was a rich silk merchant in China, and Jimmy had been sent abroad to receive an American education. He lived in Chinatown, which was just a few blocks from school, and I frequently walked him home.

Jimmy was lithe and strong, slight and broad-shouldered; he had the high forehead my great detectives associated with intelligence, and a shiny black hairdo copied from hair tonic ads and photographs of Rudolph Valentino. Jimmy Wong was further distinguished by his everyday school clothes—three-piece suits, brilliant-white shirts with starched collars, and each day a different tie. His well-polished shoes matched his hair, and cologne made him smell as nice as he looked. Jimmy should have been the envy of every American boy; instead, the other kids considered him weird, strange, scary, *too old*, and avoided him.

As a fellow outcast I was attracted to him. His spoken English wasn't as good as mine, although it wasn't much worse than the speech on any East Side market street. But I enjoyed talking to him. I always spoke slowly (which I still do, to foreigners), and I remember a busy exchange of headshaking and other gestures. Jimmy always responded graciously. I certainly enjoyed being regarded with respect, because it was new to me. Jimmy found me especially helpful, particularly when Mrs. Ehrhart asked me if I would help him with his English homework.

I did what I could to help Jimmy, and we got along fine. I corrected his work—purely by sound, because English grammar was foreign to both of us—and his grades improved. The *look* of his work was another matter. I was surprised at every paper he showed me, because his written English—while it didn't say much—seemed to have come straight from the illustrations in our penmanship textbook.

He wrote with a flowing hand, each letter precisely slanted, each word delicately balanced, each page a model of symmetry. Jimmy Wong's handwriting made my own look crabbed and careless.

Jimmy considered me his closest American friend, and I considered Jimmy Wong the most exotic person I knew outside the pages of Sax Rohmer. Jimmy had a cousin living on Mott Street who had arranged for him to come to America, but Jimmy lived on Doyers Street, by himself. I had never known a boy who lived by himself, bought all his own clothes, and ate all his meals in a basement restaurant across from his apartment. He apparently never lacked money, and since his father lived five thousand miles away, in Hong Kong, Jimmy Wong had no one to account to. I dreamed of living someday like Jimmy Wong.

One late afternoon, after we had arrived at his apartment and had gone over his homework, Jimmy invited me to have dinner with him. It was dusk by now, the neon shop signs had been lighted to comfort tourists, and I should have been thinking of leaving for home, where no doubt the evening meal would be waiting. I looked at my Bulova wristwatch and saw a flash of Daddy with strap in hand (I had already missed fiddle practice), but the prospect of eating in a Chinese restaurant with a real Chinese friend was more than I could resist, and nothing short of the threat of death could have kept me from accepting Jimmy's invitation.

We walked across the wet, black, crooked Chinatown street, entered a narrow passageway, and moved down stone steps into a dim cellar. The restaurant was all I had hoped for, had imagined: it was small, cramped, ill-lighted, stifling, frightening, and mysterious, and smelled of joss sticks and hot cooking oil. There were six or eight small tables occupied by elderly Chinese men, some drinking tea, some eating, and some just sitting. As I looked around, delighted and a little frightened, I could see no other whites. I was especially conscious of that.

I half expected to see a grotesque oriental spring out of the heart of this steamy, scented inferno, the Satan of evil impending. I just *knew* that underneath the brightly lighted streets of tourist Chinatown were the secret meeting places of the tongs, the hidden menace of opium dens, the heavy trade in the white slave market, and a thousand other conjurations of oriental mystery. I hadn't read Sax Rohmer for nothing. I had eaten in Chinatown restaurants before—in what we called the Chink's—but this restaurant was different: this was where the real Chinese ate.

Jimmy chose a small table in the corner, and soon a Chinese girl pushed through a heavy set of draperies at the rear of the room and came to take our order. She and Jimmy spoke softly and delicately in what I assumed was Chinese, but I wasn't really listening; I was thinking, and looking, and allowing myself to be enchanted. I had never seen a Chinese girl up close—so satiny, so silky. Who was she? Why was she waiting on tables? Was she actually a waitress, or was she, more likely, a courtesan? And what was behind the draped doorway? A black-and-gold joss house? An opium den? The On Leong Tong? The Hip Sing Tong? The kitchen?

I don't remember what Jimmy ordered from Anna May Wong, but I remember trying to use chopsticks for the first time, in obedience to Jimmy's instructions. I wondered whether he would be offended if I asked him about the Chinese girl, about this dimly lit cellar, and if I would be allowed to leave this den alive. But then our conversation turned to the commonplace—he told me what life was like in Hong Kong, and I leaned heavily on my summer vacations in the Catskill Mountains. I'm afraid, however, I spent too much time not looking at Jimmy but sneaking glances at the waitress as she appeared and reappeared, and at the resident Chinese diners, certain they were stealing furtive looks at *me*.

Happily, and by sheer good luck, I thought, I escaped harm that night. I wasn't poisoned or stabbed or mugged or forced to smoke opium; and I am reasonably certain that I didn't eat rats' tails or pick up any human fingers with my chopsticks. I would surely have recognized them if I had.

Nonetheless, that rather prosaic afternoon in Jimmy Wong's apartment and the immensely exhilarating dinner hour in nighttime Chinatown eventually influenced my life and thoughts more than warranted by what had actually happened. Jimmy led the sort of life which, I discovered, I coveted most: fun without responsibility. Playing grown-up without *being* a grown-up. Jimmy Wong, with his easy money, had unintentionally set me up, and my downfall was imminent.

One day a little later, our new homeroom teacher, Mr. Marx, who also taught algebra, announced a contest for the best original essay in American history written by a junior high school student. He passed out the rules for contestants. The first prize was twenty-five dollars, and I think the contest was sponsored by the American Legion. No matter. The prize money caught my eye, and I read the rules carefully: the essay was to be no longer than three handwritten pages; it was to be written in ink; it was to be submitted before a certain date; and neatness would count. The judges would include Dr. Kottmann, principal of the school, and two history teachers; their judgment would be final.

The idea of winning this American history contest appealed to me greatly, and at risk of appearing unpatriotic, I must say I had only one object in entering—to win that twenty-five dollars. I was highly motivated, and I set to work with both zeal and cunning. I had no special case I wished to plead, so I was free to roam through the lush fields of American history hampered only by the date of the deadline and the number of sources available to me in the school library and the public library on East Broadway.

I read a lot, put together a pile of heavy-handed quotes, and finally was ready to write. My subject was imposingly entitled "The Genesis of the Constitution." Ah, that was a title in a million—with a title like that, I didn't see how I could lose. When I thought of the types against whom I would be competing, I could already feel the twenty-five dollars in my kick. I couldn't see how I could lose, provided (1) the contest wasn't fixed (2) the faculty judges weren't crooked and (3) the judges could read my handwriting.

I was satisfied that no one would set out to fix a contest like this one, that Dr. Kottmann and the two history teachers weren't crooked, and that whatever I wrote would get a fair reading. But it was here, exactly, where my plan would probably collapse in ruins. I wrote a next-to-impossible hand—a set of curious symbols that combined the Palmer Method (a utilitarian handwriting the school tried to teach us) and endless hours of imitating the virile backhand style of Principal

Kottmann's signature, which I had seen on notices tacked to every bulletin board.

After some hard thinking and not inconsiderable reexamination of the rules (*Neatness counts. In ink.* Geez!) I was forced to conclude I could lose. When it came to being neat while writing with ink, I could name three or four idiot classmates who had it all over me. My twenty-five dollars—the nice amount I saw as a gambling stake—was lost before I had won it.

I stared at my textbookish essay, all three handwritten pages, and realized I was a dead duck. Page one: a pale blue inkblot at one o'clock. Page two: I had tried to make a clean erasure and three ink-measles showed between the faint blue-ruled lines. Page three: one thumb smudge just this side of nine o'clock. I had done my best, and, characteristically, my best wasn't good enough.

Once again I read the rules. *Neatness counts.* And it came to me that nowhere did the rules state specifically that the author of the essay had to write the paper himself. "Whoa!" I said. "Wait a minute. Look again!" I looked again and again. No! The words spoke for themselves: originality, neatness counts, in ink, and the rest of that stuff. No sir, there was not one word to thwart my latest and most brilliant scheme. I went to see Jimmy Wong.

Jimmy was most agreeable. It was the least he could do to repay me. Transforming my three pages of cramped handwriting into his own beautiful script was little enough compensation for the help I had given him with his homework. He didn't ask for explanations and I offered none; like most of the other kids, Jimmy had little interest in the essay contest; I had asked him, as a friend, to do a straightforward copying job for me, and he did; he was simply an innocent party to my little confidence game.

Jimmy Wong's handiwork was a delight to behold. The bastards wanted neatness, I'd *give* them neatness. And there it was in front of me, my own language uncorrupted, lovely, symmetrical, legible, and neat as a pin. Jimmy had banged the long ball down dead center. The twenty-five dollars was once again all but in my pocket. There was now nothing more I could do to ensure "The Genesis of the Constitution" would win the Big Money. I needed only to turn my essay in on time.

At last the day arrived when Mr. Marx asked the class for their essays. Would we please bring them up to him? Three girls and a boy left their seats and smugly deposited their work on Mr. Marx's desk. I folded my paper in half, the long way, as I had been taught to do by Mrs. Follmer, and slipped my essay into the stack. Mr. Marx gathered the essays together, straightened them up, and slipped them into his briefcase.

Two or three days later, in the middle of my English class, I was summoned to the principal's office. I had wondered how the prize would be awarded, and this was obviously it. I could see Dr. Kottmann congratulating me, shaking my hand, kissing me on both cheeks as French generals did when awarding medals to heroes in the Fox Movietone News, and handing me twenty-five dollars. My preview was crystal-clear. Creative imagination conquers all. I had fought the good fight (with Jimmy Wong's small contribution, of course) and victory was now in sight. I walked down the hall to the door—DR. WILLIAM A. KOTTMANN, PRINCIPAL—and entered.

I gave his secretary my name and she told me to go right in. I walked through a gate into Dr. Kottmann's inner office, hoping my expression said good student and modest winner. Dr. Kottmann, a wonderful-looking old man, sat at his desk. He had thick white hair, horn-rimmed glasses, and a full, yellow-white Kaiser's mustache. He did not look up as I entered his office, because he was reading what looked like my essay, his lips tight, as he tapped his desk with a letter opener.

Standing to one side of the desk, looking even more stern than Dr. Kottmann, was my hateful witch of the woods, the Queen of the Night, the harridan who was probably wearing a pair of Mama's beautiful silk stockings, and who was unquestionably a rotten history teacher—Mrs. Follmer—glowering, staring me down, probably sorry I had won.

Dr. Kottmann looked up. He waved a page of my paper. "Did you write this?"

I nodded. I didn't like the way this was going at all. Dr. Kottmann seemed unduly serious, and what was Mrs. Follmer's role? And why was it necessary to have her at this meeting? Could it be she was one of the judges? I may have tried a small smile, but I was suddenly more uncomfortable than a winner should be. I addressed myself to Dr. Kottmann and said I had written the paper last week. He seemed amiable enough. He removed a fountain pen from a desk set, handed it to me, and slid a memo pad in my direction.

"I want you to write the word 'Genesis,' " he said. I wrote out "Genesis," picked up the pad, and handed it back to him. He placed my offering alongside page one and compared my "Genesis" with the title of the essay. He now turned both sheets toward me. "Do these look the same to you?" he asked.

I examined the sheets very carefully. I held one finger under the "Genesis" I had just written and one finger under "Genesis" in the title. "Yes, sir," I said quickly, "they are both spelled exactly the same way."

Dr. Kottmann looked over at Mrs. Follmer, then looked down at the pages on his desk, and I now realized his usual kind expression had been replaced by what could only be described as grim impatience. He tapped angrily at the essay. "Did you write this paper—'The Genesis of the Constitution'?" I nodded vigorously. He shook his head. "Then whose handwriting is this?" he demanded, pounding page one.

"Oh," I said, "*now* I see what you mean. You mean did I *write* that paper?"

"Well, did you?"

I shook my head. "No, I didn't. A friend wrote it for me."

"What's the name of this friend?"

Here was something I hadn't counted on. I now had more than a suspicion that I hadn't won his essay contest at all, and while I could accept the idea I might have made a mistake in asking Jimmy to help, I was now being asked to squeal. To *rat* on a friend—something I wasn't going to do. "It's just somebody I know," I answered.

Dr. Kottmann looked grimmer than ever; he seemed to be trying to think of what to do next. He gestured toward Mrs. Follmer, who puffed up threateningly. She reached over, picked up a page, and waved it in my face. "This is Jimmy Wong's handwriting, isn't it?" The witch.

I stood there, stone silent.

"Answer Mrs. Follmer, young man!"

"I was just following the rules," I said, "the part about neatness counts."

Dr. Kottmann was through with the preliminaries. His face was red and his voice sounded thick. "Did you know you were supposed to write this in your own handwriting?" I tried to look chastened; hell, I was heartbroken. "Do you know that what you did is called cheating?"

Cheating! "I didn't cheat," I said, "I *never* cheat. I wrote that essay all by myself—Jimmy just copied it over."

"There!" Mrs. Follmer said. "Just as Mrs. Ehrhart said. This essay was written by the Chinese boy"—she waved the paper like a battle flag—"and it should be disqualified, and *he*"—pointing at me—"should be punished."

Dr. William A. Kottmann, Principal, studied the kid standing forlorn before the tribunal of last resort, waiting to be judged, then looked down at the essay on his desk. He stared at it long enough to make me think he was actually reading it. He looked toward Mrs. Follmer. "Some of this is really quite good," he said.

Mrs. Follmer frowned. "He *cheated*, and he should be punished."

Dr. Kottmann now seemed to have the situation in hand; he seemed calmer, relaxed now, more authoritative. "If you had written this essay in your own handwriting," he said, not unkindly, "you might have won the contest." He paused. "As a matter of fact, it *did* win the contest until Mrs. Follmer saw it; she recognized that the handwriting was not yours, and she gathered from Mrs. Ehrhart that the handwriting belongs to the Chinese boy. And so—I am sorry to say this—your essay is disqualified."

I was moved by Dr. Kottmann's speech, by his skillful handling of a dramatic conflict between teacher and student, by his graciousness, and, above all, by his fairness. Despite my wasted efforts in trying to win this dumb essay contest, I was still grateful when Dr. Kottmann pointed out that I had *nearly* won the twenty-five dollars. If he had intended to touch me, he had—and I was bewildered when tears came to my eyes, because I had no idea how they got there.

CHAPTER EIGHT

I OFTEN WONDER whether, as a teenager, I had any sense of right and wrong. Did I actually believe Jimmy Wong's handwriting would enable me to win a prize I might otherwise not have won? Or did I suspect my little con might put something over on the Establishment? Did I steal *Paradise Lost* and bring it home because I wanted to read that particular book, or was I outflanking the librarian? Or Sharkey? Did I "lose" my leather jacket so I could fit in with the rest of the boys or did I want to spite my father? Did I have some sense of what was suitable, appropriate—some sense of what was right and what was wrong?

Thinking about these questions sixty years later I'd like to believe I had a hidden streak of goodness that invariably led me down the right road, but I'm more inclined to accept Sharkey's view when he said, "That's a lotta crap! As a kid, you were never any fuckin' good!" Now I've come to believe he was right. I grew up in a milieu where the only way to be called a winner was to be strong, and strong meant ruthless. Kindness, mercy, honesty, fairness, and good manners were valueless.

Most of the principal characters in my young life were, to me, losers—Principal Kottmann, Mrs. Follmer, the East Broadway librarian, Jimmy Wong, and even Zaida. They believed in ethics, that some things were wrong because they were harmful; Sharkey and I, too, whether I like it or not (he was, after all, the most important influence in my early life), valued only winning. Those who lost didn't know how to win; they were thrown to the waiting lions because they were entangled, by *choice*, in the moral trap that certain human acts are

179

wrong. But with Sharkey's example to guide me I was safe from such wrong thinking, at least for a year or two.

Right and wrong meant as much to me then as it did to most ghetto kids; if it felt good it was good, and if it didn't it was bad. That Daddy and Mama had more money to spend than other ghetto parents obviously made it easier for me to boast a supply of things unavailable to other kids my age. I saw nothing wrong with the idea of money. Money had its special purposes—the best of which was that it made you feel good. But what other young East Side kid was required to show off his white flannels, his gold ring, his Bulova wristwatch, his Monti *Czardas?* There seemed to be some conflict here.

Scampering through the dirty streets, my gangly figure even in everyday clothes decked out like some recently arrived innocent, I created an effect I knew was all wrong. I longed to be like my chums, and whatever didn't fit under that blanket of street security—my father's wealth, his prestige, his fearlessness, his selfish concern with that part of my life that was not his to control, his demand for virtuosity—that too was dead wrong. But I didn't arrive at this conclusion without some help. I was trained by a hard taskmaster.

The story of Daddy's gun and how it fell into my trembling hands is, I believe, a fine example of that kicked-around maxim "I am of the religion of my father." Daddy, of course, had had the reputation of being a tough guy in a tough neighborhood. But Rutgers and Monroe streets were no longer Daddy's territory alone; by the early thirties the toughchiks were no longer Sharkey's toughchiks who knew Sharkey's reputation.

New gangs had been formed, and now new toughs, with little regard for or fear of their predecessors, roamed the neighborhood, wearing the same old snazzy clothes, frightening the poor, terrorizing anyone with a few bucks in his cash register, intent only on building their own formidable reputations. Sharkey did what he could to hold his position—his toughness was still best expressed with his fists— and more than one toughchik discovered, the hard way, that taking on Sharkey's saloon meant taking on Sharkey, and Sharkey was not a willing mark.

While all around the neighborhood cash boxes were looted, stores were burgled, and mayhem was the order of the day, Daddy's saloon had so far remained inviolate. By now, however, the new toughchiks had grown too numerous for one man to handle. Daddy's informants reported having sighted toughchiks in the neighborhood who didn't even live there. Pirates, and worse.

The new gangsterism now crept throughout the Lower East Side and occasionally scratched at Daddy's swinging door. He knew it had to happen, and he was worried about the tactics of these insane outsiders. As for Sharkey's saloon, they didn't respect the institution. They laughed when Daddy dropped some old names—his friends of the past. There was apparently no way to domesticate the new thieves, and Daddy sensed Big Trouble. "They look like they're all hopped up," he said to Mama one night, "they're so *meshugeh*—like they all wanna get killed."

A couple of these tough punks held up a saloon only two blocks away, and Daddy was deeply distraught over this encroachment into his stamping ground, what he thought of as "his" territory. For years he had maintained excellent relations with the old hoods and their henchmen; they respected Sharkey's "rightness," and his code of "honesty." In turn, he had respected their power and provided them with friendly but impersonal support, and everyone observed a live-and-let-live compact.

It was different now; things were changing too fast. Punks with poisoned minds seemed to mushroom all over the East Side, and what was at first a slow poison now moved faster, and in a more deadly fashion. Punks had no identifiable leaders; they formed loose, roving gangs difficult to control, to pin down, and they were impossible to reason with. And now blackjacks and strong-arming were no longer in fashion. The new punks habitually used guns.

They moved swiftly into enemy territory, scaring the hell out of everyone in sight, particularly saloonkeepers. Saloons were their favorite target, because there was always considerable cash on hand. Moreover, saloonkeepers were in no position to report a stickup or a burglary to the cops. They reported, instead, to old-time hoods with whom they were still on good terms, who solved the problem by moving vengefully against saloonkeepers outside their territory who they believed supported the new punks, and so it went. For Sharkey it was a period of crushing and undisguised frustration. Muscle, as he had always known it, was out. The new muscle, the old equalizer, was now a gun.

One night Daddy brought home a gun. I heard him drop it on our kitchen table as Mama went to prepare his glass of tea. Let it be known to *everyone*, he explained to Mama, that in Sharkey's saloon the guy who ran the joint carried a rod and knew how to use it. He would flash his new gun around the saloon, and remind his clientele that Sharkey was no guy to fool with. Soon the word would get out that he would not give up one cent to any outside gunman without a struggle. "You hafta fight fire with fire," he said grimly. "Give the punks as good as they get."

I could hear the concern in Mama's voice as she pleaded with Daddy not to carry a gun on his person or to keep it in the saloon. She reminded him of old friends who had broken the law and were still paying the price. If revenue agents or the police searched the saloon for liquor and found the gun, Daddy would be held in violation of the Sullivan Law. Mama's logic did nothing to change his mind. He insisted he would keep the gun for the next few days—just long enough to pass the word that he had one. And to remind others that he knew how to use it.

As I lay in bed listening to this conversation, I had a deep urge to see the gun. The gun must still be lying there on the kitchen table, heavy, ugly, just waiting for someone like me to see it. The object of my affection. I'd never seen a real gun—I'd seen guns in the movies, heard them bang away on the radio, and read about them in the good gray pages of *Detective Fiction Weekly*. Now here was my chance—just the other side of my bedroom door.

I pushed myself out of bed, stomped to the door, and shouldered it open. Rubbing my eyes as if I had just awakened from a deep sleep, I said, "I gotta go to the toilet," and moved toward the bathroom. Blinking sleepily, I paused and did a take. "Hey, Daddy," I said, pointing to the weapon, "what's *that?*"

Daddy picked it up; it was a gun all right, a small revolver. "What does it look like?" he said in Yiddish. "It's a gun!"

I looked at it with eyes half opened in admiration. "Can I touch it?"

"Wotsamatter," Mama put in nervously, "you never saw a gun? It's a *gun*, that's all. Go to the toilet!"

I gazed at the revolver—desire exploding all over my sleepy face. "Here," Daddy said, perhaps sensing my yearning, "touch it for a second. Then hurry up and go to the toilet and take a crap."

I took the revolver from his hand and examined it, fondled it. "Take the gun away from him," Mama said to Daddy in disgust. "Children don't need to know about guns. Go—go to the toilet!"

I went, but an unpromising future was just around the corner.

One rainy afternoon a few months later, as water ran through the streets and dripped down the rain-spattered windows, when I was alone at home and tired of reading and dreaming and dealing out hands of seven-and-a-half from which I was already a millionaire, I decided it was a good time to play my private game of grope-search. The game hinged on the invisible connection between our homelife and Daddy's illegal saloon life. What kept these two lives safely separated, what enabled all of us to live in our lovely flat instead of a large cell in the Big House, depended (according to my *Detective Fiction Weekly* mind) on possessing secret papers—hidden and controversial documents, concealed stolen goods, and buried treasure; and the six rooms of our flat, as I had discovered after several years of ransacking, were full of secret places for hiding things unlawful, strange, and risky.

Whatever treasures I had uncovered in the past were often new only to me, and lay buried in closets and drawers stuffed with old bath towels, bedsheets, tablecloths, and mothballed winter overcoats. But there were occasional surprises. For example, one gloomy day while fooling around in the dining room, I noticed that the left-hand side of the top buffet drawer could be lifted out to expose a compartment made to order for hiding secret papers. From this particular repository I learned the legal owner of Daddy's saloon was not Daddy at all, but someone I had never heard of (and I still wonder about that).

Other caches turned up in the kitchen, on the top shelf of the dish cupboard, for instance, where, in a rose-decorated sugar bowl, lay a small handful of half-dollars; sometimes I took one if the bowl was full enough. Just below the cupboard was the broom closet, where we kept our supply of good whiskey. I used to think how nice it would be if I had a secret buyer for a bottle or two—the whiskey would never be missed—but that, too, remained a fantasy. I also enjoyed pawing around the night table in my parents' bedroom—its single drawer contained a gold cigarette lighter, Daddy's diamond stickpin, and a small, square, lacquered box that held Daddy's Trojan horses.

One of my favorite spots was the top of Mama's wardrobe, stacked with a mountain of bedding that reached almost to the whitewashed ceiling. Beneath the bedding lay the family photographs: my maternal grandparents shortly before their arrival here; Daddy before he was married; Mama in a sailor dress; me on a pony, and again in a first-grade school picture, frowning. I still remember the thrill of pulling Mama's vanity bench up to the closet door and standing up on it to poke around under our winter feather comforters so I could slip out pictures of Mama and Daddy in a Coney Island gallery, Zaida in a Russian shako, and one of me perched on the branch of a tree in the Catskills. But my special surprise on this dull, drizzly day as I groped around the top of the wardrobe closet was to touch the barrel of Daddy's gun.

I guessed Mama had hidden the gun on top of the closet for safekeeping. And now *I* had it. I ran into the kitchen and bolted the chain on the front door so no one could disturb me without knocking. Now that I was safe, I took the gun into my bedroom where I could study it at leisure. It was the same revolver I had held in my hand one night, and the chambers were empty.

I pretended to play a little Russian roulette (Tom Mix, Wm. S. Hart, and Art Acord, *saludos amigos!*), and I won, of course. My next stupidity was to hide the gun under my mattress so I could take it to school the next day and show it off to the other kids. Each morning during recess, we played our own show-and-tell ("See this apple? I robbed it off a pushcart!"); the thought of their astonishment when I whipped out a real gun, the real McCoy—a genuine rod!—made the risk I was about to take worthwhile. There wasn't one chance in a million—I reasoned the odds were right—that Mama or Daddy would miss the gun before tomorrow afternoon. When I got home from school I would simply replace the gun under the comforters and no one would be the wiser. My anticipation of the next day's recess was so overwhelming I had to take the gun out and look at it again before I could fall asleep that night.

Recess was always at midmorning, and I felt a pleasant little shiver of excitement. I sat at my desk with the gun snug against my waist, under my shirt and the top of my pants. Mr. Marx, my algebra enemy, clearly intent on taking the edge off my adventurous mood, announced there would be an exam. "Get your pencils and notebooks ready while I pass out the test," he commanded.

The kid sitting directly in front of me said, "Goody," and I could have whopped him on the head; his name was Myron something. I hated algebra, I hated Captain Marx (as I called him), with his fringed bald head and the look of an old sea dog, and I hated Myron something because his right hand was always ready to semaphore the captain that he knew the right answer when no one else did.

Myron may have been the only person in the class who had fewer friends than I did. He was a Boy Scout, a wiseguy, and a show-off, and in our class that added up to three strikes. When he walked down the hall between classes, his natural adversaries used two fingers to clip him on his ass, but Myron never let on he'd felt a thing. His mother would be waiting for him in the schoolyard when classes were released, and he was bright enough to avoid anything that would bring about a confrontation with his foes. In Mr. Marx's class Myron was my nemesis; because I sat directly behind him, every time Mr. Marx asked Myron a question he could see me trying desperately to avoid being called upon. Algebra and Mr. Marx and Myron made me sick.

The algebra test was now on my desk, and I studied the questions with some irritation. Number three was a doozey. I wrote some x's and y's for questions one and two, and moved on to question number three, the tough one. I read the question twice and had no idea of even how to begin to answer it. Pondering this ridiculous question ("How old is John if his Dad will be half the age of his brother when his sister is twelve" is about how I remember it), I leaned forward and wheezed into Myron's righteous back, "Question three. What's the answer?"

Myron pretended he hadn't heard me. I poked my pencil into his spine. He shook his head as if to say no. That's the way he always reacted—the sonofabitch wanted all the good grades for himself. I checked to see whether the coast was clear. Captain Marx, I noticed, was in the back of the room, his eyes on the windows, staring at the great outdoors. I unbuttoned my shirt, reached in, hesitated not a moment, took the gun from under my shirt, and stuck the warm barrel flush against the back of Myron's neck. "Number three," I whispered fiercely. "The answer!"

Myron half-turned, perhaps wondering what object pushed against the back of his neck, and what he glimpsed brought forth a stifled yelp. I jammed the gun under my shirt again as Mr. Marx, ever alert for undue yelps, raced quickly down the aisle toward Myron's desk to ascertain why Myron's head was turned aside when he should have been looking down at the test. "What's the trouble here?" he asked.

"He's gonna shoot me," Myron wailed. "He's crazy. He's got a gun."

Mr. Marx paused, bewildered. "A gun? Who's got a gun?"

"Leroy stuck a gun in my neck. I saw it!"

Mr. Marx held out his hand to me. "Where is the gun? Give me the gun."

"*What* gun? I ain't got no gun. *Myron's* the one who's crazy!"

Myron was terrified. He kept repeating, "He *had* a gun. I *saw* it. He *had* a gun."

Mr. Marx grabbed me by the back of my collar. "Stand up!"

I stood up, the lowest button of my shirt still undone. The class watched us, fascinated. "Give me the gun."

Hell, I figured, he's probably already seen it. What could I do? What would any sensible person do? I reached into my shirt, took out the gun, and handed it to him, barrel first. "It's not even loaded," I said. "It's just a toy. I was only foolin'."

Five minutes later we stood in Dr. Kottmann's office, where Mr. Marx, holding the gun away from him as if it were a live cobra, told Dr. Kottmann why we were there. Dr. Kottmann asked if the gun was mine. I nodded, and the conversation was over. He scanned a list he took from his desk drawer, picked up his telephone, and asked for Dry Dock 1401. I knew that number well.

I didn't have to sweat long; in ten minutes Daddy arrived escorted by Smack, the hackman. I saw the fierce expression on my father's face, and I didn't like it. This wasn't Daddy—it was Sharkey. I had seen that look once when he took on three tough guys right on the sidewalk in front of the saloon; they never knew what hit them. I trembled. I had seen him angry before, and I knew what to expect as soon as he had me cornered in the back room. How could I get out of this? I knew what he'd ask: What was I doing with his gun? How did I find the gun? Why did I bring it to school? Who was I gonna kill? I had to make up some explanation—what could I tell him that he might believe? That I found the gun on the bedroom floor? No. That Mama asked me to deliver the gun to him? No. That this was not his gun but a *different* gun—Jesus, no! My guts trembled.

I didn't have long to wait. The conversation between my masters took only a moment. Daddy recovered his gun, and as we walked out of Dr. Kottmann's office Daddy hesitated briefly and removed his belt, and then I could hear it swing and strike my back. I dropped to the floor. And right in the hall, as kids came streaming out of their rooms to change classes, I received his best. If he intended to punish me in the cruelest way, he couldn't have picked a better time or a more delighted audience.

In front of Dr. Kottmann, Mr. Marx, Smack the hackman, and a horde of my wide-eyed enemies, we began a ballet worthy of the Marquis de Sade. At our opening steps, Dr. Kottmann started forward as if he wished to join in, but the intensity of Daddy's animal sounds and the opening, piercing screams of the sacrificial adolescent heard against Daddy's invective indicated the performance would be a simple point-counterpoint—not, as Dr. Kottmann had perhaps assumed, a *pas de trois*, but a true duet.

I wish I could say that some jaunty gallows humor flashed through my mind, like the lyrics of one of our favorite songs—"Play, Gypsy! Dance, Gypsy! Play, while you may"—or that I was thinking of a way to cry out, "Oh, Daddy, if only you hadn't been overindulgent by allowing me once to hold a gun, there would have been no need for overstrictness at this moment." But I wasn't thinking of anything, I was screaming and screaming.

* * *

After thirty years of working bits of Daddy into cocktail-party conversations, I have found that some aspects of his personality call for a more objective analysis than I can muster. I have finally concluded that I was forced to accept him not so much as a rational being, but more or less on faith, the way my grandfather looked upon his God: "The Lord giveth, and the Lord taketh away."

In the period of his greatest influence on me, my father did nothing to give me many good qualities of character. I cannot hold that against my father any more than Zaida would have found fault with God; as he would have said, there's no sense complaining about what God never gave you.

To talk about what my father "took away" from me in my formative years would be incorrect; what he withheld may be a little closer to the truth. But "withheld" isn't true either—he wasn't capable of teaching me to have a strong ethical sense. As it was, my father gave me good and bad qualities and some that were good in one circumstance and bad in another.

In his desire to create a son who would fulfill his ambition, my father neglected to give me a healthy sense of my importance (the gang helped show me how unimportant I really was) or self-worth (no one I knew, except perhaps Zaida, trusted me from here to the corner, and properly so); to teach me to have less concern for the opinion of my peers (which is probably why I preferred cheap woolen mittens to leather gloves); to encourage formal intellectual development (books were safer hidden in closets than lying on the table); and, finally, to teach me that to tell the disagreeable truth would forestall punishment better than a good lie. He nearly made me into a serious snob, and I discovered on my own that pretension, which was a heavy weapon of self-defense on the East Side, was ineffectual—useless.

These, then, were the particular qualities my father denied me. But he did provide me with some good qualities, several that reflected his own views, and others, fortunately, through his indifference to what he thought didn't count. Unfortunately, however, in my boyhood he filled me with exaggerated humility, a sense of my unimportance which magnified my lack of self-confidence. His tirades filled me with the kind of mortification that made even my humility seem like pride.

Moreover, he gave me a blend of condescension and insolence, especially when I was able to invoke his name and his reputation in my own behalf; I wasn't called upon to do this often, but the tactic was valuable at times. What prevailed strongly was his idea that a well-turned lie could be more plausible than the truth—and more acceptable.

What I am thankful for, however, is what he gave me, by his prohibition: a love of books, of reading, and, by extension, the awareness that knowledge was available everywhere, even on the Lower East Side. In his idiosyncratic way, my father gave me what he could when he thought the time was ripe, and the summer before I was fourteen he sent me to a whorehouse. A man of his persuasion and conviction, like a good woman, is hard to find.

Think of it! Imagine yourself a father. For *whatever* exotic reason you decide to send your son to a whorehouse, how do you broach such a subject? He is almost fourteen. Do you approach it gingerly? Do you say, "Sonny boy, may I make a suggestion?" Or do you say, "We're pals, kid, and there are a couple of girls I'd like you to meet. . . ." Remember, we're talking about a fourteen-year-old boy, a manchild in junior high school who wears glasses, Vaseline on his hair, Dr. Posner shoes, is a blaze of pimples, and is finding ways to play with himself.

Daddy managed. (After all, I did wind up in the whorehouse.) It happened during the summer. Mama and my ten-year-old sister spent the summer at a Catskill Mountains resort, and Daddy and I were expected to join them on weekends. This arrangement drew Daddy and me much closer together; we were on our own, bachelors, as it were. Mama arranged credit at the bakery, the dairy, the grocery, the candy store, and I remember gorging myself on all those delicacies—especially chocolate bars—Mama had previously permitted only in moderation.

I stayed out of Daddy's way as much as I could without trying to disestablish his authority, but I was still held accountable. I reported to the saloon for my daily practice, I still had to ask if I could go to the movies, to the park, to the roof garden of the Educational Alliance, to the Chink's. Daddy, too, seemed to take his parental responsibility more seriously. For one thing, he missed Mama. After he closed the saloon he looked into my bedroom, and if I was still awake he often chose to talk to me. Who else could he talk to?

At first, these little talks—Daddy perched on the edge of my bed, smoke curling from his Rameses II cigarette—were awkward, difficult to get started, and were, in a way, rather embarrassing. As the summer nights passed, however, we slowly discovered subjects of mutual concern: the muggy weather; my violin lessons with Cores; a runaway horse who had bolted down Cherry Street; the new saloon customers called sandhogs who were building a tunnel under the East River; whether a tough guy like Jack Sharkey would knock out that German bum Max Schmeling, and assorted small talk. He missed his late-night glass of tea and, of course, Mama.

Our relationship was reasonably happy except for the hellish moments each day when I was careless enough to allow Daddy to see me chomp away on one of my favorite Hershey chocolate bars. As I shoved the candy into my mouth, feeding an insatiable desire, Daddy saw red. Growing as angry as he could become (without actually punching me), he delivered his litany on why pimples continued to grow on my face. A son like his ought to be good looking, and instead I insisted on looking like the rest of the bums. Chocolate was my ruination! His daily admonishments, warnings, threats, horrid tales of the distant past, frustrated me no end because I ate Hershey bars (with or without almonds) the way a deep-sea diver uses oxygen.

"That crap you keep eating puts a lotta shit in your blood," Daddy said, spitting on the ground. "It makes your blood too rich—that's why you got those pimples on your face. You look like you got some kinda disease, like you belong in a hospital."

I worked hard trying to avoid having Daddy see me eating a Hershey bar. I was intent on saving our otherwise good relations. But my efforts seemed fruitless. Most of my afternoon activities were carried on out in the street, and in the summertime, particularly, Daddy sat in front of his saloon, his chair tilted back against the store window, watching the street games, nodding to friends, and holding court.

His eyes were good, and if I were where he could see me, he could tell the moment I had a mouthful of Hershey bar. I once brought him a chocolate-covered bar called Tastyeast that was supposed to be good for pimples, and displayed my great medical discovery. I thought that in that way I could satisfy Daddy by curing my acne and still eat chocolate. "Oh, you *putz!*" he said patiently. "If it's got chocolate, how could it be good for pimples? Chocolate *makes* pimples. Throw that crap in the garbage!"

Stung by his losing battle against the Hershey forces, Daddy decided to motivate me through fear. "Chocolate makes pimples on your face," he said, instructing me, "but playing with yourself *keeps* them there." I looked at him curiously, all ears. "Playing with yourself" was Daddy's euphemism for "jerking off"—an East Side boy's favorite pastime. He now realized he had my undivided attention, and he went on. "And people who play with themselves wind up in the crazy house." That was it. That was the way Daddy brought up the question of masturbation.

I was dumbstruck. I had heard Daddy use taboo sex words before, but only in passing; they were never directed at *my* childish ears. For Daddy to be talking to me about jerking off (and that was *exactly* what he was talking about) frightened me. It was okay for the gang to discuss this subject in cellars and back alleys, but to hear it from Daddy made me wonder where the hell I had slipped up. How had I given myself away? Who ratted? Did Daddy *really* know anything about jerking off? No, this was probably just his way of taking candy away from me.

I was all wrong. Daddy knew all about it. In the same devious way he had arranged to bring me before Toscha Seidel and the music critic and, eventually, a new music teacher, he now sought to arrange my sex life. One afternoon, after I had finished practicing, he reached into the cash register, pulled out a five-dollar bill, and handed it to me together with a little white engraved calling card. The card bore a man's name and an address somewhere on Second Avenue. "Go to this place," Daddy said, matter-of-fact. "You'll see a lady. Give the lady the card and the money and she'll take care of you. She knows you're coming."

I said I didn't understand what I was supposed to do. Was he asking me to deliver the five dollars to this address, or what? Daddy nodded. "Don't ask stupid questions. Just go there, and they'll take care of you."

"You mean you want me to go right now?" I asked, unbelieving. Daddy nodded. I nodded. What the hell was there left to say?

I put the card in my pocket and walked out into the street. Second Avenue. Who would believe what had just happened? I looked around for someone to talk to—with whom could I share this wild news? I reached into my pocket to feel the card again. And the fiver. Impossible. I just knew I was being sent to a real whorehouse. I had to tell someone, to elaborate upon it, I had to show *someone* the calling card—that solid irrefutable piece of evidence—to discuss its ramifications, its possibilities, its explosive *meaning*!

I had heard older fellows (who had been lucky in a crap game) talk about going to a cathouse, or a joint. Joints on the East Side were as common as clothes on a clothesline. There were one or two joints on every tenement block, and some streets, like Allen Street and those streets skirting the Bowery, had at least one joint in every building. Again, I knew from the chatter that cheap joints were a buck a head (on a cot in an empty flat), and the better joints—the so-called standard joints—were two bucks a head. But a place that charged five dollars a head had to be something special. Perhaps gangster stuff.

Nobody was around for me to talk to. Joey and Petey were nowhere to be seen. That's the way my life was. When I needed friends the most, they were not available. Even in this most trying expedition in my short and unhappy life I was required once more to be on my own, to supply my own moral support, to talk to myself, and to find my own way to Second Avenue, twenty blocks north.

As I approached the age of fourteen, my sexual experience was slight, and among my more sophisticated peers might be considered nonexistent. Oh, I knew about girls, all right, and no doubt I had heard much more about them than I really knew.

Lower East Side boys attained maturity early, if maturity meant a sort of worldliness, and worldliness meant a sort of knowledge that all girls screwed—some screwed for money while others charged nothing. The free ones were called "sure things," and the ones who charged were called "whores" (pronounced "hoors"). All East Side kids knew that, and in *that* respect, anyway, I was normal. Other kids in the gang—Muttsie, for example—no doubt had had some experiences with neighborhood girls that I had not; but then Muttsie didn't have a briefcase to carry, a fiddle to play, glasses to wear, or a mouthful of Tastyeast to swallow on the sly. Even so, neither Muttsie nor Casanova was among my heroes.

I had my fair share of female companionship, but they were mostly dream girls. Between the ages of twelve and thirteen and a half I made serious studies of three girls, and I am not at all certain they were available (with or without money), except, perhaps, the last one, whom I remember only as Adelaide the singer. The others seemed like nice girls, particularly after they had completed their many personal appearances in my day-and-night dreams.

Mae Rabinowitz was a doll-faced lovely who was both plump and tall. She was especially tall—probably about five foot seven or eight—and whatever other difficulties she may have had, being too tall headed the list. Because I suffered the same calamity, I believed we had a lot in common. And so I fell in love with her—and that's as far as it went. Mae was about fifteen at the time, and I saw her not as a girl but as a warm, ripe woman. In my meditative moments I spent a lot of time thinking of female torsos, and somewhere along the way I discovered that Mae had a more than ample bosom. Another plus.

While Mae wasn't noticeably bright or witty, she was kind and personable, and when she helped out in her father's grocery store, she was always accommodating. When I stopped in to buy something for Mama I could always count on Mae to smile at me as she fondled my lox or bagels or a pound of butter. As lovers, Mae and I never talked much, just "Gimme a canna Heinz beans," or "You want the *big* box Gold Dust or the little one?"—mundane statements, but from the heart. There was more to our relationship than that, but Mae chose to remain blissfully unaware; in reality, I thought, we were bursting with a silent yearning that must remain hidden from the world. When

I offered my unspoken love, the best she could do was hand me a canna Heinz beans. Still, I felt there was more to it than this silly reciprocal trade agreement.

In the same way, I didn't get very far with Evelyn Sachs either. Sixteen, honey-blond, sturdy, strong but feminine, Evelyn made me think of amber waves of grain and mountain majesties. She was clearly unhappy, I thought, as I watched her walk down Rutgers Street. She needed sky-high trees, rugged mountains, golden plains, a bedouin tent, and a true master—me. When I saw Evelyn from a distance I sensed the smoldering. Others might think she was tired, dragging her weary body home after a tough day in the sweatshop, but I knew differently. I knew that sun-sleepy look. I dreamed of that outdoor girl look, that Gentile look, that look so ardently athletic.

Once Evelyn accosted me on the street to ask if I had seen her little brother Moishe. I could see the weariness in her lovely face, the sagging shoulders, the strength seeping out of her glorious being. For her to be so desirable and to be wasting time looking for someone named Moishe made the world seem senseless. I told her I thought her brother was playing in the park and I would find him and bring him home, and I did. Evelyn smiled at me and ran up the stoop to her small apartment, but she was never the same after our spontaneous chat—I had shown her I *cared*. We never spoke to each other again. But we *knew*—we were not made of stone.

I was now past Delancey Street and approaching Second Avenue, and my thoughts turned, naturally, to Adelaide. My memories of Adelaide the singer are not quite as vivid as my remembrance of Mae Rabinowitz and Evelyn. I'm all mixed up about Adelaide—there were the nasty things I had heard about her before we met (at Mrs. Rothstein's junior high orchestra rehearsal), and some of those things may be mixed with what I learned about her afterward. When one has loved and lost—I mean *really* lost—then one may be forgiven for being a little mixed up.

Adelaide had dark, shoulder-length hair, a pleasant face, large eyes, a square chin, and a short stocky figure that (as I later learned) was built for group sex. She never had much to talk about. By the time she was fifteen she had been left back at least twice, but Mrs.

Rothstein discovered that Adelaide could sing, and made regular use of her strong voice in our weekly all-school assembly.

I met Adelaide when Mrs. Rothstein teamed us together in a tune from an operetta called *Frasquita*. Mrs. Rothstein played piano, Adelaide sang, and I provided a violin obbligato. It was all very high class until the program was over, the assembly hall had cleared, and Adelaide asked me to remain after everyone else had left.

Around the schoolyard I had heard that Adelaide was a girl of easy virtue, and if she was asked properly, she couldn't say no. At the time, I had only the vaguest notions of what this intelligence meant. For half an hour we sat in the rear of the darkened assembly hall. At first I was preoccupied, wondering what she might expect of me. Adelaide sat in the seat next to mine (she *had* to be there, otherwise her hand could not have reached my fly), and when she was finished, I came to realize that here was a girl I could love.

I was flattered, tickled silly, and all balled up. I finally realized the meaning of that old saw "Masturbation is the thief of time." And I could now vouch that Adelaide certainly had those qualities which lead young girls to erotic success. I was now hooked, totally committed.

Even while I sought ways to see her after school, I knew that an older guy named Sammy waited for her every day at the entrance to the schoolyard. Sammy, Adelaide told me, was her regular boyfriend. They both lived near the Williamsburg Bridge, and ever since she was thirteen he had been her steady. They had found ecstasy in the dark recesses under the bridge, and when one day Sammy brought along several friends for a Big Party, Adelaide became the most popular girl on or under the Williamsburg Bridge. But now, she told me, all that was in the past. She really liked me. And I believed her.

I never had a good look at Adelaide's naked charms. It was always too dark. Moreover, that's the way I wanted it. I was not going to have the first real love in my life spoiled by my looking at things I was not supposed to see and by fooling around with things I wouldn't have known what to do with even if I *could* see them.

What finally brought our affair to an end, broke us up, was really no sillier than what brought us together. One cold night around a street fire, which Joey and I kept alive by feeding it slats from an old orange crate, Joey picked up the conversation. Here's the way I remember it:

"Guess who I saw in school today?" Joey said to me.

"Who?"

"Angelo and his friend Big Nick."

"What were they doing?"

"I saw them in the janitor's room—the one with the washtub. Where we smoke."

"What were they doing—hitting somebody?"

"No, but they had this broad with them. I went in to grab a smoke, and I saw the broad jerkin' them off. Holdin' their cocks—one in each hand. First, she didn't see me—she was too busy. Then I saw who it was. *You* know the broad—they call her Adelaide or Get Laid or some name like that."

The street fire no longer seemed warm enough, and I ran up to my cold bed, shivered, and wept.

Compared to most of the Lower East Side Streets, Second Avenue on my way to meet a prostitute was for me the Champs Elysées, as shown in my geography book. While other East Side streets were generally dingy, dirty, narrow, cramped, and disarrayed, Second Avenue gave an impression of purposeful busyness, spaciousness, and middle-class solidity. The gray brick buildings on both sides of this boulevard were not East Side tenements as much as they were apartment houses. Second Avenue has its beginning in the interior of lower Manhattan, and it was a special place. If you were in a plane looking down on Second Avenue you'd be somewhere between the East River and the Hudson River. But Manhattan Island was so poorly planned that Second Avenue residents had no waterfront view; as compensation, perhaps, they suffered no water rats.

Compared to Rutgers Street and Daddy's saloon neighborhood, Second Avenue was a high-rent district. There, presumably rich landlords catered to presumably high-class Jews, or, at least, to those Jews interested in upward mobility—Jews who preferred the Second Avenue Yiddish Theater to neighborhood movie houses like the Dump; diners-out whose Orthodoxy went down the drain when they discovered the agreeable, five-spice scent of roast pork; and entrepreneurs who believed that Calvin Coolidge's concern for Business showed he had a good Jewish head.

The territory stretched before me, and as I came closer to the address I was looking for, I realized what lay ahead was (for me, at least) unknown, and I at once grew tense and nervous. Soon the house numbers left me no choice; twice I walked past the house, stopped on the next street corner to study my calling card, felt in my pocket for the fiver, and now, pretending I was an old Second Avenue hand, I returned to the proper doorway.

I entered the apartment house. Everything seemed so quiet. I remember walking up some stairs, stopping to check my calling card with a corresponding apartment number, studying the number on the door, and then, scared but unable to hide, knocking. Three short taps, softly, timidly, so as not to disturb anyone who might still be abed. I waited. I was still nervous, but functioning. I tried three more taps.

For the first time I noticed a grilled peephole at eye level; it had just opened and I could sense I was being observed. A woman's voice, husky and dark and sexy, asked me what I wanted. I read the name on the calling card (a name I can't remember), and told her that Sharkey had sent me. She opened the door just wide enough to take the card and the folded five-dollar bill from my sweaty fingers. The door closed, and again I waited. As my anxiety grew, the door re-opened, not a moment too soon, and now I was permitted to enter. My first cathouse.

I was greeted by a stocky, handsome woman in her late thirties. She looked every bit as old as Mama. She looked neat—I remember a plain dark dress—and when she said, "come right in," I entered the apartment, speechless. I don't know whom I had expected to answer the door. A sleek, naked girl, maybe. Or a sleazy, hard-bitten broad fresh out of a women's prison movie. But not this sedate old lady. Even though I had planned a few bright remarks to hide my inexperience, all I could do was stare at her. I never expected to be met by a woman who looked like she could be one of my relatives.

She flipped a light switch, revealing a foyer painted in some discreet dark color, while I stood stock still, as if my feet were nailed to the floor. She beamed at me. She took a step backward and looked me up and down. Such delight in her dark eyes. Such pride. I was both confused and embarrassed—and still speechless. "I'm Esther," she said, and gestured to show she remembered me when I was only *so* high. She had known Sharkey long before I was born; the *old* days. (Why were we standing here discussing old times? Was I in an old folks' home or was this really a high-class Second Avenue cathouse?) Oh, it was so nice to see Sharkey's fine-looking son. Such a big boy, so grown-up—a real *mensch*!

We stood in the foyer while I stuck around hoping for instructions, still nervous and jittery, like a colt waiting to start his first race. Finally Esther patted me lightly on the cheek and said, "Let's go see what the girls are doing." She opened a door and I followed her into the kitchen. Sitting at a table playing cards were two *women* (girls, hah!) probably in their twenties. One was blond, the other dark-haired, and, at the moment, neither of them looked especially sexy. Somewhere I had lost my voice.

"This is Sharkey's son," Esther said, beaming. The women looked me over, and smiled. "That's Renée," she said, nodding at the blonde. "She's going to take care of you."

Renée grinned. She had pretty teeth, and a sweet kind of show-business look, which only increased my fear. The truth is I was never more frightened in my life. It was like getting ready to take a test for which I was fully unprepared. Instead of being excited and anxious to get going, for a moment I wished I were back home quietly turning the pages of *Snappy Stories*.

Renée laid down her cards and stood up. The top of her head was even with my nose, and that made me feel better. At least I was taller than she was. She tightened the belt of her flowered bathrobe. Her gesture wasn't particularly sweeping, but I thought I caught a glimpse of flesh below the vee of her neckline, and it was just possible that Renée had nothing on under her robe. And she didn't, too. "Let's go, honey," she said (and she might just as well have said, "What grade are you in?").

Renée left the kitchen, and I followed meekly; the colt was now a quiet lamb. We moved through the foyer, opened a fresh door, and entered a bedroom which seemed to wrap me in a sort of red haze. The draperies seemed red, the bedspread seemed red, and whatever

furniture and doodads decorated the rest of the bedroom gave the room
a warm, rosy glow. I raised my hand to my eyes to soften the brightness
and suddenly I realized my eyeglasses had become a problem.

Do I take my glasses off? Is it safe to leave them on? Would they
get in the way if I had to kiss her, or something? On the other hand,
if I took them off I wouldn't be able to see a goddam thing. I carried
my bewilderment to the middle of the room and stood as bravely as
I could at the foot of an unusually large double bed. Renée closed the
bedroom door. "You can take your clothes off," she said, untying her
belt. I sat down on the edge of the bed as she went into a tiled
bathroom. "I'll only be a minute," she whispered.

Gingerly I proceeded to untie my shoelaces and ease off my shoes,
and I had just started peeling off my socks when she walked through
the bathroom door stark naked and sat down on the bed next to me.
Renée smelled as nice as anyone I had ever known; years later I learned
her perfume was called Lily of the Valley. As she sat next to me, in
attendance, as it were, I had a realization of how close she was, of
naked thighs and bare breasts, of my deep and childish ignorance,
and I was happy to stand up so I could unbuckle my belt—there was
no other way to get my pants off.

I was now truly spooked, afraid of the beautiful, busty blonde
sitting on the bed waiting for me. Nothing stirred. I was, I imagined,
a ball of putty. There was no urge, no craving, no appetite, and not
a smidgin of lust. Nothing. Now if I had been *imagining* this scene—
Renée waiting playfully on the edge of the bed, with me hovering
over her like a sex-crazed Percheron—there might have been something to see. The reality of the situation, however, with Renée waiting
on the bed, grapefruit breasts and all, had of course the extreme
opposite result.

But this was no fantasy. Reality was all. I still had on my sports
shirt, my newest long pants, my undershirt, and my shorts, and I
wanted to keep them on as long as possible without losing face. I had
my pants about halfway down, struggling to keep my balance, when
there was a soft tapping on the bedroom door, and I froze. Renée said,
"Come in," and for a moment I thought she was addressing me.

Madam Esther's face peered into the room, looking more than
ever like my maiden aunt, and for a moment I was half-brave with

relief. She gestured toward Renée, who slipped off the bed and trotted toward Esther like a good child expecting a reward. What followed was obviously a secret conversation. They whispered together for a moment, after which Esther smiled at me, patted my cheek, and tiptoed out of the room. Renée smiled as if she knew something I didn't (which I didn't), went into the bath, and returned quickly. She was now wearing her robe.

She resumed her place on the edge of the bed, and spoke gravely. "I think it's better to wait until you're ready. Esther says we don't want to jump the gun." I smiled weakly. Jump the *gun*! Hell, I was more like Prometheus Bound, like a slingshot unslung.

Well, I finally made it. That is, I got all my clothes off, and as I stood there, Renée removed her robe and took me in hand, I smelled the lovely scent of her Lily of the Valley, and an eternity later (where was the music? where were the stars? where were the bombs bursting in air?) love conquered all, and Daddy's purpose had been served.

I dressed more quickly than I had undressed, entered the bathroom, where I wiped my penis with a pink tincture of Renée's selection, gave Esther a goodbye handshake, and learned I was expected to return in two weeks for further instruction (I returned twice more, and then the summer, as well as my sex course, was over). High as the sky, and avoiding cracks in the sidewalk as if they existed not at all, I ambled down Second Avenue and all the way home.

The next day, locked in the bathroom, my eyes an inch from the medicine-chest mirror, I examined my face minutely. The same goddam pimples were still there. If I had known that most of them were scheduled to come and go for another decade I could have saved Daddy fifteen dollars that summer. Looking at it another way, however, he did try to add to my otherwise vicarious life, and what he did for me just before I turned fourteen was, in any case, selfless.

CHAPTER NINE

Now, THAT MAMA, refreshed and full of new energy, and my sister, tanned as a potato pancake, were back from their vacation, the summer seemed about over. The lumbering, hefty East Side sun became less oppressive as the days shortened, and Daddy, happy to have his family once again in the fold, made ready for what he hoped would be a good saloon season.

For some time now he had been worrying about potential hazards—the new hoods in the neighborhood; conversations he'd had with Uncle Mike about the too likely repeal of Prohibition; and then, of course, how he could have made my pimples disappear before Mama got home.

Since my pimples hadn't disappeared and Mama was home, there was obviously nothing further either of us could do, and Daddy finally abandoned my Second Avenue twice-a-week sex therapy. He was, therefore, once again able to concentrate on triumphing over the hoods, and what to do with his saloon if those bastards in Washington permitted people to buy drinks just anywhere. Furthermore, with the pimples question out of mind, he could now get back to work in earnest on his other career, turning me into a world-renowned violin virtuoso.

My resistance to Daddy's magic design was encouraged by his lack of interest in or indifference to *my* personal designs. Or so I believed. His frustration arose from his lack of understanding that I saw him not as my teacher, my friendly disciplinarian, my *father*, but as my adversary. As I lay half asleep in my listening-bed I often dreamed I could rule the world—rule, that is, if I didn't have to enter the ring with Young Sharkey. He was just too accomplished—too big, too strong, too experienced, too physically clever, too brutal.

What saved our protean relationship until I ran away from home a year later, what enabled us to function at least part of the time as father and son, was a lesson he inadvertently taught me through the years, the message I touched upon earlier—that, for Daddy, any plausible lie would beat the plain truth a million ways. It's too bad I adopted this awful principle, because the more adept I became at handling its tricky nuances the less there was for us to share.

Certainly some of my lies were justified, and if they weren't justified . . . well, I thought they were, and the result was just as satisfactory. Perhaps the rhythm of blows across arms, legs, thighs, and backside was not, by itself, enough to mold a fifth-rate (but persistent) liar; but when these raps, slaps, stinging jabs, and smarting leather clouts became a regularly scheduled series of appointments in the meager light of my back-room cell, the truth lighted my path: to lie was to survive. Lying wasn't only easier to do, but was almost always less painful. And, eventually, with constant practice and a desperate imagination, I found not only that lying enabled me to live to lie again, but that inspired lying was fun.

Inspired, or fancy, lying had its moments. In my time I lied to Daddy about my whereabouts after dark, the money missing from the sugar bowl or the disappearance of currency left lying around the house, my shaky and declining academic performance at school, my scrapping of clothes I hated to wear, the cost of eating out on busy saloon nights, and a small catalogue of lesser lies not worth describing but part of my survival gear.

I can't say I regret telling Daddy all those lies. There is, however, one lie, one big lie, that I do regret. My work with my violin teacher, Michael Cores, was for Daddy a hope that something great—something perhaps even beyond his dreams—would happen to me. I was too young at the time to wonder whether my welfare was Daddy's first consideration in his desire to make me a musical "somebody," or whether I was being used to further his own well-being, to show me off as his success.

At this moment, of course, it no longer makes any difference, but sixty years ago, although I didn't know it, my future was to be determined by my weekly lessons with Michael Cores and the lies I told Daddy about our wretched relationship. I never said to Daddy, "I'm not your kind of fiddle player and I never will be. Why don't you give up?" (I comfort myself nowadays with the idea that even if I had known it and had found the courage to say it, he never would have believed it.)

Still, it was inevitable that Daddy would eventually catch hold of the shaky wire that maestro Cores and his reluctant student walked together. During one bitter, confused, and hateful hour in Cores's studio on Riverside Drive, Daddy would see his hopes dashed, his plans for our future shattered, and his dream become a nightmare. Later, I would have been unable to explain to him why I had lied if, indeed, he had asked me to, nor could I offer him another plausible lie to mitigate the first—a lie so inconceivable, so monstrous to Daddy's natural mind, that I don't believe he ever thought I could have invented a lie like that. But I did.

It was a Saturday midmorning toward the tail end of summer, the sunshine cool on the saloon swinging door as I went through the barroom to pick up my fiddle and briefcase in preparation for my regular session with Cores. On my way in I had noticed Smack and his cab parked just outside the saloon, waiting to escort me according to Daddy's earlier instructions, to what I had come to think of as my angst-ridden hour at my weekly Riverside Drive inquisition.

On my way out of the back room, fiddle case under my arm, Daddy stopped me. I thought he intended to play one of his let-me-look-you-over scenes; instead, he suggested joining me at my lesson. I nodded my head, although I couldn't believe he was serious about his proposal. Saturday afternoons the saloon was busy; I saw no one behind the bar to take his place. But, most important of all, he had never actually heard Cores give me a lesson.

Cores and Daddy had met briefly when lesson arrangements and fees had first been discussed, but from that point on what Daddy knew of Cores's methods of instruction, messages to students, and (worse) messages to parents came directly from my imagination, from what I thought Daddy would enjoy hearing.

While Daddy and I talked and I tried to divert him from this dangerous notion, Pietro the bartender entered the saloon and I learned Pietro was starting several hours earlier than usual because his brother was getting married that evening and Pietro had to be there. Daddy, ever the good sport, had agreed to this special arrangement and decided, on the spur of the moment (since this was as good a time as any), to listen to his virtuoso son take one of his five-dollar lessons. Pietro had provided Daddy with several free hours, and he was ready to forgo his usual afternoon nap because, as he put it, he felt fresh as a rose, and he had long been planning to hear Cores give me a lesson.

I had no choice. I knew what Daddy was looking forward to, and I had lied about this subject for so long that no matter what I might say at this moment, nothing would prevent Daddy from making this major journey. What Daddy expected, of course, was to hear Cores tell of my remarkable accomplishments, to bask in the warmth of Cores's congratulations to a severe but caring father, and, in turn, for Daddy to remind Cores that behind every boy virtuoso was a parent who, in his own way, was also a virtuoso.

We left the saloon, got into Smack's cab, and headed uptown. Daddy was dressed for the expedition. He wore his favorite salt-and-pepper tweeds, his obviously expensive white-on-white shirt, and one of his good ties fastened with a small diamond stickpin. These weren't Daddy's usual Saturday-morning wear, and suddenly it struck me he had known about this trip much longer than I thought he had, and I felt even worse. He was looking *forward* to this meeting.

I must surely have wished I were dead, or at least going up to Riverside Drive alone. Cores's normal reactions to my playing were bound to mystify Daddy, whose knowledge came from my own reports, and at the very least he was in for an unspeakable surprise. I wished Smack would run his taxi into one of the el pillars along the way and save us all an endless hour of grief.

Unfortunately we arrived at the Riverside Drive address on time. With fifty trips under its belt, Smack's taxi could have made the journey on its own. Daddy and I entered the building and rang Cores's bell, and his eighteen-year-old piano-playing daughter opened the door and smiled. I smiled with some effort, introduced her to Daddy, and hoped her father wouldn't call upon her to accompany me in the

Vivaldi. The concerto didn't go well and had of course never yet met with Cores's approval, and I didn't relish being put down in front of Daddy *and* Miss Cores. Either one was one too many.

We made ourselves comfortable in Cores's waiting room and listened to the violin sounds coming from his studio. They sounded pretty good to me, and while Daddy sat bolt upright on a straight-back chair totally unimpressed, I leaned back on a small blue sofa and fumbled through the pages of a book I had picked up off the end table. The dust jacket said, in giant letters, LION FEUCHTWANGER, and I wondered why *my* name could not have been Lion. Meanwhile, Daddy, to remind me that I was on the threshold of a master lesson, as well as to express his own view on reading indiscriminately, continued to throw me small, exasperated, but nonetheless dirty looks.

After several minutes the studio door opened and a young man came out, said goodbye, and I hunched myself to my feet. I told Daddy I'd see him right after the lesson. I tried to persuade him to remain in the waiting room and talk to Cores *after* the lesson. I said that Cores didn't like to have outsiders in the studio when he gave a lesson. Maybe Daddy would like to go for a walk and return in half an hour; maybe Smack could show him the sights on Riverside Drive. Maybe this. Maybe that. I supposed I sounded panicked, because I was. But Daddy stood firm.

He hadn't got himself all dressed up just to parade up and down Riverside Drive. He had made the trip uptown to meet the master teacher, to receive fresh instructions, fresh ammunition, fresh confirmation; the firmness of his expression said he had come to hear the good work, to be catered to, to be indulged, and at five dollars per, he was entitled to this action. And not in the waiting room, but *inside*. In the sanctuary. Where the action was. Where important decisions were made. Where his life's work hung in the balance. He bounced off his chair and followed me into the studio.

Cores was making a note in a small notebook in which I assumed he kept his accounts. As we entered the studio he looked up and seemed surprised to see Daddy. He smiled his mustache smile as if to say so nice of you to come, shook hands, then removed a batch of music from the top of the piano bench, moved the bench to a corner of the small studio (a baby grand piano and bench, a wooden chair for Cores, a small escritoire, and space for two music stands; violin cases were usually left on top of the closed piano, and there was no place for a student to sit down), and with a wave of his hand indicated it was to be Daddy's seat.

Daddy seemed to enjoy this arrangement, and as I removed my violin from its case and tightened the hair on the bow, I prayed, and hoped my plea to God would carry, if not the day, at least the next hour. But my prayer was destined to go unanswered. I knew that nothing untoward was likely to happen as long as I played well (which I never did for long), because Cores would simply nod his head and listen. For him, that was approval. The trouble would start when I made my first mistake (usually in the first ten seconds), and then the Russo-American lecture would begin, accompanied by small but stinging physical reminders with his bow. All of which scared me stiff. Daddy knew nothing of this.

Perhaps the Lord doesn't pay much attention to supplicants who are scared stiff. No doubt it is written somewhere that paralysis shows a lack of faith. Well . . . I could hope. Daddy took his chair and settled back, expectantly. I was thankful he could watch only my back; but that meant he would be facing Cores's little mustache and big mouth head on. In any case, I wouldn't have to watch Daddy watching.

I placed my thin stack of music on the stand and waited. Cores picked up his bow, the better to chastise backsliders whose elbows were too flexible for his taste, and in a voice unmistakably intended to mean "Play ball!" bawled out "A major!" I heard him. Loud and clear. This was his day to ask for scales. The basic scale is called the diatonic scale, of which there are twelve major ones. Good fiddle players are familiar with at least ten of these scales, and Cores's opening message was simple: Starting with the tone A in the G string in the first position, play an A-major scale through three octaves, ascending and descending without pause, four quarter notes to each up and each down stroke of the bow, in four-four meter, at a tempo no slower than allegretto, with perfect fluidity and impeccable intonation—the sort of thing Menuhin did every day. That was what Cores meant by "A major!"

I took a deep breath, tucked the fiddle under my chin, bit my lower lip to stop its quivering, lifted my bow, and took a chance—

zing-smooth-*zing-zing-zing*, again and again and again. After I had zinged all the way up to my proper climax and plunged down again (although not quite as smoothly as I would have liked), I realized I was still upright, still on my feet. From experience I knew the best thing I could do now was remain motionless, fiddle under chin, eyes straight ahead, bow at the ready. Poised. The picture of confidence.

I could feel Daddy's intense boredom on the back of my neck. Daddy hated scales, perhaps even more than I did, and for years I avoided practicing scales because Daddy didn't consider them music. Scales were something you warmed up with; nobody actually walked around whistling scales. Playing scales was like warming up by punching the light bag before you entered the ring; but it was in the ring that you came up against the real meat.

And then Cores showed why some people—Toscha Seidel, for example—thought he was worth five dollars a lesson. "Clean, young boy!" Cores nagged. "You must be *clean*! I teach you to go up scale *clean* and come down *clean*, and you slide. Why you *sliiiiiiide?*" With the edge of his bow he tapped my right elbow. "Now," he commanded, "play again!"

I tried again. I knew what he had in mind, but I couldn't do it; what he was asking, the elimination of the slide, took practice, and for the twenty dollars a month Daddy paid him for my lessons, he knew he had the authority—the right—to assume I practiced whatever he decided was good for me. In the viola section of the New York Philharmonic his word was law, with formal sanction by the St. Petersburg Conservatory, and what was good enough for them ought certainly to have been good enough for me.

It would have been beyond Cores to conclude I didn't practice my assignments; he would have assumed my failure to follow instructions wasn't plain willfulness (he couldn't have conceived of that either), but was pure musical empty-headedness. Thus, Cores and Daddy shared an innocent eccentricity—neither could understand why anyone wouldn't *want* to obey their orders.

When I came to the end of the scale, I knew I had failed once again to do what Cores had ordered. I went up and down that fucking scale as if my life depended on it. Which it did. In fact, I knew I had missed the lifeboat when I was halfway down, when I shifted from the A string to the D string, where I always slid a little because it gave the scale so much more feeling.

Cores shook his head, all perplexity. "The young boy slides," he said to Daddy. "I say play clean and he slides." He was talking to Daddy, but only because he was there. I shifted my stance so I could look back at Daddy for a moment to acknowledge that Cores was addressing him, not me. Daddy reacted calmly; he appeared to be listening carefully to Cores's words, but without emotion—the way one listens to a carpenter as he explains why the swinging door doesn't swing easily. Actually Daddy seemed interested but not especially upset—so far he hadn't heard any music. He was waiting for the meat.

Getting no rise out of Daddy, Cores said impatiently, "All right. Now the Kreutzer." Thank God the scales were over, I thought, as I opened the book of Kreutzer études resting on the music stand. Cores checked through the lesson dates he had marked in the page margins, and pointing to one of the études I despised, tapped his bow against the page and said, "Play!"

I bit my lip and began my down-bow. I had barely got the étude going when he once again tapped the page with his bow. I understood his tapping only too well. It meant "Stop!" I stopped. I waited. He stared at the étude, perhaps translating something to himself from Russian into English, and with his bow scratched at the first line like a cat clawing a sofa. Then his rasp: "Fingers must fall on strings like hammers. Not like pussycat. Like hammers." *Bang! Bang!*—he hit the page. "Make yourself com-*fort*-a-bull! Now play again!"

For the next forty minutes Cores earned his money. His black three-piece suit (his teaching uniform), his mustache, and his obvious difficulty in making verbal points in a foreign language against an aesthetic illiterate in any language made his forehead drip sweat. He was not looking his best as he continued to push this rag of a fiddle player through the wringer. Sweat ran down my face and hands, and while Cores could wipe his forehead with a handkerchief, *my* sweat dripped off the palms of my hands and landed on my Dr. Posner's. The process sounds disgusting, and it was.

Although I couldn't look at Daddy, I felt his presence as surely as if he were holding me by the throat while reading the future in my sweaty palms. If only he would say something—anything to change the atmosphere, to remind Cores I was just a dumb kid trying to get this fiddle lesson out of the way, and that he, Sharkey, would know how to beat the truth into me later on. Instead, Daddy chose to remain silent, and silence wasn't Daddy's main strength.

In the past, when Cores spoke I always managed a "Yes, Mr. Cores," "No, Mr. Cores," "Okay, I'll try it again," anything that might show I was paying strict attention; perhaps my usual hangdog responses would help calm down his righteous but wasted anger. Now, however, I could say nothing. My heart raced, my balance wavered, my tongue was dry, and the sweat wouldn't stop. When I was forced to play a phrase over and over I simply bit my lip harder and began to welcome the bitter obligatory final scene—Sharkey and I dancing around the back room.

Cores glanced quickly at his wristwatch, and his spirits seemed to fall. He stood beside me, his head down and his fingers picking at the pages of the Kreutzer. Then, in a moment of resolve, he slammed the book shut, and with his usual forcefulness said, "Now the Vivaldi." Not one of Daddy's favorites, but for Cores the Vivaldi Concerto for Violin in A minor was a *piece*. The grand finale of the lesson. A rich and just reward. A baroque dessert for young men who ate all their scales and arpeggios in three-octave courses.

At the moment, Vivaldi couldn't help me at all. What would have saved me was to watch Cores disappear before my very eyes. The Vivaldi was not so much a piece as still another arrangement of broken scales and arpeggios, all of which had to be played with perfect intonation, clean hammer strokes, and, to sound reasonably authentic, no sliiiiiiding. If Cores had wished to choose a piece that would have satisfied Daddy's idea of music (as well as my own) he would have, at this stage, avoided the Vivaldi. But Cores, unlike Daddy and me, had little regard for other people's tastes. There wasn't a hope in the world that I could play any part of the Vivaldi concerto right. After all, where did my musical taste come from?

There is a section in the first movement that moves along at a pretty good clip, a section Daddy often heard me practice because I imagined he would like the pace, anyway. But that section was still some distance away, and the true opening of the Vivaldi (which I was immediately engaged upon) was completely unfamiliar, untuneful, and by his standards without pizzazz.

I thought I could hear Daddy shifting in his chair, and I was certain that his reflectiveness (as reflective as I ever saw him) was about worn out. He had been sitting there now for some three-quarters of an hour, and it must have occurred to him that he had traveled all the way up to Riverside Drive only to hear his son berated and insulted and to see him gently tapped with a bow—all old hat to Daddy.

Up to this point he hadn't heard much of what he had planned to hear, and he hadn't even had a chance to discuss my future musical career. He liked Cores, he told me later on. He liked Cores's teaching style, his obvious concern for perfection, his authority, his toughness. So like his own. Fiddle players were no different from boxers. They had to do a certain amount of roadwork, jumping rope, punching the bag, shadowboxing; but these were only preliminaries. Now, as he sat waiting, he was ready for the main event, and he hoped it would be something challenging, exciting, flashy, something like the *Czardas*, say. He could see that I was all rosined up now, ready to move to the center of the ring, and he expected me to come out fighting.

Meanwhile, back in Cores's cat-and-rat cage, I was by now a little way into the Vivaldi concerto. I knew Daddy was waiting for something to happen. Where was the suspense? the excitement? the roar of the crowd? the knockout? I could sense his patience, his forbearance, his close listening, and I fought Vivaldi even harder. Still nothing happened. Scales and arpeggios. That's all. Daddy by now must surely have thought he was mistaken: perhaps this wasn't the main bout after all.

I came to a cadence and Cores stopped me. Impatiently he made a few bowing marks on the music, gruffly indicated that the Vivaldi needed a lot more practice, and, plainly exasperated, now laid his bow on top of the piano—his usual signal that the lesson was over. Daddy, of course, was unaware of this subtlety. He was still waiting for the main show to begin. I removed my packet of music from the stand, and with the violin still tucked under my chin, I reached toward my violin case resting on top of the piano.

"Mr. Cores," Daddy began confidently, "can I hear my son play the *Czardas*?"

The fiddle was still under my chin, pressing against my Adam's apple, choking the life out of me. I closed my eyes and wished I were dead. All my fears were aroused and ready to devour me. This was why I didn't want Daddy here to meet Cores, to talk with him about my performance or lack of it, what I should have been practicing regularly in the back room, the lies I had told him about the wonderful things Cores had said about me.

When I opened my eyes again Cores was shaking his bald head. "What *czardas*?" he asked. "The lesson is over. No *czardas*. *Czardas* good for Gypsies. No *czardas*."

The trouble with Cores was that he didn't know about Daddy— who he was, his reputation, his position on the Lower East Side, the saloon, his toughness. He was innocent of Daddy's temper, his disdain for the appropriate, his fearlessness, his habit of swinging first and asking questions afterward.

Daddy's salt-and-pepper suit and his diamond stickpin must have seemed to Cores like the resplendently gaudy uniform of a hardworking but successful East Side Jew, the symbol of his success, which explained how he could lay out twenty dollars a month for a would-be fiddle scratcher. Cores couldn't possibly have imagined Daddy in action, could never have seen how quickly Daddy could dispatch anyone who crossed him. As far as he knew, Daddy was simply the overdressed immigrant father of a not especially prized pupil.

For once, Daddy's position was curious. He knew how to take a guy out with a roundhouse to the kisser, but short of that, he didn't know how to handle anyone who didn't fear him to begin with, who had never observed at first hand a demonstration of his physical superiority. So far, as the two faced each other, Cores had not yet recognized (as I had) the set of Daddy's jaw, the hard line of his mouth, his cold, wary eyes, the tautness of his heavy shoulders.

"Your son," Cores pushed on in his Bolshevik accent, "plays like a Gypsy. Not like violin player. I try to teach him to play *clean*. But no, he don't practice! He *wants* to be Gypsy."

Daddy curled his lip at me. "You mean my son don't *listen* to you?"

Cores shook his head slowly, as if to say that Daddy was incapable of understanding plain English, that Daddy didn't get the point at all. "When young boy comes first time to me he play like Gypsy. I try to make him com-*fort*-a-bull. Impossible! He still plays like Gypsy. When your son first comes to me he can't hold violin, he can't hold bow, he is"—he searched for the right word—" he is, how do you say, a *cripple*."

Cripple! The word slashed at Daddy like a long knife. He stood there, shoulders hunched, his face showing his pain, stunned by this ugly, dirty word made even dirtier, more personal, because it meant physical weakness, and that he could not tolerate. *Cripple*! Why in God's name had Cores chosen to use this word? Daddy, I remembered, had called me many things in the past, words in English and Yiddish and Polish that were supposed to show me I was ungrateful, lazy, conniving, weak, lackadaisical, shiftless, feeble, wobbly, bungling— but *cripple*? Never.

And to hear this filthy word now, from this Russian bigmouth, this total stranger, to have *cripple*! thrown in his face by this high-class bum in his three-piece suit, to have it said without apology, without fear, without fancy language, spoken straight out without misgivings, as if Cores were a hanging judge, must have been as frightening to Daddy as if *he* had been called a cripple.

Never having seen Daddy on the ropes before, but having seen him stretch out three guys on the sidewalk in front of his saloon, having seen him use his weight against the new gun-toting hoods in the neighborhood, I wouldn't have been surprised to see Cores hit the deck after one of Daddy's impulsive, lightning-fast one-twos. The heavy atmosphere was right, Daddy's temper was right, and he looked right.

Yet he did nothing. He stood there, stunned. Perhaps he realized he wasn't on Rutgers Street, Cores wasn't just another bum, but this poor fiddle teacher wasn't even a worthy opponent. Daddy seemed to sag, to tire; the iron went out of him; he had been punched around, almost knocked down. But wait! He was still on his feet. He wasn't out by a long shot. Nobody had called *him* a cripple.

He took a deep breath, as if to keep the old fire burning, looked without expression at Cores, and nodded slowly. The truth came to him finally. The crushing, painful intelligence, this tragedy of his had now hit home. But Daddy had outlasted Sharkey. "My son is a cripple," he said softly. "I thought I could teach him to play the violin"—he turned up his hands in resignation—"and now I find out he's a cripple." He smiled sadly at Cores. "Ain't that a joke?"

I closed my fiddle case, carefully snapped the lock on my briefcase, and when Cores opened the door of his studio, Daddy and I left like retreating soldiers, softly, quietly, obstinately silent.

Outside we spied Smack's taxi, and we walked toward it together along the quiet, gray street. Both of us got into the back seat and Smack set off for home. Several moments passed and Daddy and I had yet to speak to each other, and his silence frightened me. I didn't know what to expect—rage and blows perhaps. My experience with him had been in lesser matters, and I knew, as we used to say, that I was in for it. After what Cores had told him he had a right to be bitter, to threaten, to damn—a right to all of his anger repertoire. Instead, I was now faced with his unaccountable and awkward silence.

An image of what I thought would happen to me when he once got me into the back room brought tears to my eyes. Daddy spoke to me in Yiddish: "Why are you crying?" My tears increased. I sobbed, and shook my head.

He placed his large hand gently on my shoulder. "*You're* crying?" he asked, a kind of jokey quality back in his voice. "*I'm* the one who should be crying." I looked at his seamed face, and I could see tears in *his* eyes.

"Don't cry," he said, pulling out his silk handkerchief. "It's nothing to cry about."

Smack stopped for a light and Daddy bent forward as if he had dropped something on the floor. A moment later, as the taxi moved forward, he seemed once more in full control. Apparently he had found what he was looking for. He pushed his handkerchief into my hand. "We won't tell Mama anything that happened. Not a word. Understand?"

I took off my glasses and wiped my eyes, but the tears wouldn't stop. I nodded anyway, to show I understood that, finally, we were in something together.

My lessons with Cores were over. I don't know how Daddy explained it to Mama—Cores was sick, Cores had moved to Chicago, Cores had gone back to Russia, some such lie—but Mama seemed satisfied. "I never trusted him," she said. "I had better things to do with the money than give him those twenty-dollar checks."

Daddy, never one to give up easily, later arranged for me to play a private audition for Frank Damrosch. Frank Damrosch had accomplished the affiliation of the Institute of Musical Art with the Juilliard School of Music. He and his brother Walter appeared regularly on radio; all music lovers, including even some of Daddy's saloon customers—along with Toscanini, Horowitz, Stokowski, Deems Taylor, Lawrence Tibbett, Lily Pons, and other celebrities—were fully aware that Damrosch was indeed Very Big. And just before Frank Damrosch retired as dean of Juilliard in 1933, he consented to the audition. As I said, Daddy didn't give up easily.

I had little or no notice of this latest sortie of Daddy's and by that time I had not touched the violin for weeks. This pleasant interlude lasted only until Daddy told me I was to play for an important radio figure who would tell us whether I was talented (and for "talented," read "crippled").

Accordingly, we stopped in to see Frank Damrosch one day. My best recollection tells me he was a gracious and perceptive old man, somewhere in his seventies. He asked me to play something for him, and I played the *Czardas*. I was confident with little else, and besides, I had no idea the audition was to be so important to Daddy. I played the *Czardas* as well as I usually did, while Damrosch sat at his desk in a big chair, and, I thought, listened carefully. When my audition was over, I put my violin away and proceeded to wander around the office studying various paintings which brightened the walls, while Damrosch and Daddy must have discussed my performance.

Despite what Daddy told me afterward as we rode home in Smack's taxi, it is clear to me now that Damrosch was indeed a kind and good man who understood the nature of this curious and outlandish audition, and was able to provide Daddy with the confidence, assurance, and justification he deserved after he had suffered so many years of unremitting hope and so little progress.

Damrosch and Daddy (as Daddy told it) stopped before an art masterpiece and while Damrosch pointed out its extraordinary features, he further explained his own great love for this work; he then pointed out to Daddy that he would never, himself, undertake to paint a work of this kind—much as he would like to—because he lacked the God-given talent necessary to create such a masterpiece.

Daddy paused to jolt me gently in the ribs with his elbow. "He was talkin' about you, you know that?" He smiled, as if he had just discovered irony. "I never thought God would have a lot to say about playing the fiddle!"

Damrosch, he continued, went on to say that I would never be a great violinist, but if I continued to work hard—I was, after all, just barely fourteen—one day I could become an "accomplished" violinist. Daddy like that. He repeated the word "accomplished" to me as fluently as if he had learned to use the word in Bialystok. When he heard that word he knew he had what he came for; he left his meeting with Damrosch with the key word. He enjoyed saying that delicious word "accomplished," tasting its flavor, distinguishing its syllables like the lyrics in a good song, letting it fall in harmonious morsels, showing his . . . well, happiness.

Daddy liked his newfound word, and he remembered Damrosch saying, "In two years, when your son finishes high school, bring him back to me," and his kind words brought Daddy a great deal of comfort, even though he didn't dream I wouldn't have a high school diploma until I was twenty-eight. Damrosch's courtesy justified Daddy's confidence in me and in himself. I wish Daddy's affairs had not just then taken a turn for the worse, so that he might have found some reason to be proud of me, but his world was scheduled to fall apart, and my fiddle playing was to become the least of his concerns.

By the end of 1933, Daddy was broke. He had been sent to the hospital with a serious stomach ailment, and by the time he was released the State of Utah had ratified the Twenty-first Amendment, and Prohibition was repealed. Whatever businesses Daddy owned, or had a piece of, depended for their trade on the sale of illegal booze. He had invested heavy money, Mama later told me, in buying well-located saloon space, paying what was called "key" money for what was, in effect, an okay from a landlord to run the place as a saloon. Most of these places had been cheap restaurants, empty lofts, or vacant stores barely good enough to be rented out to Gypsies.

Daddy borrowed money to furnish them, to install helpers, bar-tenders, waiters, cooks, entertainers, and musicians, and pay the nec-essary police protection. On Uncle Mike's say-so, and because Daddy had been suspected of bootlegging, each place was, for the record, owned by a willing confidant (some even saloon bums) who for a little cash would sign away his life. With the repeal of Prohibition all of Daddy's ventures became worthless almost overnight (most of the collapse occurred during the two weeks he spent in the hospital), and when he was finally back on his feet, Mama—who had continued, foolishly as it turned out, to pay the weekly police protection, the medical bills, and all other expenses—was forced to explain to Daddy that they were nearly penniless.

Unless Daddy was willing to pick up where he had left his earlier life and go out looking for old acquaintances who were still in the money, there was little he could do to support Mama and us children. He now found himself, for the first time, in the same position as thousands of other Lower East Siders, with cash going out for rent and food but nothing coming in; his reputation in his old saloon world was now worthless, and like other rough, tough Prohibition saloon-keepers in the slums, he didn't fit into the new legal saloon trade and no one would hire him. He drifted for nearly a year, wearing his good clothes as often as he could, staying out late whenever anyone asked him to, looking around for what might turn out to be Smart Money; but the new hoods, who were half his age, had little use for a forty-five-year-old has-been toughchik.

Daddy got his first break from an old acquaintance who had opened a brewery in Brooklyn, and who, while he would have been ashamed to make the old Sharkey such an offer, suggested he could use a driver for one of his beer trucks. A driver's qualifications un-fortunately included the ability to read and to write up accounts, which Daddy was incapable of. Luckily, there was a job open for a driver's helper, and Daddy accepted it. The money wasn't what he had hoped for, but as the East Side saw it, a job is a job.

I was all set to run away from my Rutgers Street home, although I suppose I could easily have been talked out of it. Mama's plans to move the family to Brooklyn so Daddy could be near his work hastened my decision, and I left home for good, shortly after we moved. Leaving the East Side and setting up house in a new world was, for Mama anyway, no easy matter. The price of this move was formidable, and until Mama could lay her hands on two hundred dollars we were stuck on Rutgers Street. How Mama got the money together to end our East Side life wasn't unusual, but the origin of that money was odd enough to be pretty typical of the East Side, and, I believe, worth recounting.

At the center of this story is Mama's mother, Chana, whose grandchildren called her Bubba. She was a stocky, strong woman, and caring for her eight children (one had died in infancy) didn't shake her placid acceptance of her mandatory household and shopping duties. When she occasionally sat down to rest—she was careful to set aside a little time for this—she often allowed herself a small, tired, satisfied smile.

She often spoke with her eyes or her hands. She spent most of her time on family chores—making beds, sweeping, cooking, shopping, scrubbing—and since she never owned more than half a dozen words in English, I thought she must be lonesome. I spent some time as a boy helping her prepare dinner, helping her clean house for the Sabbath, and carrying her shopping bags, much of which we did in dead silence. I suppose I just assumed that people who didn't talk much were lonesome. It never occurred to me that Bubba may have valued silence. Talking used energy, and she needed hers for more important things, like watching over Zaida and her large family.

She did, however, enjoy the company of two friends. Whenever we went shopping together, she'd stop in around the corner on Monroe Street to spend a few minutes with Rivke, who ran a tiny remnant shop stacked floor to ceiling with curtain fabrics, with an aisle down the center so narrow that Rivke and a customer couldn't stand side by side. Bubba and Rivke grew up neighbors in Kovno, they bore a certain resemblance to each other, and they discussed what they remembered of the old days—I should say that Rivke "discussed," because Rivke almost never stopped talking; she was held in very high esteem by the women in the neighborhood because when she had been widowed some years earlier she opened her little shop and seemed to make a go of it entirely on her own. Mama paid Rivke the highest East Side compliment when she spoke of her as "a business lady."

Bubba's second friend was a fellow Kovner, Sam Bicowich, a tall gangly man with a gray mustache who operated a small jewelry workshop in the kitchen of his flat on Madison Street, a five-minute walk for Bubba from Rivke's shop in the Monroe Street pushcart section. Bicowich made specially ordered pieces and did repairing for other jewelers. He lived in the ground-floor front of an ordinary tenement, and across his window a small sign in gold leaf said, discreetly, "S. Bicowich." Perhaps he didn't want strangers to know his kitchen was frequently stocked with gold and silver settings for precious gems, and what Bubba called "dymints."

Through Bicowich, Bubba became preoccupied with diamonds —cut, polished, unset, small diamonds. Collecting them became Bubba's secret passion. Since World War One, Bubba had been saving money. How East Side women saved is, to this day, some sort of loaves-and-fishes miracle, and Bubba grew up with her miracle buried between her heavy breasts.

All East Side women chiseled money—even pennies when they could—from the tiny amounts they had to work with. Bubba would walk four blocks to save a penny on a pound of tomatoes or a quart of milk, and walk a dozen blocks to Hester or Orchard Street to save a few cents on a pound of meat or a piece of fish. Like women pioneers the world over, she made her own aprons, dishtowels, and head scarves, and she saved burned-down matchsticks, heaven knows what for.

Bubba could save money from Zaida's pay. For years his reputation for honesty as a housepainters' foreman had brought him fairly steady work, if less than substantial pay. But Bubba didn't need much, and year after year she tucked away cash in a small cloth bag that hung from a string around her neck and snuggled securely between her breasts. Bubba had never gone inside a bank and had no intention of ever doing so. She changed saved-up coins for paper currency, and later exchanged small bills for large ones.

Soon, all but one of her children were married and able to make weekly contributions to Bubba, not to keep her from starving but out of the traditional Jewish gesture of contributing to the support of Mama and Papa. My own parents contributed generously, because Bubba not

only fed our family each Sabbath and holiday, but fed me all week
and served as Mama's baby-sitter.

The money that Bubba saved through the years—*kishke gelt*,
which means, loosely, gut money (after its hiding place)—may have
become cumbersome to carry. I don't know. What I do know is that
one day her friend Bicowich persuaded her to turn some of her cash
into a few small, good diamonds. She understood she could keep them
in a small cloth sack around her neck, and that they were less bur-
densome to keep than cash.

Bicowich and Bubba agreed on the price of the diamonds, and
by the time Mama needed two hundred dollars to take her family out
of the East Side, Bubba—the last person in the world Mama would
have expected could spare two hundred dollars—showed Mama her
little sack of diamonds for the first time. Mama guessed they were
worth a couple of thousand dollars at least. Bubba then selected two
of them and presented them to Mama as a loan. Mama gave them to
Daddy, who had no trouble selling them for two hundred dollars, and
we were able to pay our East Side tradesmen's bills and move to
Brooklyn.

Later I learned that several years after the move to Brooklyn,
Bubba had been taken sick and eventually went to the hospital, where,
after several hard weeks, she died. Mama was with her toward the
end, and Bubba managed to tell her that she had left the bag of
diamonds, for safekeeping, with her friend Rivke, the remnant-store
lady. If anything happened to Bubba, Mama was to pick up the diamonds and distribute them equally among herself and her two sisters.
The diamonds would be their inheritance.

After Bubba's death, Mama told Daddy the whereabouts of the
little bag of diamonds, and they went back to the East Side to see
Rivke. The remnant store, they were surprised to find, was closed—
it had been closed for over a week, they were told—and Bubba's great
friend, Rivke, was nowhere to be found. They tracked down her place
of residence and discovered a dingy flat crammed with old furniture,
but no one they asked had seen Rivke for at least a week. Daddy spoke
to the police, but their search was fruitless. Rivke had vanished, along
with Bubba's dymints. True to her reputation in the neighborhood,

Rivke was indeed a clever business lady. No one ever learned where she had decided to spend her old age.

Daddy became a lifelong member of the truckers' union, Mama became a full-time housewife, I ran away from home and became interested in jazz and took a job playing piano in a small-time bar and grill in Brooklyn. I joined the army in World War Two, was discharged in Washington State, made my way through graduate school on the G.I. Bill, and, sometime in the fifties after I had received tenure in my teaching job, I thought it would be both proper and interesting to see Daddy and Mama.

Daddy was now in his sixties, and Mama wrote that he had begun to think of retirement, he enjoyed reminiscing, and he hoped I was doing even half as well as I said I was in my infrequent letters home. It was a good time to see my family. I said *au revoir* to my wife and daughter and set out for Brooklyn to see whether I could go home again.

On a bright Sunday afternoon Daddy and I sat out in the backyard of their house in Canarsie, smoking cigarettes and having a drink while indoors Mama worked on my welcome-home dinner. She had asked me to avoid any arguments before dinner (I was reminded of the kitchen in Rutgers Street), and I'd promised I'd be a good boy. "When Daddy meets some of his old friends when he's delivering beer and they ask about you, he tells them you're way out somewhere in Washington. He says, 'He's got some kinda racket out there.' He's really proud of you. Don't get him all worked up!" I promised.

Daddy poured us another drink and looked at me with a leathery, wrinkled smile. He seemed a little shy, I thought. I hadn't known Daddy could be shy. "How'd you get here—fly?"

"Yeah," I said, "on United."

"Didja get a round-trip ticket? If you didn't we could help you out." I grinned and said it was okay, the ticket was all taken care of. We sipped at our drinks, stuck, I thought, for conversation, waiting for Mama's dinner signal. "Tell me," Daddy said slowly, as if he had thought about the question for a long time, "exactly what is it you're doin' out there in Washington?"

"I'm a teacher," I said. "I teach music."

"I know that. But what is it you teach? Violin? Piano?"

"No," I said, hesitating. "I teach . . . well . . . it's something called theory."

"Teery? What in the hell's teery?"

I tried again. "Well, Dad . . . it includes things like harmony, counterpoint—stuff like that."

For a moment he looked flustered. He thought about what I had just said for another moment or two. "Teery, eh?" he repeated. Then his face lit up. He got up from his chair and walked to where I sat. Grinning to beat the band, he slapped me on the back and winked conspiratorially. "Teery, eh?" he said proudly. "Leave it to *you*, son!"

The last time I saw Daddy alive was in 1970 on his eighty-first birthday. We were still smoking cigarettes and having a drink. Talking about our lives on the East Side, he said, "What the hell, son, we had a real good time in those years, didn't we?"

I said we sure did.